REPUBLIC STUDIOS:
BETWEEN POVERTY ROW
AND THE MAJORS

Richard Maurice Hurst

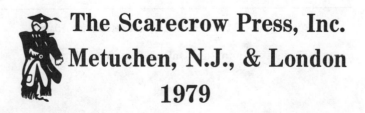 The Scarecrow Press, Inc.
Metuchen, N.J., & London
1979

Library of Congress Cataloging in Publication Data

Hurst, Richard Maurice, 1938-
    Republic Studios.

    Bibliography: p.
    Includes index.
    1. Republic Pictures Corporation. I. Title.
PN1999. R4H86   384'. 8'06579494   79-19844
ISBN 0-8108-1254-1

TABLE OF CONTENTS

PREFACE

Almost everyone acknowledges the effects of movies on culture but their specific role in American popular culture varies depending upon the source cited. Writings about film fall into two broad categories--fan and academic. The fan publications are usually unabashedly nostalgic and attempt to revive the pleasures that movies brought to audiences in their youth. Examples would include Alan Barbour's The Thrill of It All, dealing with B Westerns, and Jack Mathis' Valley of the Cliffhangers, dealing with Republic sound serials. 1* Academically, the cinema can be viewed historically, anthropologically, psychologically, cinematically, or sociologically.

All approaches tend to find a significance in the movies which Hollywood rarely acknowledges. Historically, the importance of film in any given era has usually been recognized but has not often been analyzed since the historian frequently views film as an undeveloped art form whose role in culture is difficult to categorize. Some of the inherent dilemmas caused by this cautious approach are covered in Paul Smith's The Historian and Film. 2 The anthropological school is perhaps best represented by Hortense Powdermaker3 and tends to view film's effect on modern culture as a mass produced technical development filling much the same role as folklore and ancient religions did in past cultures.

From the psychological viewpoint, movies are viewed as unconsciously reinforcing basic cultural patterns and, at the same time, influencing and directing these patterns through the emphases of successful films which affect audience behavior. The main thrust of this approach is perhaps best represented by Martha Wolfenstein and Nathan Leites in their Movies: A Psychological Study. 4

The cinematic approach has gained popularity in the last decade and says essentially that movies are a major

---

*Notes to the Preface begin on page viii.

force in history and should be studied both as a mirror to the period and as a factor in the overall history of a given time. This approach views film as an art but acknowledges its roots in economics. One of the more successful studies of this type is Garth Jowett's Film: The Democratic Art, [5] which is similar to works of an historical nature except that the author is devoted to the study of the cinema and emphasizes film as a major force in modern history rather than treating film as only one incidental factor in the larger pattern of historical development.

Finally, movies can be viewed academically from the sociological approach and, in this case, are usually studied in relationship to what the filmmaker was trying to impress upon his audience through the film. Of course, all films carry some message in the mere act of telling a story but the message film as sociologists think of it is the subject of David Manning White's and Richard Averson's The Celluloid Weapon: Social Comment in the American Film. [6]

All of these approaches have two things in common. First, they concentrate on the A film, the major production, and not the much more numerous and far more widely seen B film, that shorter economically produced type of unpretentious entertainment made from 1935 to the mid 1950s to fill the double bill and to enable the small neighborhood theaters to stay open seven days a week and provide an hour or two of diversion for the general moviegoing public. Secondly, these studies normally accept the basic premise that movies influenced their audiences and through them the general culture but they rarely attempt to draw insights from this concept. They do not usually study a genre or a studio in detail and then draw conclusions as to what the effects might be. The failure to take this last step is because sometimes it is felt that the conclusions are obvious and, even more important, because there is no sure way to measure these effects.

This study of the influence and significance of the major B studio, Republic Pictures, on the American scene utilizes aspects from all these schools of thought but probably falls closest to the cinematic historian's approach. By studying certain genres produced by a studio which specialized in the B format, key messages of these films will become apparent and their relationship to and effect upon the American scene will be documented. It will be shown that the studio was not interested in art but in economics, that in order to be profitable the movies had to entertain, and that in entertaining they also influenced and reflected the American culture as they saw it. The results, while unintended, were nonetheless important. Although there is still no way to measure these effects, the following chapters attempt to show that the B film generally and the output of Republic Pictures especially did have a significance to the study of American history from the mid 1940s to the mid 1950s.

To some moviegoers, the collective B film provided a barometer by which they, the individual members of the audience, succeeded or failed far more than the major pictures with a more obvious attempt to moralize--such as King Vidor's Our Daily Bread (1934) or Frank Capra's Mr. Smith Goes to Washington (1939). Republic was a major producer of quantity and quality B films. Perhaps the studio's quality made a difference in the success of the unintended lessons in their B films. But whether Republic was in a category with other B producers such as Monogram and Producers Releasing Corporation, or whether they were in a class by themselves, their pictures did influence their audience and perhaps to a greater degree of significance than the A picture which is so often discussed in this context. This influence may not have been as immediate or impressive as that of a blockbuster production but it was perhaps of greater depth, longer duration, and thus more substantive as a whole.

To substantiate this hypothesis, the first chapter is devoted to an overview of the history and economic structure of Republic for those unfamiliar with the subject. A more detailed survey of film scholarship as it pertains to Republic follows, while the third chapter develops the importance of various B genres as represented by this studio. The following chapters are devoted to a discussion of significant Republic serials, three representative Republic B Western series, three comedy series from the studio, and finally a brief coverage of non-series B movies from Republic. The last chapter summarizes the messages in the studio's films, their possible relationship to the appropriate eras in American history, and the studio's contributions to the movie industry.

Many Republic files proved to be unavailable though other sources were extensively utilized. Loans from collectors of pressbooks and other studio public relations materials were helpful. Some primary Republic sources existed in the New York Public Library, the American Film Institute in Los Angeles, the Margaret Herrick Library of the Academy of Motion Picture Arts and Sciences in Los Angeles, the University of California at Los Angeles Library, and the library at the University of Wyoming. Over two dozen interviews with Republic personnel and authorities conducted by the author proved invaluable. Also film viewings, taped film soundtracks, and scripts contributed to an understanding of the Republic product. Monographs, newspapers, and other published sources were of course consulted. Finally, fan publications, while not analytical, contained extremely valuable material such as interviews and filmographies.

Acknowledgments are in order but it is hard to know where to begin. Historians and popular culture scholars Professors Milton Plesur, Mel Tucker and Michael Frisch of the State University of New York at Buffalo, and Frank Hoffmann of the State University College at Buffalo, were very helpful and provided perspective and objectivity. Republic personnel both in front of and behind the camera contributed much as will be seen. Fans and film scholars such as Don Miller, Francis Nevins, and Jack Mathis offered valuable suggestions and materials. The National Museum Act provided a grant which greatly eased the various research trips and purchase of materials. Finally, and most important, there were my wife Jolene and children Ruthann and Michael, who gave support throughout the whole process. All of these people and many others unmentioned have assisted me in trying to show that the Republic B film has an important place in the understanding of American history and culture. Where I have succeeded, they share in the contribution. Where I have fallen short, I of course accept responsibility.

September 1977   Richard M. Hurst

Notes

1. New York: Collier Books, 1971 and Northbrook, Illinois: Jack Mathis Advertising, 1975.
2. New York: Cambridge University Press, 1976.
3. "An Anthropologist Looks at the Movies," Annals of the American Academy of Political and Social Science, CCLIV (November, 1947), p. 80-87.
4. New York: The Free Press, 1950; reprint ed. New York: Hafner Publishing Company, 1971.
5. Boston: Little, Brown and Company, 1976.
6. Boston: Beacon Press, 1972.

Chapter I

THE RISE AND FALL OF REPUBLIC:
AN HISTORICAL OVERVIEW

The year 1935 was not an auspicious time to begin a
new company and certainly not a film studio. Despite an initial optimism brought on by the New Deal, the country remained in the throes of the economic turmoils of the Depression, a situation which persisted until the sound of military
drums in Europe brought economic recovery. Moreover, in
contrast to popular legend, the film world did not glide
through the thirties on fat profits from the tickets purchased
by millions of entertainment starved citizens. 1* True, attendance was good but the film industry was affected by the
competition of radio and other factors. The big, established
movie companies weathered the era, made excellent films
for an appreciative audience, solidifed their gains, stabilized
their business and artistic techniques and laid the foundations
for the great profitable and successful days of the early to
mid-forties--at least from the movie makers' point of view.
But the Depression era was not so kind to smaller, shoe-
string, independent film concerns. Many fell by the wayside.

In spite of this or perhaps partially because of it, in
1935 Herbert J. Yates founded Republic Pictures. Yates,
once an executive in the American Tobacco Company, entered the motion picture business in 1915 when he became as-
sociated with Hedwig Laboratories, a film processing concern.
In 1918, Yates financed Republic Laboratories and in 1924
consolidated several processing plants and crystalized his
holdings into Consolidated Film Laboratories, a complete film
laboratory service. 2 In 1927, Nat Levine had founded Mascot Pictures and launched a long career with the serial production, The Golden Stallion, 3 a ten episode serial with stuntman Joe Bonomo which proved to be a satisfactory entry in
the serial genre. From the beginning, Levine's company
was financed predominantly by Yates' Consolidated Film

Laboratories. During the next eight years, Nat Levine's
Mascot Pictures built a reputation for producing competent
action pictures and serials.

In 1935, Yates approached Levine with the offer of a
consolidation. Yates wished to expand Mascot's ailing feature film and Western program, while retaining its serial
production schedule which led the industry in the genre.
Thus, in 1935, the two joined W. Ray Johnston and Trem
Carr, both of Monogram Pictures, and other independents
to form the new Republic Pictures Corporation. The new
company made its headquarters at the old Mack Sennett
Studios on Ventura Boulevard at Colfax and Radford Avenue
in North Hollywood which Mascot had leased periodically.
By using Levine's production experience and Monogram's exchanges in thirty-nine cities, the new corporation felt that it
could dominate production outside of the major companies
market.

The pressbooks for the 1935-1936 season were a confusing combination of logos--what with final releases from
the combining companies and "new" releases from the parent company--with Republic and Monogram predominating.
However, an overview of the situation showed that the cast
of Republic's direction was already formed. Twenty-two
films, predominantly mysteries such as The Spanish Cape
Mystery, melodramas such as The Return of Jimmy Valen-
tine, and adventure pictures like The Leathernecks Have Landed,
headed the list. These were followed by "8 John Wayne
Greater Westerns, " "8 Gene Autry Musical Westerns, " "5
Action Dramas, " and "4 Republic-Mascot 1936-1937 Serials."[4]

One of the first moves in the campaign to capture the
action market was to expand a series of top quality Westerns
for which there was a ready audience. John Wayne, under
contract to the studio, was put into a proposed series of
eight Westerns beginning with a relatively expensive film entitled Westward Ho. This was the most costly picture for
Wayne since his starring debut in The Big Trail (Fox, 1930)
and cost nearly $18,000. Some sources credit the film with
grossing over $500,000 although this is a much inflated es-
timate.[5] On the basis of this and other successes, Republic
was now a power with which to reckon.

However, everything did not go completely smoothly.
In less than two years, Variety headlined, "Carr, Johnston
Leaving Outfit."[6] So in less than a year W. Ray Johnston

and Trem Carr withdrew from the company feeling that Monogram had gained little in the consolidation. Johnston later
reorganized Monogram. Carr's position as Republic's production chief was taken over by Nat Levine. In their first year,
Republic grosses were over two and a half million dollars.
Flush with the new company's success, Levine was quoted as
saying that Republic was spending $6,750,000 on twenty
Westerns, twenty-four features, four serials, and eight "special" productions. 7

But it was Yates who was the guiding force behind Republic from the beginning--both financially and in terms of
artistic emphasis and economic patterns. Although Yates and
Republic periodically attempted to break free of the B picture
mold, they were never really successful and remained first
and foremost a B studio--the best perhaps, but nonetheless
subject to the fortunes of the B picture.

The B movie was definitely a creation of the Law of
Economics. Although the economic organization of the studio
is not the major concern of this study, a brief summary of
the economics of the B film and of Republic's approach is
therefore necessary for the sake of completeness.

Beginning in 1935 and continuing into the early forties,
the American moviegoing public came to expect the double
bill, although small towns would frequently show single films,
both A and B. Also, prior to the epochal Supreme Court
Decision of 1949, United States versus Paramount Pictures,
Inc., the major studios owned their own theatre chains and
knew that they had a guaranteed audience for their products.
Now, that monopoly was ended but previously, regardless of
the cost and merit of the picture, it had a guaranteed booking. These two factors contributed to the rise of the B
film.

The major studios, however, were committed to the
A production and, while each maintained a B unit well into
the forties until rising costs caused them to play down this
aspect of production, they preferred to stay with the high
quality film which brought in most of the profits because of
guaranteed distribution and percentage contracts. But the
audience wanted that second feature. B pictures were therefore produced to fill the bill inexpensively and for a fixed
rental rate. The profits, while not spectacular, were predictable provided the costs were kept down. The majors
were not geared to filling this very real need so the lesser

studios led by Republic stepped in to fill the gap. Most of
these studios relied on State's Rights distribution wherein
film packages, often in blocks of six or eight, were provided
to a wholesale distributor who handled them exclusively in a
region frequently made up of one or more states. However,
Republic and Monogram were large enough to set up exchanges
similar to the majors in large cities.[8]

It should never be forgotten that Republic, as well as
every motion picture producer, was governed first and foremost by the profit imperative. Time after time, the following chapters will refer to the ideas which Republic films
represented. But it must be realized that Republic was not
really concerned about ideas in its films. Republic was concerned not about influencing its audience, youthful or mature,
simple or sophisticated. Rather the studio was concerned
with making an exciting, entertaining, and therefore, it hoped,
profitable product for a certain type of theatre and audience,
which product would meet with the approval of the Motion
Picture Association of America and various religious and
local censors. Since Republic's chief market was in the Midwest, the South, and the Southwest, this resulted in the local
censors being a bit more demanding and thus made Republic's
"message" more conservative and traditional.

The point is that the conscious attempt of Republic to
reinforce traditional values can be traced to the simple fact
that it was profitable for them and they were in the business
of providing good action pictures inexpensively and depend-
ably.[9] Most academic and popular writers have recognized
the potency of the profit imperative, but do not give it the
emphasis which the industry feels it deserved. For example,
Robert Sklar notes it in reference to silent films but, if anything, it increased in the Depression era. "Of the feature
films exhibited in such picture palaces, and at every other
movie theater large or small throughout the country, no more
than a tiny number were produced without the expectation or
at least the strong hope of reaping a profit. This made the
movies unique among the arts."[10] Sklar also points out that
the creators in other fields such as literature, dance, and
theatre were often dedicated and willing to break even or accept some losses. Critics used to this approach attacked
movies for their lack of aesthetics not understanding their
basic commercialism.

Because of this frequent blindspot on the part of
critics and scholars, and because of the importance of economics to Republic, it must be emphasized that the studio under-

stood its foundations from the beginning. First, its founder
and guiding genius was above all money-oriented. "Yates ...
was interested in a healthy balance sheet. The fact that his
studio was considered the horse opera center of the film industry did not matter in the least. He was neither proud of
it nor embarrassed by it. He was first and foremost a
businessman."[11]

Perhaps the most telling example of Republic's dedication to the profit motive can be seen in a special merchandising section in the Hollywood Daily Reporter published
separately and devoted to the studio in 1938. Under the headline, "The Stability of Republic Pictures," it is stated, "The
people behind Republic have been identified with the financing
of motion picture production for nearly twenty years."[12]

> The principle behind Republic is as financially
> sound as the dollar received from the exhibitor.
> Just as long as it supplies the exhibitor demand,
> so long will be the health of its success. ... Quali-
> ty Without Waste ... so long will black ink dominate
> the red on its ledger.
> In fact, there is little about Republic Pictures
> that is not built upon a cold "business" basis. The
> barometer of its bank balance is truly the box-
> office.[13]

While disclaiming any ambition to make major epics,
the studio argued that it made good pictures but kept the exhibitor's cost in mind. "It is simply a formula whereby
every picture must measure up to the Republic standard of
consistency ... the highest point of excellence in production
quality, made within a budget cost that will permit the most
reasonable of rentals when it reaches the exhibitor."[14]

Of course, Republic expected sound business practices
to pay off for the studio as well as the exhibitor. The Hollywood Reporter agreed and offered the opinion that, since Republic films had shown steady improvement in the studio's
first two years, Republic was likely to become an industry
leader within five to ten years.[15] Republic personnel were
chosen for their business acumen as well as their artistic
sense, the writeup claimed. The technical facilities were de-
scribed--they were superior from the beginning because of
the Consolidated Laboratories and the Sennett Studios--and
a typical production scene was included ending with the ad-
monition, "It is all a part of the scheme of things at Republic. Economy--to the nth degree--but without waste.... A

lost hour, Republic officials know, means many lost dollars.
All of which would blast the business slogan and the very
basic premise of Republic Pictures."[16]   Stressing quality
with economy, Republic quickly became the leading B studio.

    In order to realize and maintain these heavily em-
phasized economies, the studio utilized efficient and often
clever means to save money.   Republic relied heavily and
very professionally on such devices as expert use of stock
footage (action sequences of merit good enough for multiple
reuse), inexpensive character actors and actors on the way
up or down, re-releases, strict budgets and shooting schedules, and no-nonsense writing and directing.   However, the
income factor remained dependent upon flat rentals, and, as
production costs rose during World War II and after, profit
margins declined.   Yates therefore early created four cata-
gories of productions to hopefully maximize profits: 1) Jubilee pictures were basically Westerns with a seven day
schedule and $30,000 budget (later $50,000).   Two per
month were normal.   2) Anniversary pictures were Westerns, action/adventure and musicals with a two-week schedule and budgets up to $120,000 (later $200,000).   3) Deluxe
pictures dealt with varied subjects with twenty-two-day schedules and $300,000 (later $500,000) budgets.   They were frequently directed by house director Joseph Kane.   4) Premiere pictures were directed by top names such as John Ford
and Fritz Lang with shooting schedules of approximately a
month and million-dollar budgets.[17]   Films in the latter cata-
gory were Republic's premiere productions, meant to compete with the major studios in the A market, and to build
Republic into a major studio without surrendering their lead
in the profitable but limited B area.   Some later well-known
examples include: Ben Hecht's Specter of the Rose (1946),
Frank Borzage's Moonrise (1948), Edward Ludwig's Wake of
the Red Witch (1949), Orson Welles' Macbeth (1950), Fritz
Lang's House by the River (1950), Allan Dwan's Sands of Iwo
Jima (1950), John Ford's The Quiet Man (1952), and Nicholas
Ray's Johnny Guitar (1954).   All of these men were well
known creative people who also worked at major studios
during their careers and several have even become cult figures in the seventies.

    While it was sometimes claimed that Yates did not
understand these films[18] or was not allowed to control
them,[19] he backed them because he was hoping to break into
the A production percentage rental market while remaining
active in the B categories.   But the B's continued as the back-

bone of the company, economically as well as artistically and
philosophically. The Jubilee and Anniversary categories were
consistent and grossed approximately $500, 000 each into the
fifties while the latter two categories were variable or sus-
tained losses. Despite Yates' public statements to the contrary, [20] the economic imperative began to catch up with Republic in the fifties. Audience tastes changed and attendance
shrank. Television proved especially competitive to the B
market. Production costs drove profits down. Republic also
had legal difficulties with the Screen Actors Guild concerning
residuals on films released to television which resulted in a
boycott. The expense of the Premiere productions proved a
critical monetary drain which was greater than the return
either in prestige or profits. In other words, Republic could
not compete with the majors in the final analysis. This, and
the other factors, broke the studio economically. The following chart from Kings of the Bs summarizes the economic
story of Republic:[21]

Republic Pictures, Inc.
Financial Data for Year Ending October 31

Year	Gross Revenues	Net Profit/(Loss)
1958	$33, 464, 482	$(1, 487, 337)
1957	37, 899, 826	(1, 362, 420)
1956	42, 236, 206	758, 401
1955	39, 621, 099	919, 034
1954	37, 962, 359	804, 202
1953	37, 265, 035	679, 217
1952	33, 085, 511	759, 604
1951	33, 409, 613	646, 404
1950	30, 310, 748	760, 574
1949	28, 086, 597	486, 579
1948	27, 072, 636	(349, 990)
1947	29, 581, 911	570, 200
1946	24, 315, 593	1, 097, 940
1945	10, 016, 142	572, 040
1944	11, 137, 125	561, 719
1943	9, 465, 338	578, 339
1942	6, 700, 358	504, 351
1941	6, 256, 335	513, 451
1940	7, 235, 335	590, 031

In the thirties Republic's net profit stabilized in the

$500,000 to $1,000,000 range. In the forties the gross profits increased but, due primarily to economic factors, the net
returns actually decreased. Backlog sales to television helped
keep up and even increase profits in the early fifties, but by
1956 Republic was in the red and dying as a film producer.

With the economic organization and the pervasive influence of the profit imperative at Republic Pictures firmly
established, it is necessary to describe briefly the studio's
early period, its most creative time, and examine the type
of product Republic provided and the niche it occupied so
well in the late thirties and into the late forties.

Technically Republic quickly proved to be top rated
even in its early years. Consolidated Film Laboratories
ranked as the best sound laboratory in Hollywood and, together with Radio Corporation of America sound recordings,
gave the Republic films a polish that other independent productions lacked. [22]   The quality of the Republic product soon
came to fill a void between that produced by the major studios and the variable products of the independents. [23]   Camera work at Republic was considered to be exceptional. The
best camera trucks, good composition, rapid panning techniques, and the use of numerous studio dolly shots all gave
Republic productions a feeling of movement that was not
found in most of the films of the major studios. In the musical department Republic scored to the hilt. Most of the
other companies, even among the majors, let long dramatic
and action scenes run without music in the thirties, but Republic filled most of their pictures including the serials with
a nearly complete musical sound score. [24]   This attention to
detail paid off in a quality product. Republic combined no-
nonsense straightforward direction, professional camera work,
and skilled editing with these good musical scores to produce
a highly competent, attractive set of films.

Republic technicians were considered to be of the
highest caliber. Action directors such as Mack V. Wright,
Ray Taylor, Joseph Kane, William Witney, and John English
all turned out top-rated films for Republic in the late thirties and early forties. In the early forties, Lew Landers,
R. G. "Bud" Springsteen, and Spencer Gordon Bennet among
others joined the Republic directorial ranks. Top stuntmen
such as Yakima Canutt, David Sharpe, Tom Steele, and Dale
Van Sickel were invaluable given Republic's emphasis as were
special effects geniuses Howard and Ted Lydecker and their
able assistants. Cameramen such as Jack Marta, Bud

Thackery, John Alton, and William Bradford contributed a
great deal which often went unnoticed outside the profession.
And the musical scores, already mentioned, were handled
by men such as Stanley Wilson, Victor Young, William Lava,
Paul Sawtell, Cy Feuer and Mort Glickman. Finally, credit
should be given to staff writers such as Ronald Davidson,
Barry Shipman, and Sloan Nibley to mention only a few. [25]

Republic embarked upon an extensive program of
Westerns, serials, and second features, or program pictures
as they were called. Oddly enough, aside from the serial
field where they excelled, Republic never entered the area of
movie shorts with any enthusiasm. As film writer Leonard
Maltin says:

> Most of the B picture factories had little regard
> for short subjects, although judging from the
> speed with which they made feature films, they
> probably could have turned out a two-reeler in
> an hour. Republic did have the short-lived
> "Meet the Stars" series in the early 1940's,
> but aside from this and occasional one-shots,
> Republic, Monogram, and their peers steered
> clear of short subjects. [26]

But in the area of B action features, Westerns, country musicals, and serials Republic found a place. Since most products of both independent and major studios in these areas of
programming were lacking in quality, Republic's well planned
specialization created a firm and respectable niche for the
studio. Whereas the products of the independent producers
of this period were often cheap and crude and the films of
the major studios which were made to reach the "lower levels" frequently missed the mark, the Republic product found
a ready market both among the exhibitors and the audiences,
especially among the secondary theaters in large cities
throughout the country and in general theaters in smaller cities throughout the Midwest and South.

Moreover, Republic's market was all the more
firmly established by the fact that the studio consciously
played to the middle America audience. They found their
audience not only with the type of material they produced but
also with the themes they emphasized. And, as shall be seen
in the following chapters, this was to be the importance of
the Republic product. They hit a chord. Michael Wood recognizes the significance of this factor for audiences when he

says the public can be "extraordinarily resistant both to rub-
bish and to masterpieces, when they fail to strike the right
chord.   It is worth recalling ... the essential structure of
the industry in its great days; settled financiers on the East
Coast were investing in uprooted adventurers on the West
Coast because of their supposed expertise on the subject of
what the Middle West really wanted.   The movies ... dreamed
up an America all on their own, and persuaded us to share
the dream.   We shared it happily, because the dream was
true in its fashion--true to a variety of American desires. ..."[27] The dreams had to strike a chord and the Midwest was generally where it--the audience and therefore the
chord--was to be found.

        This point was especially applicable to Republic.   The
studio's films were often not reviewed by large city papers
at all and when they were, their appeal to non urban interests
were frequently emphasized and not always positively.   For
example, Don "Red" Barry was a leading star of Republic
Westerns in the forties who, while appearing in an occasional
A film, was basically a cowboy hero with his audience in the
Midwest and South.   A contemporary New York reviewer of
a Barry Western noted this fact with a negative twist when
he stated in his review of The Sombrero Kid (1942):

> "The Sombrero Kid," doubled at the New York
> Theatre, is a Don "Red" Barry item in which Don
> does his usual act.   He, you know, is the cow
> chap who frequently has to pretend to be an outlaw
> himself, thus consorting with the villains, in order
> to turn them over to justice at the end.   He does
> it here, too, with his usual skill of fist and gun.
>   The picture makes one point, another familiar
> of the Westerns, which is worth pursuing for an
> inch or two.   The prime or master villain behind
> the scenes is the town banker.   This happens too
> often in Westerns to be mere coincidence.   There
> is some ground for the belief that the makers of
> Westerns, operating upon stringent budgets, have
> deep in their subconscious minds a resentment of
> people who control money.   They take it out in
> their libellous portraits of that great fraternity of
> money lenders, the bankers.
>   Now, although Westerns in a big city draw their
> audiences from among the children and like-minded
> adults, back where the grass grows long the gen-
> eral populace is entranced by them.   And since

many a Washington legislator hails from these
same sticks, the influence of the Westerns on
banking legislation in the United States is probably
greater than you have ever suspected.
This is only a thought inspired by "The Sombrero Kid". These Westerns do leave a lot of extra time for thoughts, don't they?[28]

Although these comments are delivered somewhat
tongue-in-cheek and with an obvious air of superiority, the
big city newspaper was in effect acknowledging Republic's
domain.

Action became a class item at Republic and, with its
audience and profit ratio firmly in mind, the studio continued
to grow throughout the early years. In April, 1939, the
New York Herald Tribune proclaimed: "Republic Pictures
Plans 50 Features in Season: Four Serial Films to Complete
1939-'40 Output."[29] Later that year Variety stated "30
Writers Working at Repub, New High".[30] And the next year
the New York Times heralded "62 Feature Films Listed by
Republic: Studio's Schedule for 1940-41 Includes 'Deluxe'
Releases, Westerns, and 4 Serials."[31] For the next season,
the New York Morning Telegraph noted, "Republic Sets Biggest Slate: To Spend $15,000,000 During Season for Fea-
tures, Westerns, Serials."[32] In February, 1942 Yates
announced plans to spend $2,500,000 to add land and new
buildings to the complex.[33] And so it continued throughout
the war years and into the late forties.

Yet another indication of Republic's success was its
decision to join the Hays Office in September, 1941. The
Hays Office, or Motion Picture Producers and Distributors
of America, was the official censorship arm of the industry
and membership therein gave a stamp of legitimacy.

In part, the Times said:

IN THE BIG TIME

Unless blackballed by some class-conscious studio,
Republic will become a member of the Hays organization during the coming week. When the independent concern began to show an awesome profit
the rushing by the Hays sorority began; on Monday
the ten members will pledge Republic. While it is
officially gratifying to be deemed worthy of the

honor, the elevation provokes a certain distress
in the hearts of the studio staff.
Membership implies a dignity they don't like.
Republic is one of the few remaining members of
the school that operates on the Stern Brothers'
theory that "a tree's a tree and a rock's a rock;
shoot it in Griffith Park."
Now they will not be able to charge persecution
on the part of the Hays group. In the past the
publicity department had delighted in dropping bits
of information showing how they were being tor-
tured. ... But the press agents are philosophical
about it; they say they might as well be Hays members if they are forbidden, anyway, from carrying
on the noble tradition of the elemental life. [34]

As was pointed out in discussing the profit imperative,
the fact that Republic had a straightforward no-nonsense entertainment oriented philosophy is one of the points which is
crucial in analyzing its influence on its audience.

Republic achieved early success with its serial production program and with series Westerns beginning with the
John Wayne, Bob Steele, and Gene Autry series, as well as
the group oriented Three Mesquiteers movies, and carrying
on with a multitude of similar series into the early fifties.
After the first few years of providing quality action program
pictures, Yates decided to actively expand Republic in the
direction of large budget major features. Two early examples of this type of production were Man of Conquest (1939)
with Richard Dix and Dark Command (1940) with John Wayne.
Republic had hoped for major status from the very beginning
but it took a few years to lay the firm foundation of pre-
eminence in the B market.

In its very first year the following lead in to a report on the company appeared in the New York World Telegraph:

FILM PARTNERS IN QUICK RISE
Republic Pictures Corp.   Enters "Major" Field
with Capital of $2,000,000

With many of the so-called "independent" motion picture companies increasing and improving
their product so that they are rapidly taking their
place in the "major" field--vide Columbia Pictures,

which started out as an independent producing con-
cern--it is interesting to trace the rise of the
Republic Pictures Corp....[35]

In the following year, the New York Times reported,
"Republic Pictures is aspiring to bigger and better things and
hopes, within the next year, to enter the ranks of the majors."[36]

In mid-1938, Republic seemed to make its first big
move. In the New York press, the event merited feature
coverage with some depth:

> The first problem of the producer ... is to find
> some way to take the gamble out of picture making.
> Perhaps the best formula has not been found, but
> Herbert J. Yates, founder of the three-year-old
> Republic Pictures Corp., does seem to have hit
> upon a thoroughly feasible plan. At any rate, it
> has worked, and worked well, for Republic.

CONCENTRATED ON WESTERNS

> Three years ago, when Republic made its debut
> in the industry, the company announced a complete
> program of varied photoplays, feature pictures,
> Western dramas, and serials. The program was
> completed on schedule and was generally well ac-
> cepted, but actually Republic concentrated its
> greatest efforts upon its Western drama....

START ON SERIALS

> With his first goal reached, Yates turned to new
> fields in the company's second year. Continuing
> the policy that made Republic dominant in the
> Western field, Yates planned to bring his organi-
> zation to similar eminence among producers of
> serials....
> Now, Republic has declared itself in the fight
> for leadership among producers of features.
> "Army Girl," ... is Republic's most pretentious
> feature production and is offered as a herald to
> the company's coming bid for popular acclaim in
> this new field.[37]

Frankly, Army Girl misfired as an attempted A pic-

ture but it proved to be a B feature of merit and featured
some outstanding stunt work. [38] Moreover, the tenor of the
publicity campaign as engineered by Republic represented in
the foregoing article did show that the studio was expanding
its horizons beyond its beginning borders.

Man of Conquest, a highly fictionalized action oriented
account of the life of Sam Houston, was Republic's first real
A, and special attention was provided by Rose Pelswick in
the New York Journal American: "A million dollars is a tidy
sum, even in Hollywood, and it's perfectly natural therefore
that Republic Pictures should be Pointing With Pride to its
first million dollar [the actual cost was somewhat more than
half this public relations figure] production--'Man of Conquest.' " She pointed out that in its four year existence Republic had built a reputation for serials, Westerns, and action melodramas, inexpensively but efficiently produced. She
claimed that in the process the studio had been the salvation
of many small theaters. "But while most of its films are
neither intended for nor reach the 'A' theaters, this unpretentious product means a good deal to thousands of small exhibitors throughout the country. Many a mortgage has been
saved for a small town operator." Pelswick concluded that
Republic was expanding but appreciated its already established
market.

As a matter of fact, the company has no intention
of departing from its present distribution. It is
proud of its reputation as the "King of Serials" and
the good will it enjoys. Only by this time Republic
figured it was time to step out, to produce a couple
of million dollar items and widen its distribution to
gain class as well as mass response. [Emphasis
added.][39]

Actually, as Peslwick implied, Yates had already determined to straddle the fence. He and the Republic organization wanted the status and respectability of A productions
but he realized that Republic's foundation lay in producing
good B's. Previously Variety had stated, "Yates Wants
Better B's from Republic,"[40] and the New York World Telegraph reported Yates' prediction that "Republic Will Turn
Out Escape Films."[41] In this very telling article Yates gave
in its basic form the essential philosophy on which the Republic success story (and eventual demise) was based. He
stated, "The kind of entertainment that we, at least, will
stick to will veer away from heavy dramatics or pictures of

war.   They will have to provide an escape ..., and until
new things develop the company will stand pat on its present
plans."

Yates conveniently overlooked Republic's commitment
to one service serial per year and its various patriotic and
preparedness films which were frequently war pictures.
However, "its present plans included continuing A productions
on a limited basis," Yates concluded.   In another interview,
Yates elaborated on his policy as well as his problems concerning A films:

> And about twice a year, ... we will come forth
> with our big-scale contributions....
> [I]t's especially difficult for an independent stu-
> dio to cast important films because the "name"
> players, for some reason or other--even if we pay
> them top salary and our money is as good as any-
> body else's--feel as though they're lowering them-
> selves by working for us.   Once they get going,
> however, they change their viewpoint.
> Many a fine actor has gotten his real break
> through working in independent pictures.   At Re-
> public, we don't attempt to develop personalities.
> We'd rather farm out our promising players to
> other companies and let them do the experimenting.
> Take John Wayne, for instance.   He's in our West-
> erns--which are cleaning up doubly because we
> loaned him to Wanger for "Stagecoach."[42]

Republic's own house organ, The Republic Reporter,
reflected Yates ambivalence.   During this same period, it
noted "Republic's Rise in Industry," ran newspaper quotes on
Republic as a major studio, proudly emphasized Republic's
competition with other film companies for advertising space
and trumpeted both Man of Conquest as a major production
according to famed Hollywood columnist Louella Parsons,
and headlined Dark Command, a fictional treatment of Quantrill's Raiders as an A picture.   At the same time, the company periodically pushed its serial production values, stressed
Gene Autry's popularity, openly acknowledged the importance
of Republic Westerns to the studio, and pointed out the family entertainment values of the B ranked Higgins Family
series.[43]   Republic, quite reasonably, wanted the best of
both A and B worlds.

In retrospect, Yates' decision to stay with Republic's

strong areas at this point and venture only occasionally into
A productions seemed wise. Man of Conquest was a good
beginning but a flawed one. Released in 1939, it was Republic's first serious attempt at the A movie and press releases from their house organ reflect this. Nonetheless,
Man of Conquest retained a kinship with Republic's major line
of productions. The music was good but reminiscent of
countless action films released and to be released by Republic. The action sequences were spectacular but strangely
enough seemed to lack the personal involvement, frenzy, and
spontaneity of the B Westerns and serials. The cast with
Richard Dix, Gail Patrick, and Joan Fontaine, along with
several non-studio character actors was adequate, but even
here Republic stock players such as George "Gabby" Hayes
and Max Terhune plus many bits by people like Ernie Adams,
the small "weasel" of countless B films, were in evidence.

     And the plot, despite any pretentions, boiled down to
action/adventure melodrama with even more patriotism and
honor than in the B Westerns thrown in if anything. About
three-fourths of the way through, Andrew Jackson is con-
fronting Sam Houston who is on his way to take over Texas;
Jackson delivers a no-holds-barred speech about his relation
to the United States, Houston's relation to Jackson, and
Houston's relation to the United States which, although a bit
longer and more pretentiously written, matches any morality
speech given in lesser Republic productions.

     Later, the film includes a bit of unconscious male
chauvinism. Margaret, Houston's love interest, complains
soulfully that Houston is riding off to battle and she wishes
she could do the same to which Houston romantically replies
that if she did so, he would not be able to ride back to her!

     Perhaps Otis Ferguson, noted film critic for The New
Republic, best summed up both the failure and significance of
Man of Conquest:

          Its story of Sam Houston and the grabbing off of
          Texas is perhaps less prettied up than is true of
          the run of screen epics, but its importance to the
          trade is that it was made by one of the "small"
          companies. Republic is, of course, getting larger,
          but there is always the dazzling hope that someday
          some outfit too small to tremble with such mighty
          fears as shake Metro will take on a subject that is
          not good movie taste, and do it up brown. Man of

Conquest is done brown enough--it scandalizes
history with the best of them. [44]

The film was recognized for its attempt to break into
the majors but possessed the same "flaws" of the majors'
productions without really being unique. And like the majors,
Republic and Yates had the same "fears"--or perhaps beliefs--
that the majors had. Republic could not have handled the
story of Houston any differently. It was flag waving and patriotism to the hilt as were Republic productions on all levels.
That was a major part of Republic's style.

Thus, Republic in its first time out really failed to
break free of the strictures of the product at which it did
best. Man of Conquest, for all its merits and its high budget, remained essentially in all aspects a good, expensive B
production.

And the same held true for a great many Republic A
productions through the years. John Wayne felt that Republic
could not deliver a true major production. [45] Sloan Nibley,
a writer at Republic, offered the following opinion to the
author: "Republic was never considered a 'major' lot although they did make three A's, Wake of the Red Witch,
Sands of Iwo Jima, and The Quiet Man (which was entirely
the product of John Ford and the writer Frank Nugent)....
What Republic did better than anyone else was good, fast
action shows for a price."[46] While the statement is a bit
harsh, perhaps it has an element of truth. Republic controlled A's usually lacked the class of A's produced by others
and released by the studio.

Throughout the life of Republic Pictures until a final
lingering illness in the late fifties, Herbert J. Yates ruled
the studio with an iron hand. [47] To his credit, the fact remains that his studio was a success for nearly two decades
within the parameters of its endeavors. [48] Nat Levine, the
serial genius, left within eighteen months of the merger to go
to Metro Goldwyn Mayer Studios and thence into relative ob-
scurity. [49] However, it is Levine who established the serial
format which helped make Republic the important action studio that it was and for that contribution he retains credit.
Neither Carr nor Johnston had any lasting effect on either the
Republic philosophy or production techniques and emphases
although the Monogram exchanges undoubtedly helped establish
Republic distribution.

Perhaps the best way to gauge the progress, success, and hopes of Republic is to look briefly at the rather magnificent and somewhat overpowering Tenth Anniversary brochure the studio published on itself in 1945.[50] This was the year before the motion picture industry as a whole hit its zenith in attendance and perhaps popularity. Like the entire industry, Republic was buoyant and full of high hopes. The sixty-four page booklet covered the whole spectrum of movie production, promotion, and distribution but obviously emphasized the "stars." Republic listed eighty-nine, running the gamut from John Wayne and Susan Hayward to character actors such as Tom London, sheriff, grandpa or badman in over four hundred movies, and Edward Everett Horton, bewildered comedian of sophisticated farces. Republic candidly recognized the fact that their list of "stars" included contract players and lesser lights and stated under the heading "Read Your Fortune in the Stars":

> A box office name is a name that attracts people to your theatre or a name that adds to the value of a production or a name that grows greater with each new appearance. In the eighty-odd pictures on the following pages, you will find some in each group. A few have pulling power on their own, such as John Wayne, Roy Rogers, Gene Autry, Ann Dvorak, Constance Moore, Vera Hruba Ralston, Joseph Schildkraut, Tito Guizar, names which go above the title ... real marquee names now. Then there are the featured players, the addition of whose names to any billing adds selling value to the picture. And finally the young players, the shooting stars of tomorrow. In the past Republic discovered many young players only to lose them to bigger studios. Today in our 10th Anniversary Year Republic is a "bigger" studio in its own right ... and today Republic will discover new stars ... and hold them for Republic pictures.[51]

The company recognized the importance of its foreign markets--serials and Westerns were very popular overseas and in South America where the action easily surmounted the language barriers--and pointed out, "Europe ... Asia ... South America ... Pan-America ... the Middle East ... everywhere Republic's 10th Anniversary is a big event.... Hundreds of picture-wise people in every department, all bound together by the common language of the American motion picture in general and Republic pictures in particular, enthusiastically face a future of brightest promise."[52]

In the area of product, the copy acknowledged the studio's past successful year in the area of general releases. "Last year, Republic Pictures turned out sixty-six full length feature pictures, including such honeys as 'Brazil,' 'Earl Carroll Vanities,' 'Flame of Barbary Coast' and others. Most of the scenes ... indoor and outdoor ... musical and dramatic ... costume or western ... were shot on these 135 acres ... every costume and property passed through Republic's shops and property rooms."[53] But they quickly zeroed in on the two areas for which the studio was best known.

The first was of course the serials:

> But wait ... we almost forgot the boys and girls
> who add so much bounce and zest to your theatre
> program ... those action-mad menaces, those
> thrill-tingling tanglers, those cliff-jumping, dare-
> devil, death-defying deemsters who make the hair
> stand on end and the hero get the gal ... the se-
> rial makers. To be specific, the Republic serial
> makers. The lads and lassies who put serials
> back on the "come-hither" map when they went
> into the lush comic strip field and came up with
> "The Lone Ranger" and "Captain Marvel" and
> "Dick Tracy" of hallowed ticket-selling fame.[54]

Oddly enough, Republic had made its last serial using a comic hero, Captain America, the year before. But the writers had no way of foreseeing that Republic was to forsake comic characters and turn its serials to other areas for sources so they pointed with pride to an accepted successful development.

The second area of strength was obviously the Westerns:

> And you and your box offices know that it is Re-
> public which dominates the western field. With
> Gene Autry, we started westerns back on the high
> road to fame and fortune. Now with Roy Rogers
> at the top of his stride, with Wild Bill Elliott,
> Allan Lane, Sunset Carson, "Gabby" Hayes, Bob
> Nolan and The Sons of the Pioneers, and others,
> we mean to keep them that way ... one small but
> very profitable part of Mr. Herbert Yates' 10th
> Anniversary Plan to put Republic at the top of the
> heap in 1945.[55]

The anniversary booklet concluded hopefully and forcefully:

> Watch Republic. Watch its list of big directors
> grow. Watch its list of star box office names grow.
> Watch its list of top-flight pictures grow. For
> we're headin' for the top spot in the motion picture
> industry in 1945. [56]

Ironically, while Republic specifically and Hollywood
in general had every right to expect an expanding and pros-
perous future, events were to take them in the opposite direction within another decade. The next few years did seem
to justify their optimism. But forces were in motion which
would affect the whole moving picture field and Republic was
not destined to be an exception. Some production cutbacks
in the late forties were only a slight indication of what was
to come in the fifties. Although adverse factors were to
change the entire motion picture industry, Republic, which
was a borderline case, was one of the first to feel the trem-
ors which were eventually to prove fatal. [57]

In the fifties, Republic suffered a series of setbacks
which eventually led to its demise as a producing unit. One
fact was undeniably the emergence of Vera Hruba Ralston
(later Vera Ralston). Herbert Yates attempted to make Ralston, who became his wife, into a leading star. While she
was not as poor an actress as some critics felt she was,
she simply did not have star caliber and the attempt to push
her pictures upon the exhibitors gradually discredited Republic to some degree. [58] One author summarized the situation:
"From 1941 to 1958, a Miss Vera Hruba Ralston, the wife
and perennial protégée of Republic's President, Herbert
Yates, made twenty-six indescribably inane pictures, all for
Republic, a feat of conjugal devotion (on her husband's part)
romantically credited with dispatching Republic into receiver-
ship." [59] Ralston also influenced Yates to back at least one
class production per year, such as Orson Welles' Macbeth
and John Ford's The Quiet Man. [60] These prestige productions were not always financially successful. Ralston herself
admits that, "We [she and Yates] attempted to upgrade ...
to do better things ... but it didn't always work out." [61]

It all began in 1941 when the New York Morning Tele-
graph began a story, "Figure Skating Bug Hits Republic
Head." [62] Ironically enough, the tenor of the article was that
Yates was interested in making ice pictures after seeing the

"Ice Capades" starring a Dorothy Lewis. While "Vera
Hruba" was mentioned, she was not the main thrust of the
article and her future position of influence was unforeseen.
However, she was a Czech refugee and ice skating star who
became the favorite of Yates[63] and he set out to make her a
star. By 1946, the New York Post's Screen News and Views
identified her as, "It's Vera Ralston Now - Republic's Queen
Takes 'Rib'"[64] in reference to the dropping of her Czech last
name which she had been using as a middle name. The same
article cited her as "Queen of Republic Pictures. She's the
high-budget gal, and the big box-office bambina." Ralston's
favorite director was Joseph Kane. "He is so gentle and so
understanding--and I don't react well to temperamental peo-
ple--directors, players, or anybody else." By 1953,
when she had become Yates' wife, columnist Louella Parsons
queried her, "Has being married to the owner of Republic
Studios made any difference in your career?" She replied,
"No, I don't think so, ... I've always worked hard because
I knew I had a lot to learn."[65]

Unfortunately, Republic stockholders felt differently
and in 1956, the New York Times noted, "Investors Sue
Yates: Charge He Used Film Company Funds for Wife's
Career."[66] The Herald Tribune was even more specific and
stated, "Allege 18 Vera Ralston Films Flopped."[67] At this
point she had appeared in twenty films. The Daily News chose
to headline the odds, "Suit Calls Film Tycoon's Wife 9-1
Floperoo."[68] Ralston was to go on to make six more pictures through 1958 when another suit was instituted charging
that Yates operated Republic "as though it were a private
family-owned business."[69] This he had done from the beginning although during the years of profit, it was accepted.
These lawsuits were symptomatic of the problems Republic
faced. While Ralston's lack of box-office appeal did contribute to the situation, it was only a part of the setbacks which
beset the studio.

It is true that many actors resented working with Ralston and that superstar-to-be John Wayne even then had the
clout to refuse additional pictures with her. This oft re-
peated charge was commented on by Maurice Zolotow, Wayne's
biographer: "Determined to make his movie about the Alamo,
Wayne was beset by problems with Yates. Already Yates was
looking for ways to make his dearly beloved, Vera Hruba
Ralston, a co-star of this epic. Wayne rebelled at making
pictures with Vera Ralston. She had made twelve pictures
for Republic since 1945, and only two showed a profit, the

ones with Wayne."[70] Ralston did not appear in The Alamo, made later and away from Republic. But she did appear in the Wayne produced The Fighting Kentuckian which hastened the break between Wayne and Republic. Wayne is quoted as saying, "Yates made me use Vera Hruba.... I don't want to malign her. She didn't have the experience. She didn't have the right accent.... Yates made me cast her. It hurt the picture.... I've always been mad at Yates about this because we lost the chance to have one damn fine movie.... Yates was one of the smartest businessmen I ever met. I respected him in many ways, and he liked me. But when it came to the woman he loved--his business brains just went flyin' out the window."[71] It was the last picture Ralston made with John Wayne.

Nonetheless, Ralston was not the sole downfall of Republic. She herself feels that she was the victim of poor material.[72] Perhaps the last word on the Ralston controversy belongs to director Joseph Kane who helmed nine of her twenty-six pictures:

> She was very nice to work with. She was in the same sort of position with Yates as Marion Davies was with William Randolph Hearst. So, if she'd been that sort of person, she could have made it rough for everybody. Naturally, when you're in that kind of position with the boss, you can do anything you want. She never took advantage of that situation. She was always very cooperative, worked very hard, tried very hard.

> But, you know, the public is a very funny thing. The public either accepts you or it doesn't, and there's nothing you can do about it. If they don't go for you, well, that's it.[73]

Another factor in Republic's demise was the competition of television. Republic had the knowledge, the facilities, and the technical ability to make good competitive television series. In fact the company won an Emmy (television's version of the Academy Awards Oscar) for its Stories of the Century television series.[74] This was one of the few television series which the studio attempted. Utilizing years of exciting stock footage, the series offered Western action in a pseudo historical setting with different famous desperadoes meeting justice each week. Nonetheless, Republic really failed to meet the competition of television. The

popularity of Stories of the Century proved to be an exception
and, after a few less successful series, Republic used its
television arm as a means of releasing old movies to television. When the studio did not develop an active television
production unit in its own right to any appreciable degree,
other television units took over Republic's specialty. Com-
plicating the problem was the fact that Republic also sold its
extensive library of old films to television in the fifties.

Yates early realized the potential advantages of selling
Republic movies to television. He used the Hollywood Television Service (Republic's television division) not only to
make series for the medium but also to handle the leasing of
Republic's old product which was a natural for the youthful
industry. However, difficulties quickly arose. In October,
1951, Roy Rogers sued to ban the showing of his old features
on television for commercial purposes arguing that it implied
product endorsement and therefore damaged his professional
name. The courts found in his favor. But then in May,
1952, the courts decided against Gene Autry in a similar
suit thus throwing the whole controversy into a state of total
confusion. [75]

However, Republic went ahead with plans to make its
product available to television and late in 1952, Variety reported, "200 G Rep Deal Releasing 104 Pix for TV Seen
Breaking Log Jam," but noted that the Autry-Rogers films
were still questionable. [76] (It was not until 1960 that the
complete package was made available.) [77] But, in making
this move, Republic was one of the first large, active studios to make a deal with television.

Three years later, Republic went the rest of the way.
In a story entitled, "Republic to Rent Top Films to TV:
Studio to Offer 76 Features, Valued at $40,000,000--Plans
No Outright Sale," it was pointed out that, "the studio has
made some 300 of its old 'B' products and low-budget Westerns available to TV in the past." [78] Ironically, four months
later the same source included a story, "Republic Starts
Cutback in Staff." [79] This undoubtedly contributed to the next
development.

In January, 1958, the Screen Actors Guild and the
Writers Guild of America threatened to strike Republic over
the question of residual payments to post 1948 films released
to television. [80] The next month the writers did vote to
strike and Republic was eventually forced to give way on the
issue of residuals. [81]

        The decision to provide their old films to television
proved a misjudgment on Republic's part in yet even another
way in retrospect. This sale represented one of the first
such major packages to be sold to television. Unfortunately,
this move tended to discredit Republic in the motion picture
exchanges so that their theatrical productions did not get
proper circulation. [82] Another competitive factor was that the
major studios, noting the success of Republic over the years,
finally began to compete with that studio on the same ground
in making low budget action films utilizing the techniques,
the lessons, and sometimes even the personnel of Republic. [83]
The majors were always better able to circulate their now
competitive product in the theatrical markets than Republic,
especially given Republic's mishandling of the television issue. [84]

        The final factor in Republic's collapse is more difficult
to document but perhaps ultimately it was the greatest factor of
all. Scholar Francis Nevins hits on it briefly. "My conversa-
tions with Bill Witney and Dave Sharpe, my reading of such
reminiscences as those of Joseph Kane, and my general
gestalt of what was going on at Republic have led me to conclude that what killed Republic was not competition from the
majors; it was Herbert Yates' obsession with sinking all his
profits from the action picture into super-productions starring
Vera Ralston, combined with the fact that the rise of TV
ended the traditional Saturday matineegoing habits of America's
children, combined with post-WWII inflation and union demands
[emphasis added]. "[85]

        Besides providing a nice summary, Nevins also voices
an additional important point. Republic was tops at escapist
fare--Westerns, serials, series, and country Western musicals and this was what the audience thrived on in the Depression thirties and the war years of the forties. By the fifties
middle American values prevailed, luxuries were more abun-
dant, and the audience preferred harsh realism and downbeat
excitement in their movies. Interest in the old escapist fare
was relegated predominantly to television. The Saturday
Matinee died.

        Republic just did not adapt. The need for change in
B film subject matter to meet audience demands was covered
by Joe Solomon, active B and exploitation film producer of
the seventies, in an interview in Kings of the Bs. [86] To
survive, the B film producer anticipated or quickly followed
the latest audience fads in what had become a market with
accelerating changes in popularity Solomon felt. With a few

mately fifty to sixty pictures a year in its prime but only
twenty-six in 1957, seventeen in 1958, and five in 1959.
Most of these were produced elsewhere.

Herbert J. Yates authored a column in 1953 in which
he summarized Republic's position and his plans for the future. In view of Republic's increasing difficulty concerning
the competition for distribution and exhibitors, as stated
above (p. 24), the article takes on an added interest.

> There is no one person who has all the answers
> to the problems which must be faced in 1953; but,
> at least from Republic's viewpoint, I have formu-
> lated a definite program for our business platform.
>   Republic for the past two years has streamlined
> its production organization. We have economized
> in our studio costs, but not at the expense of en-
> tertainment values appearing on the screen. In
> fact, our cost-per-picture-produced is higher than
> ever, because of increased production magnitude,
> best casts, and the public demand for pictures in
> color. We will make at least 20 deluxe pictures
> for the new season, at costs ranging from $750,000
> to $1,500,000. Our production budget will be tri-
> ple the amount that Republic has ever spent on any
> season's product.
>   From our experience with pictures like "The
> Quiet Man," we know that few pictures gross what
> is regarded as abnormal business. However, the
> average deluxe picture, costing up to $1,000,000,
> has a hard time recouping its negative cost. A
> few super-grossing deluxe pix can't keep the pro-
> ducers in business, nor can they sustain the large
> number of 'A' theatres that depend upon this type
> of product.
>   Thus, the problem represents a triple responsi-
> bility for producer, distributor, and exhibitor. If
> the producer makes marketable 'A' pictures that
> the public will buy, and the distributor merchan-
> dises the picture in such a way as to arouse au-
> dience interest, it still remains for the exhibitor--
> the most important link in the Hollywood to the
> public chain--to bring people into the theatre by
> solid promotion which takes advantage of intrinsic
> audience value and national preselling.
>   The production of a program of 'A' pictures is
> the gamble that Republic is taking in 1953, and it

exceptions, Republic tried to continue to provide the same
quality, but outmoded, entertainment to an audience who had
either outgrown it in the fifties or absorbed it for free on
their home television. By way of illustration, Ed Bernds
who directed B's for Columbia, Allied Artists, and American
International during his long career, and who has provided
valuable contrasting viewpoints said that he and other Columbia directors referred to Republic "as the home of entrenched
mediocrity" and felt that "Yates made the Republic personnel
so conservative that they didn't adapt" thus leading to the
failure of Republic. Bernds felt that Yates was very loyal
but stifled initiative in his staff. [87]

Needless to say, Republic workers interpreted the
situation somewhat differently. Albert S. Rogell, Republic
director and leading cameraman/second feature director
from the twenties to the fifties, felt that Yates' tight budgets
caused his people to be very imaginative and to create good
films under adverse conditions and rigid deadlines. [88] Others
voiced variations on the opinion that Republic was resource-
ful in its day but acknowledged that Republic played itself
out in the early fifties. Perhaps Sloan Nibley, Republic
writer after World War II, best capsulized it when he said
that "Republic had the right formula at the right time ... it
was an unconscious success ... Republic had it at the right
time but didn't even know it. "[89] When the times changed,
Republic did not change the formula--at least not enough.
Perhaps the studio was too busy trying to cope with other
more concrete problems it faced in the fifties. Perhaps it
just lacked imaginative leadership.

The decline was of course a gradual process, and
there were continuing hopeful signs but it was just so much
whistling in the wind. The following headlines from the
New York Times are indicative of Republic's prolonged
"last Hurrah":

> Republic Is Adding Four Sound Stages
> Republic to Offer Independents Aid
> Republic Studios Continue to Grow
> Republic Raises Production List
> Republic Studios to Resume Work
> Republic Studios Expanding Plant. [90]

Production was suspended several times in the mid-fifties
and periodically announced as resuming thereafter but finally
ceased in 1956. Republic had produced and released approxi-

is the gamble that every other producer in Hollywood will have to take. How many pictures will
be produced in 1954 and how many theatres will
continue to operate will depend on what returns the
producer and the theatre will receive on the majority of 'A' pictures produced for 'A' houses in
1953. We are selecting our stories not only for
their entertainment but for exploitation values as
well.

   Competition from television will increase. In
areas that have television, more stations will be
added. In many cities that have not had television
competition in 1952, there will be stations in 1953.
But I believe Republic's large investment in 1953
is justified and reasonable business risk. If I
weren't, I wouldn't be in the picture business. [91]

His assessment of the condition of the motion picture industry was accurate for the time. His projection of Republic's
future was not.

   In late 1957, Republic resigned from the Motion Picture Association and the Motion Picture Export Association.
Variety noted, "Republic bowout is said to be based on economical considerations since the company is folding its overseas setup and plans to retain only a few territorial operations."[92] Considering the popularity of its product in the
foreign market, this move was especially indicative of what
was developing. In February, 1958, it was rumored Republic was going to close its remaining domestic branches and
it was pointed out that it had "virtually dissolved its distribution organization" and had lost $1,362,420 in 1957.[93]

   At the annual stockholders meeting in 1958, Yates announced, "We have one problem--getting out of the motion-
picture business." One anguished stockholder inquired, "What
happened to your vision, Mr. Yates?"[94] But Yates who was
tired and ill no longer had the interest or the vision.[95] He
had lost his enthusiasm for film making and with his exit the
producing end of the business ceased.

   On July 1, 1959, Yates relinquished control of Republic to Victor M. Carter, California banker and real estate
operator. For all practical purposes Republic was declared
dead as a motion picture studio. An article in Variety headlined, "Fading, Fading--One-Man Rule, Yates' Republic Exit
Latest Instance," and indicated that Carter and his associates

paid Yates and his family "slightly under $6,000,000."[96]
The Carter administration decided not to continue to make
new films for theatres or television. The Consolidated Film
Industries would be operated as in its beginning. It would
be a processing and releasing organization, and the studio
would be made available for television and theatrical production rentals from other firms. The studio's first major
rental was Dick Powell's Four Star International, Inc., a
major television producer.

With new administrative operations in effect, the company was once more on solid ground. Old films were made
available for televiewing and theatrical releases. But the
Carter regime was not committed to film. The conglomerate
had other priorities as indicated by the following headline
from Variety: "Plastics the Charmer in Bettered Earnings
Picture for Republic."[97] Under those circumstances, it
comes as no surprise that on May 4, 1963, it was reported
"C. B. S. Gets 10-Year Lease on Coast Republic Studio."[98]
The property valued at close to ten million dollars had been
taken over by the Columbia Broadcasting System with a ten
year lease and an option to buy after that time, which was
exercised in February, 1967.[99] The studio, now known as
Studio Center, is presently the West Coast production headquarters for the C. B. S. television network. Republic still
exists on paper but the past glories of the studio are no more
except in ever increasing revivals. National Telefilm Associates, the legal owner, repository, and distributor of most
Republic films and related material, reports that not only
are Republic packages for television in demand, but Republic
pictures are also continually circulating in foreign theatres
throughout the World.[100] Interestingly enough, after the deal
with the Columbia Broadcasting System was concluded it was
generally confirmed and acknowledged within the industry that
the technical facilities of Republic Studios were still far superior in all respects even to those of the major studios.[101]

Opinions on Republic seem to vary and frequently reach
extremes. Those who are critical give Republic and Yates
no credit. Fans tend to be overzealous, nostalgic, and de-
fensive. Walter Abel, well known character actor and Paramount contract player active in movies in the thirties and
forties, was a professional of wide experience and some objectivity. He did a two-week B feature, Who Killed Aunt
Maggie?, at Republic in 1940. As an outsider without an
axe to grind or special interest in the studio his opinion
represents a reliable middle ground. Abel contended that

Yates did not regard himself or his studio as inferior in the
Hollywood system, noting that he did not keep a stable of
name actors but produced his own kind of pictures and had
his own small distribution setup. Abel regarded Republic
as "better than poverty row" and Yates as "a small scale
Harry Cohn ... [however] he was considerate of actors but
he had to work like hell." Abel did not resent his stint at
Republic and indicated "it was just another job." The picture was "a great hit in the South," and "a damned good
little mystery ... but would have been great at another studio." Abel also credits Yates for urging him to accept the
Paramount contract offer. [102] His characterization of Yates
and Republic sums both up well--a successful Hollywood executive whose studio made a quality product within limits
which was aimed at a specific audience to make a profit
with no further pretensions.

Notes

1. Robert Sklar, Movie Made America: A Social History
    of American Movies (New York: Random House,
    1975), p. 162
2. 1956 International Motion Picture Almanac (New York:
    Quigley Publishing Company, 1956), pp. 446-47
3. Gene Fernett, Next Time Drive Off the Cliff! (Cocoa,
    Florida: Cinememories Publishing Company, 1968),
    p. 143
4. Republic 1935-36 Attractions Now Available! (Los An-
    geles: Republic Pictures, 1935).
5. Sam Sherman, "Hollywood Thrill Factory, Part I,"
    Screen Thrills Illustrated, I (January, 1963), p. 28.
    Allen Eyles, John Wayne and the Movies (Cranbury,
    New Jersey: A. S. Barnes, 1976), p. 45 lists the
    cost as $37,000 but agrees with Sherman on its prof-
    itability and significance to the Wayne series.
6. December 18, 1936.
7. New York Sun, May 4, 1936
8. The birth of the B picture is covered in depth in King
    of the B's: Working Within the Hollywood System:
    An Anthology of Film History and Criticism, Edited
    by Todd McCarthy and Charles Flynn (New York: E.
    P. Dutton and Company, Inc., 1975), pp. 13-32.
9. Republic personnel consistently played down the artistic
    aspects of their films preferring to emphasize that
    they did their best to provide entertainment for a
    profit. Of the twenty-four persons interviewed only
    one played down the profit motivation but she acknow-

ledged its existence. Telephone interview with Vera
H. Ralston, Republic actress, Santa Barbara, California, May 10, 1976.

10. Sklar, pp. 86-87.
11. Roman Freulich and Joan Abramson, Forty Years in
    Hollywood: Portraits of a Golden Age (Cranbury,
    New Jersey: A. S. Barnes, 1971), p. 114.
12. "Republic Pictures Studio," The Hollywood Reporter,
    1938, p. 5. Extensive correspondence with the news-
    paper has failed to uncover the actual date of publi-
    cation although the supplement is clearly identified as
    a product of The Hollywood Reporter. The supple-
    ment was located in the Republic clipping file at the
    Margaret Herrick Library of the Academy of Motion
    Picture Arts and Sciences.
13. "Republic Pictures Studio," p. 5.
14. "Republic Pictures Studio," p. 5.
15. "Republic Pictures Studio," p. 17.
16. "Republic Pictures Studio," p. 21.
17. Sample budgets in each category are reproduced in
    McCarthy and Flynn, pp. 26-29.
18. McCarthy and Flynn, p. 30.
19. Letter from Sloan Nibley, Republic writer, January 19,
    1976.
20. See the Yates authored article, pp. 26-27, supra.
21. Source: Motion Picture Almanac, 1941-1959 cited in
    McCarthy and Flynn, p. 32.
22. Sherman, "Part I", p. 28. Morris R. Abrams, while
    admitting the technical excellence, has an interesting
    viewpoint. He feels that the quality of Republic B's
    was strictly an economic factor. The studio devel-
    oped technical sophistication because speed was
    needed to compete in the low budget field. Thus a
    need to "keep jobs" caused the studio to improve
    techniques to best the competition and incidently lead
    to a quality product which resulted in a "brand iden-
    tification"--that is, Republic's B's stood out. (Inter-
    view with Morris R. Abrams, Republic script super-
    visor and assistant director, Los Angeles, California,
    May 17, 1976.)
23. "Republic Pictures Studio," p. 25. "Republic fits that
    unique niche of being a coordinating, producing com-
    pany rather than a competitive one." In other words,
    Republic took up the slack and filled a need ignored
    by the majors.
24. Don Daynard, "The Film Music of Stanley Wilson", The
    New Captain George's Whizzbang, no. 17 (n. d.), p. 15.

25. Most of these men were craftsmen who remained active
    in their fields following the demise of Republic. Most
    moved into television and some remain active today.
    The latter include William Witney, David Sharpe, Bud
    Thackery, Barry Shipman, and Sloan Nibley. A few
    such as Yakima Canutt, Victor Young and Cy Feuer
    achieved fame in their areas of expertise beyond Re-
    public.
26. Leonard Maltin, The Great Movie Shorts (New York:
    Crown, 1972), p. 27. Although essentially accurate
    in spirit, Maltin's statement does overlook a brief
    series of world travelogues from Republic entitled
    This World of Ours (32 entries, 1950-1955), a similar
    series of United States travelogues entitled Land of
    Opportunity (four entries, 1950), and other diverse
    short subjects. Republic's total for short subjects
    has been listed as 78 and a few more have been dis-
    covered in recent years.
27. Michael Wood, America in the Movies, or Santa Maria,
    It Had Slipped My Mind (New York: Basic Books,
    1975), p. 23.
28. New York Post, September 30, 1942.
29. April 6, 1939.
30. August 16, 1939.
31. May 30, 1940.
32. March 4, 1941.
33. New York Times, February 18, 1942.
34. September 7, 1941.
35. April 7, 1935.
36. August 30, 1936.
37. New York Herald Telegraph, July 13, 1938.
38. Bob Thomas, "Hollywood's General of the Armies,"
    True XXX (July, 1966), p. 87.
39. April 23, 1939.
40. February 22, 1939.
41. September 9, 1939.
42. New York Post, May 2, 1939. Compare this statement
    as it concerns contract players with the Republic
    philosophy on the same subject six years later (see
    p. 18).
43. The Republic Reporter I (April 25, 1939), p. 1. I
    (May 16, 1939), p. 3. I (August 19, 1939), p. 4.
    I (September 6, 1939), p. 4. I (January 9, 1940),
    p. 1. I (June 28, 1939), p. 2. I (August 4, 1939),
    p. 1. I (August 4, 1939), p. 2. I (September 18,
    1939), p. 5.
44. Robert Wilson, ed., The Film Criticism of Otis Fergu-

son (Philadelphia: Temple University Press, 1971), p. 259.

45. Maurice Zolotow, Shooting Star: A Biography of John Wayne (New York: Simon and Schuster, 1974), p. 154.

46. Letter, January 19, 1976. Republic did make other A films of course. Vera H. Ralston claims that Yates did have input into the scripts for all major Republic productions. (Telephone interview, Santa Barbara, California, May 19, 1976.) In the case of The Quiet Man, however, Ford did retain more control than normally allowed at Republic.

47. Variety, July 8, 1959.

48. Sam Sherman, "Hollywood Thrill Factory, Part 2", Screen Thrills Illustrated, I (October 1, 1963), p. 13.

49. Fernett, p. 137.

50. 10 Years of Progress: Republic Pictures Corporation: 10th Anniversary, 1935-1945 (Los Angeles: Republic Pictures Corporation, [1945]), unpaged.

51. 10 Years, [p. 24].

52. 10 Years, [p. 39].

53. 10 Years, [p. 49].

54. 10 Years, [p. 51].

55. 10 Years, [p. 51].

56. 10 Years, [p. 51].

57. These events, which are covered to some extent in the text, are covered more in detail in "Exit (As Expected) of Republic From MPEA [Motion Picture Export Association] First in O'Seas Body's History," Variety, December 11, 1957 and "Fading, Fading--One-Man Rule: Yates' Republic Exit Latest Instance," Variety, July 8, 1959. A copy of a short history of the studio prepared as a five page manuscript in 1963 for publicity use in studio rental and leasing was provided to the author by Ernest Kirkpatrick of National Telefilm Associates and previously in Republic's business division. In covering the studio's switch from active production to rental to outside producers, the document refers to the early decline of Republic as a movie producer. History of Republic Pictures, p. 3. Mr. Kirkpatrick did not know who wrote the manuscript.

58. Harry Sanford, "Joseph Kane: A Director's Story, Part 1 and Part 2", Views and Reviews, V (September, 1973), pp. 21-28, and V (December, 1973), pp. 17-25.

59. McCarthy and Flynn, pp. 50-51.

60. Interview with Anthony Slide, then of the American
     Film Institute, January 18, 1975.
61. Telephone interview with Vera H. Ralston, Santa Bar-
     bara, California, May 10, 1976.
62. June 14, 1941.
63. Diane Scott, "Memory Wears Carnations," Photoplay
     LXXII (May, 1949), pp. 34-35.
64. June 4, 1946.
65. New York Journal American, February 8, 1953.
66. October 30, 1956.
67. October 30, 1956.
68. October 30, 1956.
69. New York Post, August 20, 1958.
70. Zolotow, p. 251.
71. Zolotow, p. 252.
72. Telephone interview with Vera H. Ralston, Santa Bar-
     bara, California, May 10, 1976. She said in part,
     "I was satisfied with Republic as a studio but not
     satisfied with the material. I had no decent chance.
     The material didn't fit me.... Yes, the writing was
     not good but I was under contract and [had to] do what
     was required."
73. McCarthy and Flynn, p. 322.
74. Sherman, "Part 2," p. 15.
75. New York Times, May 15, 1952. The Times headlined,
     "TV-Movie Tie-ins Remain Confused." On June 9,
     1954, the Wall Street Journal noted, "Republic Pic-
     tures Upheld in Autry, Rogers Suits."
76. December 17, 1952.
77. Variety, October 12, 1960.
78. New York Times, January 13, 1956.
79. New York Times, May 23, 1956.
80. New York Times, January 22, 1958.
81. Variety, February 19, 1958.
82. Sherman, "Part 2", p. 16. Also Variety, June 13,
     1951. In an article entitled "Myers, Renbusch Blast
     Rep on Plan for Selling to TV," Abram F. Myers,
     Chairman of Allied State Association, is quoted as
     saying, "No doubt, exhibitors will be very bitter to-
     ward Republic." Truman Rembusch, President of the
     exhibitors organization, expressed similar opinions
     calling Republic's move "foolish."
83. It has been already noted that Republic personnel often
     went to major studios upon leaving Republic. How-
     ever, some Republic personnel worked major studios
     simultaneously with their work at Republic. Mark
     Hall interview with David Sharpe, Republic stuntman,

August, 1976, American Film Institute Oral History
Program, American Film Institute, Los Angeles,
California.

84. Interview with Anthony Slide, then of the American
Film Institute, January 18, 1975. See also foot-
note 82.

85. Letter, January 20, 1976.

86. McCarthy and Flynn, p. 144.

87. Interview with Ed Bernds, Los Angeles, California,
May 6, 1976.

88. Interview with Albert S. Rogell, Los Angeles, California, May 5, 1976.

89. Interview with Sloan Nibley, Los Angeles, California,
May 4, 1976.

90. June 16, 1953; September 11, 1953; August 7, 1954;
February 3, 1955; January 8, 1957; June 14, 1957.

91. "Top Cost Pix Shed," Variety, January 7, 1953.

92. December 1, 1957.

93. Variety, February 12, 1958.

94. Time Magazine, LXXXIX (April 14, 1958), p. 56.

95. Interview with Albert S. Rogell, Republic director,
Los Angeles, California, May 5, 1976; Roland
"Dick" Hills, Republic office manager, Los Angeles, California, May 13, 1976; and Morris R.
Abrams, Republic script supervisor and assistant
director, Los Angeles, California, May 17, 1976.
All indicated that Yates was ill, that his attitude
changed in the last years of Republic, and that this
was a major factor in the studio's failure to adapt.

96. July 8, 1959.

97. October 12, 1960.

98. New York Times.

99. New York Times, February 24, 1967.

100. Interviews with Rex Waggoner, National Telefilm Asso-
ciates, Publicity Director, and Ernest Kirkpatrick,
National Telefilm Associates, Technical Services,
May 12, 1976. Also Variety, July 17, 1974.

101. Sherman, "Part 2," p. 16.

102. Interview with Walter Abel by Milton Plesur, Professor
of History, State University of New York at Buffalo,
New York, New York, March 1, 1976.

Chapter II

FILM STUDIES AND REPUBLIC

The predominant theme of the following chapters is
basically that the movies during their period of greatest
strength were not interested in art or influence but in profits,
that quality productions nonetheless did have a very basic impact on the audiences, and that the B films, which were routine
programmers inexpensively produced, by the very fact of being unpretentious and extensively viewed especially in the
rural and urban neighborhood areas, did carry more effectiveness in reaching the audience with straightforward messages than has been previously acknowledged or credited to
them.

This hypothesis relies on primary material relative
to Republic Pictures, perhaps the best of the B studios, and
on film writing in both scholarly and fan publications. With
this in mind, a survey of these works as they relate to the
theme to be presented will be helpful. The goals, methods,
and capsulization of the conclusion will be outlined in con-
junction with a survey of previous studies.

First, there are the popular or fan treatments which
tend to emphasize some combination of nostalgia, reminiscences specifically on Republic Pictures, B movie recollec-
tions, or anecdotes on serials and Westerns. These are
normally non-academic, enjoyable, sometimes quite factual
and informative but completely unpretentious and should be
used guardedly due to varying standards. The second category is scholarly works which stress the place of the movies in history, the influence of the cinema, and which tend
to emphasize the A picture or occasionally the "sleeper"
B--a "sleeper" B being a routine inexpensive program filler
which due to critics and unrecognized quality is elevated to
the position of a classic film after release. While some film
scholarship strains for significance, several academic works
do reach conclusions which can be applied to the B film in
general.

Small as the Republic Pictures studio was and limited
as its product emphasis chose to be, there is enough of interest in the Republic story to fill a multivolume series dealing with the history, production techniques, limitations, personnel, and goals of this leading smaller studio. This study
is aimed at explaining the audience influence and the industry
significance of Republic as represented in the studio's most
successful products. To accomplish this goal, appropriate
ideas from both fan and scholarly publications have been combined with information from the files of Republic as well as
contemporary observations.

Rapid movement became the key to Republic's
success. Despite scripting deficiencies, the head-
long pace and exemplary action sequences were soon
realized as the crowd pleasers, and the sort of thing
the Republic crews accomplished best. Nor was it a
small accomplishment. Action sequences are tough,
time-consuming to stage, and were usually not fully
appreciated by audiences for their worth. A film
without lags, even an action film, is a rarity; pacing
is one of the hardest aspects of film making to overcome. Credit or blame is shared by writer, director,
cutter, producer. And to their credit, Republic pictures began early to move, and fast.[1*]

Republic had moved up fast to become contenders.
Their more elaborate films were good and solid.
But the studio subsisted on the bread-and-butter movies, and after the attempt at versatility in the beginning, turned inexorably toward the action, mystery,
adventure type of mass-audience budget job, sure to
please the paying customers if not the critics. None
of them were world-beaters, and more than a few
would have been better off buried in quicklime in the
dark recesses of some back lot. However their average was good and the pictures accomplished what they
set out to do.[2]

These two quotes perhaps best summarize the mystique
of Republic Pictures Corporation both for the fans of action films
and students of the B cinema. There has been a series of volumes, both amateur fan publications and commercial professional treatments, which pertain at least peripherally to B films,
action pictures, or Republic. And Republic was synonymous

---

with B films and action pictures.   Yet none of these really
captures the flavor of Republic productions which gave them
their significance.   The preceding statements neatly capsulize
the essence of Republic but the work from which they were
taken is an overview of the B film with only two chapters
devoted to the studio in question and the author does not attempt to delve into the potential significance and influence of
the best of the B studios. [3]

Alan G. Barbour, an ex-businessman turned fan and
commercial publisher of film material, has for many years
been attentive to Republic. [4]   But his works are basically
photographs, ads, pressbooks, and other studio releases fla-
vored with brief, nostalgia-laden, introductory texts which,
while they occasionally turn a good phrase or hit lightly on
an important point, are not meant to be scholarly cinema
studies--nor has he ever claimed otherwise.   They do have
the merit of preserving intact and making available valuable
studio material.

Gene Fernett has written two episodic studies relating
to the B films.   The first, entitled Next Time Drive Off the
Cliff, [5] was on Mascot Studios, an immediate predecessor of
Republic responsible for the studio's serial emphasis, and
contained some interesting information concerning Republic
pre-history.   The second, called Hollywood's Poverty Row, [6]
was made up of individual chapters on various studios who
located at least temporarily along the famous, or to the elite
studios infamous, Gower Gulch--so named because independent producers of Westerns located often on Gower Street in
Hollywood.   Here again, the section on Republic contains a
few informative statements.   However, Fernett's books lack
depth and consistency and must be used cautiously.

Several publications have been completely devoted to
serials--often with emphasis on Republic serials.   The jour-
nals and books range from good to poor but all are intended
to be popular and are aimed at the fan market.   Robert Malcomson, a fan publisher, put out twenty-nine chapters of
Those Enduring Matinee Idols[7] totaling well over four hundred
pages.   Although TEMI was a "fanzine", it was well done
and published a great deal of value including the transcripts
of interviews with and panel discussions involving Republic
personnel.   However, with only a few significant exceptions,
TEMI was not analytical or interpretative. [8]   The same can
be said of Jeff Walton's Serial World[9] which is still being
published.   It is a newer fanzine and as yet lacks the polish

or even depth of TEMI. It does, however, include valuable
information and interviews.

Kalton C. Lahue has published two books on silent
serials which refer only occasionally to Republic.[10] Jim
Harmon and Donald F. Glut wrote The Great Serial Heroes[11]
and, while the book is an undocumented popular treatment
aimed at the general audience, it makes some telling criticisms of individual Republic productions. The same cannot
be said of Ken Weiss' and Ed Goodgold's volume, To Be Continued.... This is an encyclopedia approach, summarizing
all 231 sound serials, which unfortunately is riddled with er-
rors and poor editing.[12] There is no interpretative coverage
save a short introduction. The sole book dealing with sound
serials which lays any claim to the scholarly approach is
Raymond William Stedman's The Serials: Suspense and Drama
by Installments.[13] Stedman covers not only movie serials,
both silent and sound, but also radio and television serials.
While having scholarly pretentions, the work is a surface
treatment and ends up more popular than academic. It still
has some merit for light reading purposes and as a very
general overview.

In many respects, the most interesting book in the
area of Republic serials is Jack Mathis' Valley of the Cliffhangers.[14] Privately published, this book is massive, over-
sized, and expensive ($66.00). It is sumptuously laid out--
Mathis is in the advertising profession--and includes an abun-
dance of information on Republic serials. Mathis interviewed
numerous Republic people, did extensive research in primary
sources, and developed a detailed chronological coverage of
Republic serials. Mathis had access to the Republic business
files and extensive references are made to them. The major
drawback to the Mathis study is his inclusion of excessive detail on minor points in the serials and too much emphasis on
source materials such as historical incidents, novels, comics,
rather than the serials themselves. Still, his volume provides
a wealth of primary references and he and his collaborators
have salvaged important data before they were destroyed by
time, neglect, and disinterest on the part of their owners.
The work is objective, documentary, and apparently aimed
at the hard core fan as opposed to subjective, interpretative,
and scholarly. He includes nothing on the influence or significance of the Republic serials except by inference. Mathis
is currently gathering materials for an objective overview of
Republic tentatively entitled Republic Confidential aimed for
1982 but he has stated that there is to be little on the sig-

nificance of the Republic product--and that will not be interpretative.[15]

There are of course innumerable books devoted to the
Westerns but none exclusively to Republic. A series of B
Western filmographies which frequently relates to Republic
Westerns has been edited by Les Adams and is entitled Yesterday's Saturdays,[16] but these are basically documentation
without any analysis. The various volumes devoted to the
Western in general either ignore Republic save for an infrequent A production or acknowledge the studio's superiority
in brief chapters devoted to the B Western. Most tend to
go no further than to mention the Gene Autry-Roy Rogers
musical Western series, often in a critical way. Don Miller's Hollywood Corral, mentioned above (p. 37) is one exception. William K. Everson, a film scholar equally at home
with popular treatments, is another outstanding exception in
clearly singling out Republic for its production values.[17]
Everson's acknowledgment of Republic stems from his willing-
ness to accept the importance of the serial and the B film
to the general history of cinema development especially in
Hollywood. Other writers on the Hollywood Western prefer
to emphasize the art of the A production. These general
treatments on the Western film are included in the bibliography and where appropriate in the text but will not be indi-
vidually covered in this introduction since their importance
to this study is peripheral at best.

There are also many articles relating to various Republic series, actors, directors or other personnel in such
diverse periodicals as Views and Reviews, Screen Facts,
Captain George's Whizzbang, Film Collector's Registry,
Film Fan Monthly, and even Playboy to mention only a few.
These are invariably popular pieces and with the exception
of an occasional article by a fan, fail to consider the importance of the studio or even to pinpoint its uniqueness in the
B film field.

Even the frequently praised anthology of interviews,
essays, and filmographies compiled by Tod McCarthy and
Charles Flynn[18] fails to do justice to either Republic or the
value of its output. While there are several references to
and acknowledgments of the general superiority of Republic,
this anthology is aimed more at defining, explaining, and
analyzing the philosophies of B films and recording the opinions of B film personnel. There are some perceptive statements concerning the importance of the B's in McCarthy and

Flynn which will be utilized in the present study but essentially the drift of their book is broad, and as such, it does
not really focus on Republic satisfactorily.

The influence of the motion picture industry as a
whole and the artistic and sociological interpretation of various aspects of the Hollywood film have been frequently treated
from the academic viewpoint increasingly in the last decade
although some of the better studies came earlier. None of
these studies, early or recent, has concentrated on Republic
or any phase of the B film. In fact, they have made no
more than passing mention of Republic or its type of product
in most instances. Nonetheless, they have provided points of
discussion relating to the B's and Republic just as have the
popular treatments discussed above.

Disregarding for the moment most of the psychological
interpretations of the movies (these are more appropriate to
Chapter III), one of the earlier academic studies which related heavily to film falls more into the common sense school
of thought and is quite sympathetic in tone to the general
themes which are to be developed. Robert Warshow's The
Immediate Experience[19] makes much of the point that when
the critic places psychological, sociological, or other intellectual interpretations between himself and the film, he is
missing the impact. Lionel Trilling aptly summarizes this
most important point in introducing Warshow's posthumous
book in pointing out that "Warshow speaks ... of those critics who deal seriously with film either in the aesthetic way
or in the sociological and psychological way and who, by one
intellectual means or another, forbid themselves 'the immediate experience of seeing and responding to the movies as
most of us see and respond to them.'... He meant, of course,
that the man watches the movie with some degree of involvement and pleasure in it.... And of himself as the man who
watches the movie, Warshow says that in some way he takes
'all that nonsense' seriously."[20] A man involves himself in
the fantasy of the movie and not in an analysis of it. As
shall be seen, a great many film historians and critics fall
prey to this analytical approach which Warshow criticizes and
it undoubtedly has contributed to a near universal blindspot
among film scholars regarding the strictly entertainment oriented B picture as epitomized by Republic.

Warshow himself zeros in on the dispute between "fans"
and "intellectuals" in discussing the primacy of the "immediate experience":

This is the actual, immediate experience of seeing
and responding to the movies as most of us see
them and respond to them. A critic may extend
his frame of reference as far as it will bear ex-
tension, but it seems to me almost self-evident
that he should start with the simple acknowledge-
ment of his own relation to the object he criticizes;
at the center of all truly successful criticism there
is always a man reading a book, a man looking at
a picture, a man watching a movie. Critics of the
films, caught in the conflict between "high culture"
and "popular culture," have too often sought to e-
vade this confrontation. [21]

He specifically criticizes the sociologist's emphasis
upon the audience and the aesthetic's emphasis on art as
missing the personal importance of the film to the individual
involved in viewing it. [22] To Warshow the movies are not
something apart to be dissected. "The movies are part of
my culture, and it seems to me that their special power has
something to do with their being a kind of 'pure' culture, a
little like fishing or drinking or playing baseball--a cultural
fact, that is, which has not yet fallen altogether under the
discipline of art." [23] This is the position which any fan and
most workers on a Republic picture could applaud. Their B
pictures were made to entertain and to reach certain basic
emotions. Sociological and artistic implications were totally
secondary, if that. Republic pictures were indeed "the immediate experience."

Warshow also makes a subsidiary but telling observa-
tion concerning negative versus positive values in the movies.
In his opinion, the elitist critics assume that art must in-
volve social criticism and thus "negative social images" are
more important as a "truer reality," while the lower cultural levels emphasize "positive images" of home and reli-
gion to obtain automatic approval. [24] Warshow concludes,
"So much of 'official' American culture has been clearly optimistic that we are likely almost by reflex to take pessimism as a measure of seriousness. Besides, the element of
pessimism is often for educated people an aid to identifica-
tion." [25]

Although the point is made using A film with intellectual pretentions as his example, the appropriateness to the
B film is obvious. The Republic B film was on the lower
cultural level, stressed positive images, and was optimistic

in tenor. These factors frequently automatically cut off the
Republic product specifically and the B film in general from
serious consideration by the educated upper levels of cul-
ture--hence the academics' frequent failure to even consider
the B's. But in doing so these same students of the film
were missing the contributions which these films were making
to the lives of the viewers because of their positive images,
their optimism, and their basic understanding of "the immediate experience".

Andrew Bergman's We're in the Money: Depression
America and Its Films, [26] a study of the film in the Great
Depression, brings forth another theme to which Republic
and the B's were to make a significant contribution. One of
Bergman's basic ideas is that Hollywood helped America survive the Depression. "Hollywood would help the nation's fundamental institutions escape unscathed by attempting to keep
alive the myth and wonderful fantasy of a mobile and classless society, by focusing on the endless possibilities for individual success, by turning social evil into personal evil and
making the New Deal into a veritable leading man."[27]

While Bergman goes farther and contends that the
Depression films of the major studios unconsciously reflected
the needs of the people regardless of their surface intent,
were subtly critical of the system, and without realizing it
provided complex answers to their criticisms which require
deep analysis, it can be pointed out that Republic's goals
were straightforward and contributed much to the comfort of
the Depression audiences. Bergman does not mention Republic but the studio did just what his basic theme implies. Republic films, due to Herbert Yates, President of the studio,
various organized pressure groups, and the prevailing concepts of the writers, supported the traditional American ideals and reflected what the studio felt their audience needed
and wanted on a conscious level. Republic's policy was a
consistent reinforcement of the American way of life and the
values of heroism. They were very much the "guys in the
white hats" for reasons which will be examined in detail in
the following chapters.

In a related vein Bergman points out that the movie
audience is given more of the type of film which it accepts
and comes to expect. [28] This factor--generally acknowledged
and in many respects a truism--was especially true of the
B studio like Republic where formula and generic films make
up the preponderance of production. Hence when they found

a message which was acceptable to their public, they hammered it home in film after film as long as the audience bought it.

In discussing G-men and cowboys, Bergman again develops an idea which is representative of Republic's philosophy and contributed to the studio's success. "And simultaneously with the emergence of the federal lawman as hero came the re-emergence of the cowboy as a vital force in the movies... As for the westerns, their epic nature unleashed some powerful, if elderly, myths about the law as a great national, creative force ... cowboys making the West a 'fit place to raise a family'...."[29] The year he is discussing is 1935, the year that Republic came into existence. That Republic contributed to the revitalization of the Western as a force for law and order and to the audience acceptance thereof is discussed in Chapter V.

On the other hand Bergman also makes much of the concept of shyster throughout his book[30]--that is the plot motif wherein the villain is someone in a position of authority-- the lawyer, the banker, the sheriff, the mayor--who is using his power to take unfair advantage of the average citizen. This was a favorite theme in Republic pictures and was a natural plot device given the audience acceptance of the situation. The villain had to be powerful to be a fit adversary for the hero--which seemed to be a continual crowd pleaser in that the average viewer preferred to think the worst of the power figures and enjoyed seeing them brought to justice.[31]

In his conclusion Bergman sees Hollywood at the end of the Depression as having "made a central contribution toward educating Americans in the fact that wrongs could be set right within their existing institutions. They did so ... by reflecting aspiration and achievement. They showed that individual initiative still bred success, that the federal government was a benevolent watchman, that we were a classless, melting pot nation."[32] That conclusion applies not only to the efforts of the major studios but also to the B film as represented by Republic.

Stephen Louis Karpf's The Gangster Film: Emergence, Variation and Decay of a Genre 1930-1940[33] is sometimes contradictory in its coverage of the films it emphasizes and somewhat more negative in its interpretation than Bergman. However, it has some application to a study of Republic especially in providing contrast. That is to say it emphasizes

some negative factors involving gangster pictures and A productions which can provide a positive insight into Republic
films. For example, Karpf feels that the gangster picture
as a genre was extremely critical, even subversive, of the
American way of life: "The gangster film questioned the
very foundations of American society. It was and is popularly held that an individual can become a success in America by studying and working hard, being thrifty and having respect for family and institutions.... Mixed in with this general
outlook is an adherence to the Ten Commandments or some
similar set of moral values. The gangster film in its fullest
development represents anarchy in the above scheme."[34]

It is of interest to note that Republic made very few
gangster pictures and that the genres wherein their strength
existed--serials, Westerns, country musicals--tended to neu-
tralize the message which Karpf sees in the gangster movies.

Along the same lines, Karpf does explore four films
produced by Warner Brothers which have positive values.
"These films are optimistic in tone.... They have a quality
which points to a problem in American society and suggests
solutions based on traditional values already inherent in the
country."[35] His examples include The Story of Louis Pas-
teur, The Life of Emile Zola, Juarez, and Dr. Ehrlich's
Magic Bullet and his discussion delves into political implications in the films. The point is that these were all A budget,
historical biographies, long on dialogue and possible political
parallels, but short on action and pacing. Therefore, whether they were positive or not, whether they really had an intended message or not, it is likely that they were not seen
by the youth and young adults and where they were seen they
made little or no lasting impressions. In comparison, as
shall be discussed in Chapter III, the effect of a Republic
action piece would be to make an impression on the younger
audience even if such were not the original intention. And
the impression was generally positive.

Basically then, both Karpf and Bergman were frequently negative in their interpretation of the messages and themes
imparted to audiences in major productions.[36] In comparison,
Republic was both consciously and unconsciously positive in
stressing the traditional standards of the audience at which
they aimed and unconsciously reinforced these standards by
an unfailing reiteration over a long period of time in series
films.

Michael Wood's America in the Movies,[37] an interesting volume on the significance of the film, is similar to Warshow in some respects and adds yet another interpretation
which can be applied to the Republic type of movie. Wood
early expresses his conviction that the movies are overdone
intentionally and that this must be taken into consideration
when analyzing their effect: "This sense of the overblown
is not a question of hindsight or changing tastes.... It is a
question of the exact tone of these movies, of their being
simultaneously hammed up and just right, pitched at their
own chosen level of swagger and exaggeration. It is the
movies, an independent universe, self-created, self-perpetu-
ating, a licensed zone of unreality, affectionately patronized
by us all...."[38] This description is again particularly true
of the B film as represented by Republic wherein certain
ground rules were recognized and accepted by the audience.
In the chapters on Republic serials, Westerns, and series,
it will be seen that Wood's "licensed zone of unreality" is
immensely recognizable and efficiently effective. It will be
shown that such ready acceptance and recognition of the Republic style and pacing made the audience even more receptive to both the story and its implied moral.

Wood also sees the film as having an unconscious effect on the audience but not in the deep symbolic meaning
psychological studies frequently claim. "We translate and
interpret and transfer from films back to life, but we do it
instantly and intuitively, working at a level of awareness
somewhere just below full consciousness."[39] This is probably a good description of where the lasting impact of Republic films hit the audience. The messages did not necessarily
lie on the surface in the stories. Nor were they deep and
complex. But they did make an impression in this area
which Wood describes and in much the same way, by an in-
tuitive transfer--especially when absorbed effortlessly over
a long period of time as in series films.

In essence then, Wood feels that the movies did mirror the American mind "... that virtually any Hollywood movie, however trivial ... can be seen as a text for a rather
special kind of social history: the study of what might be
called the back of the American mind."[40] And this is one
of the major hypotheses to be developed in the following chap-
ters--namely that the Republic product did represent certain
values accepted by the American audience and that this helped
explain the success of Republic. Moreover, this "mirroring

effect" made these films all the more effective in their influence on the viewer--it was a two-way street.

In concluding his small volume, Wood summarizes his
position--"the movies, then, offered structures of thought
and feeling to an almost inconceivable quantity of people ...
especially when we didn't give them a second thought."[41]
This is indeed the way that the films of Republic were viewed.
The youthful audience rarely gave their exciting entertainment
a second thought for it was just that--entertainment. Yet the
message was there. Wood's work sees all Hollywood films
as a force in America's social history.

The same can be said of Robert Sklar's Movie Made
America.[42] But Sklar's approach is entirely different and
his conclusions vary, so that the value of his book in regard
to understanding the significance of Republic Pictures lies
more in his concern with economic factors.

Sklar's book is a general treatment of the history of
American cinema with a heavy emphasis on the industry being
controlled economically and philosophically by the underdogs,
the minorities, and by men who came out of the lower and
lower-middle classes. Such men thus understood the traditional values of the movie-goer and appealed to the mass audiences. At the same time, these men feared criticism
from the upper classes and elitist critics and defended themselves at various times against charges of catering to the
basest instincts of the lowest common denominator, of films
espousing suspect political philosophies, or of any emphasis
by critics on the disproportionate power of movie leaders.
Sklar is concerned with the influence of the movies, who controlled that influence, and some of the implications of the influence. However, Sklar, like so many other scholars, continues to emphasize the major productions and personalities
and gives only a passing nod to the factor of the B picture.
Nonetheless he makes some telling points which are equally
applicable to the B's.

For example, Sklar emphasizes the importance of the
profit motive in the film industry and from it the ultimate
power of the public over film content.

> One reads with skepticism the many works written
> by movie-industry insiders that claim the movie-
> going public holds the real power over motion pic-
> tures. Yet there is some truth in it.... Awesome

as the power and profit of the movie moguls became
in the 1920's, they never ceased to depend on their
ability to please the public.[43]

Sklar is actually speaking of the silent era in this statement
but it proved to be just as true in the thirties and forties.
Republic realized it was governed by just such a consideration and found a product and an audience and put them together. Republic was doing the right thing at the right time for
a segment of the audience and it gave the studio a significance which was unrecognized at the time.

Sklar also summarizes the traditional view of movie
historians, critics, and popularizers concerning the upsurge
of the influence of the cinema in the thirties.

The heavenly gates swung open, and American motion pictures, so their chroniclers have universally
proclaimed, entered their golden age: Hollywood
took center stage in the culture and consciousness
of the United States, making movies with a power
and elan never known before or seen again. Not
only did the movies amuse and entertain the nation
through its most severe economic and social dis-
order, holding it together by their capacity to create unifying myths and dreams, but movie culture
in the 1930s became a dominant culture for many
Americans, providing new values and social ideals
to replace shattered old traditions.[44]

Sklar then goes on to point out that this interpretation has
many salient points but that it is oversimplified since Hollywood also was severely influenced by the Depression. Sklar's
summary of the era differs from Bergman's in that it emphasizes the creativity of Depression Hollywood. This fact
is important in that Republic was indeed founded in this unstable but creative period, that they of necessity quickly
found an approach which suited them, and that, whether
it was intended or not, their product did serve as a unifying
force and did uphold traditional values, shattered or otherwise. Republic's role in the movie culture as "a dominant
culture for many Americans" is worthy of exploration.

While not referring to Republic, Sklar further isolates
yet another factor which contributed to the success of the
studio and the good timing with which it came into existence.
"So in 1933-1934, spurred by the changes in national mood

brought about by the New Deal and prodded by the Legion of
Decency, Hollywood directed its enormous powers of persua-
sion to preserving the basic moral, social and economic ten-
ets of traditional American culture."45   This, on the eve of
the founding of Republic, could well be the tenet upon which
Republic was to base its existence.   When these circumstances
changed after the war, Republic did not, and that began the
decline of the studio.   Sklar declares the peace between Hollywood and its political critics was accepted because it gave
the motion picture industry more opportunity for profits and
prestige.   This too could be applied to Republic's whole-
hearted acceptance of the role of cultural guardian.   However,
there were also other factors.

     Sklar provided yet one more theme which is important
to the success of Republic.   In analyzing the change in the
movies in the late forties, he recognizes the importance of
the formula picture:

>   What Hollywood had learned to do supremely well--
>   comedy, musicals, genre Westerns and crime pic-
>   tures, melodramas, popularizations of classics--
>   did not provide many lessons for a new era of
>   seriousness and responsibility.   Hollywood's tri-
>   umph had been overwhelmingly a triumph of formu-
>   la, and the novelty and freshness of American com-
>   mercial movies had come from the inventive new
>   ways in which formulas were reshaped to meet the
>   times.   Formulas worked beautifully in their place--
>   and continue to do so--but formulas and significant
>   social themes did not mix effectively.... 46

This point is also seminal to an understanding of the Republic contribution.   With one exception, all of the people con-
nected with the studio who were interviewed for this study
acknowledged that Republic was strongest in the area of the
formula picture. 47   Also significant is the fact that the decline of Republic dates from the late forties and early fifties.

     In discussing the various background works, both fan
and academic, several themes relating to the role and significance that Republic and its pictures had in the pattern of
American social history have emerged.   How do these themes
fit together to form the hypothesis which will be developed
throughout the following chapters?

     Film as art is a legitimate topic.   However, the stu-

dio product of the thirties, forties, and fifties was rarely
concerned with film as an art form. This was true of all
studios, but especially of those which specialized in the B
film. Of these studios, Republic was undoubtedly the finest.
This type of motion picture was created to entertain in order
to be profitable. The B picture and the serial, especially at
Republic, were, however, frequently quality products and, as
a result, had more influence on the industry and the moviegoing public than was intended or realized at the time but
not because of artistic or sociological pretentions. Of course
many B's even at Republic were of lesser quality but the
overall average was better than has been realized. Con-
versely such films did have artistic merit occasionally but
such occurrences were accidental and of minimal interest to
those involved.

Republic learned early to produce economical films
which had top quality and which appealed to the small theatres in large cities and to a variety of outlets throughout
the Midwest and South. Other small studios could not match
the Republic quality and the major producers normally viewed
such films as throwaway products upon which they spent little
time. They each had their B units but were committed to
A products first and foremost. However, Republic's success
in the B area resulted in the smaller studios attempting to
upgrade their films while the majors took notice by upgrading
their B's and by utilizing Republic personnel even into the
present. Thus Republic did have an effect on the film industry which is worthy of examination.

However, Republic's position within the industry was
secondary to the other and perhaps more important role of
the studio. The general quality of the Republic product
proved to be important in the studio's relationship to its motion picture audiences. The Republic "attention to detail" resulted in a greater public acceptance of the type of film in
which the studio specialized. This positive effect in turn increased the significance of the Republic product on American
social history in that it contributed to, reinforced, and/or
reflected the audience viewpoint. In other words, the films
influenced the "public mind". The films of Republic were
seemingly especially important to young audiences in the Midwest and South. The extent of this influence is difficult to
measure but its existence should be acknowledged, documented, and examined. The audience was entertained but at the
same time it was painlessly influenced.

In order to examine these suppositions with an emphasis on the second point, this work will concentrate on 1) the Republic serials, 2) the Republic B Western series, and 3) other less genre oriented Republic products such as the country musicals and general action features since these were really Republic's bread-and-butter and where their greatest success occurred. A passing examination of a sample of the Republic A films was made in Chapter I on Republic's history for the sake of completeness, but since this area is not the source of Republic's significance, further reference to Republic A's will be only in relationship to the B's.

In no way did Republic's occasional venture into A productions pose a threat to the majors. Although these big productions did not directly hurt Republic until the declining years, they rarely benefited the studio greatly either in terms of profit or prestige, ironically the studio's greatest area of concern. This budgetary drain plus the other factors which were examined in Chapter I proved too much for Republic. Perhaps under different guidance, the studio would have survived and adapted. For example, Monogram did just that, becoming Allied Artists. However, Republic was besieged by a variety of problems in the late forties and early fifties and did not adapt.

Regardless of the causes for the passing of Republic as an active studio, the fact remains that the care and quality of its technical facilities and its personnel especially in the thirties and forties resulted in a superior product of its kind. The importance of this superiority will be the main thrust of this study. The movies of the period under discussion had a direct influence on the life styles, moral codes, and ethical patterns of the viewers. These films gave them a simplified but quite consistent, understandable, and usable life model couched in the terms of period pieces and fantasy to increase the entertainment value and therefore the profit ratio. Moreover, since the audience was more frequently and consistently exposed to the B movies, serials, and shorts, these products, while not as "significant" as the larger and classier major productions, had an appreciable influence on several generations of young and impressionable minds. And the surface messages of these productions, because they were formula pieces, were easily and painlessly absorbed by their willing audiences. There may have occasionally been deeper and more disturbing messages, but the major import of these films does not lie in subliminally subversive interpretations-- rather accurate or inaccurate. Finally, because of their ap-

preciably higher quality as well as their admitted quantity,
the Republic Pictures products are perhaps the best and
leading example of the importance of this type of film on the
regular moviegoing audience of the period which was the heyday of the sound film. [48]

Notes

1. Don Miller, B Movies (New York: Curtis Books, 1973),
    p. 113.

2. Miller, p. 112.
3. Miller has also published an interesting, unpretentious
    but reliable survey of the B Western, Hollywood Cor-
    ral (New York: Popular Library, 1976), which de-
    votes considerable space to Republic.
4. Barbour's fan publications through Screen Facts Press
    can be found in the bibliography. The commercial
    volumes include Days of Thrills and Adventure (New
    York: Macmillian Company, 1970), A Thousand and
    One Delights (New York: Collier Books, 1971), and
    The Thrill of It All (New York: Collier Books,
    1971). His recent Cliffhanger: A Pictorial History of
    the Motion Picture Serial (New York: A & W Publishers,
    1977), is basically a continuation of Days of Thrills
    and Adventure and unfortunately repeats much of the
    same material.
5. Cocoa, Florida: Cinememories Publishing Company,
    1968.
6. Satellite Beach, Florida: Coral Reef Publications,
    1973.
7. Mt. Clemens, Michigan: privately published, 1969-
    1974.
8. One exception was Jon Tuska "Overland with Kit Car-
    son--A Cinematography" in Those Enduring Matinee
    Idols, II (June-July 1971), pp. 146-48 and II (Au-
    gust-September 1971), pp. 163-65 in which Tuska
    finds significant symbolic parallels between this Co-
    lumbia Western serial starring Wild Bill Elliott and
    Moby Dick among other literary works.
9. Los Angeles: privately published, 1974-present.
10. Continued Next Week: A History of the Motion Picture
    Serial (Norman, Oklahoma: University of Oklahoma
    Press, 1964) and Bound and Gagged: The Story of
    the Silent Serials (New York: Castle Books, 1968).

11. Garden City, New York: Doubleday & Company, 1972.
12. New York: Crown Publishers, 1972. Don Daynard in
     the letter column of TEMI, II (June-July 1972), p.
     246 states "The book is so full of errors, omissions,
     and false information that I spent one full hour making
     corrections in the picture captions and even then, I
     didn't get them all!!!"
13. Norman, Oklahoma: University of Oklahoma Press, 1971.
14. Northbrook, Illinois: By the author. Jack Mathis Ad-
     vertising, 1975. This book is a valuable reference
     work.
15. Letter from Jack Mathis, April 26, 1976.
16. Lubbock, Texas: privately published, 1972-present.
17. A Pictorial History of the Western Film (New York: Cit-
     adel Press, 1969), pp. 140-53.
18. Kings of the B's: Working Within the Hollywood System
     (New York: E. P. Dutton & Company, 1975).
19. Garden City, New York: Doubleday & Company, 1962.
20. Warshow, p. 19.
21. Warshow, p. 19.
22. Warshow, p. 27.
23. Warshow, p. 28.
24. Warshow, p. 179.
25. Warshow, p. 181.
26. New York: Harper & Row, 1972.
27. Bergman, p. xvi.
28. Bergman, p. xvi.
29. Bergman, p. 83.
30. See especially Bergman, Chapter Two, "The Shyster and
     the City".
31. Interview with Sloan Nibley, Republic writer, Hollywood,
     May 4, 1976.
32. Bergman, pp. 167-68.
33. New York: Arno Press, 1973.
34. Karpf, pp. 212-13.
35. Karpf, p. 237.
36. For example, Karpf sees the gangster as finding himself
     more honest and less hypocritical than his betters who
     cheat within the law. Karpf feels that this was a bas-
     ic message of this type of film. p. 151.
37. New York: Basic Books, 1975.
38. Wood, p. 8.
39. Wood, p. 16.
40. Wood, p. 126.
41. Wood, p. 193.
42. New York: Random House, 1975.
43. Sklar, p. 148.

44. Sklar, p. 161.
45. Sklar, p. 175.
46. Sklar, p. 280.
47. Interview with Morris R. Abrams, Republic script su-
     pervisor and assistant director, Hollywood, May 17,
     1976. Mr. Abrams feels that there was continuous
     change in Republic pictures to adapt to the audience
     and the formula designation is oversimplified.
48. Due to the fact that the story of Republic has not been
     previously documented or its possible significance
     even acknowledged beyond fan oriented publications
     and because the Republic "bread-and-butter" product
     was infrequently discussed by the critics, this study
     relied on over two dozen interviews and extensive
     correspondence with Republic personnel and others
     knowledgeable on the subject. In addition some Re-
     public records and press releases were available as
     well as newspaper and periodical reports on the com-
     pany, its president, and its business affairs. The
     repository for the remaining Republic files is Nation-
     al Telefilm Associates, Los Angeles. These records
     are currently unavailable. Fortunately, much Repub-
     lic material has been deposited in and collected by
     three major theatrical libraries--the University of
     California at Los Angeles, the Margaret Herrick Li-
     brary of the Academy of Motion Picture Arts and
     Sciences, and the American Film Institute, Los An-
     geles. A quantity of additional material of merit is
     in the theatrical section of the Library and Museum
     of Performing Arts in the New York Public Library
     at Lincoln Center.

Chapter III

INFLUENCE, THE MOTION PICTURE, THE B MOVIE,
AND REPUBLIC

As has been discussed, the B picture was low budget,
intended to make money with a minimum investment, and usually relied on a generic structure and formula plots. This is
not to denigrate such films--many had more value than major
productions, they are worthy of study, and as Charles Flynn
says in Kings of the Bs:

> Finally, we go to the movies for great experience,
> not for great ideas. Our aesthetic response to a
> movie is inevitably linked to our movie experiences.
> And, for quite a while, the s/k/h [schlock, kitsch,
> hack--read B movies] movies were America's mov-
> ie experiences.
> Obviously, today's moviegoer may find it diffi-
> cult to develop a taste for the s/k/h movie. But
> these movies constituted the preponderance of Hol-
> lywood's output for so long that they are not only
> a part of movie history, but also of American cul-
> tural history. [1*]

The movies as a whole were a force in American history.
The B's were a major aspect of that influence. And Republic began and remained a B picture studio.

Historically, the influence of the movie industry was
increasing during the thirties. Doubt and discouragement in-
duced by the Great Depression generated the psychological
imperatives which gave the movies a new role in the nation's
emotional economy. There was a need for distraction and
entertainment as well as for reassurance. As Arthur Schlesinger, Jr., put it, "With the American dream in apparent
ruins ... people longed to hear again an affirmation of individual identity, to see again a chance for individual possibility, to feel again a sense of individual potency."[2] Movies

---

*Notes to Chapter III begin on page 73.

were not always better in the Depression but they were important to the audience. [3]

Movies may have had more importance than ministers
in this era. In their well known sociological study of "Middletown" in the thirties the Lynds even go so far as to im-
pute the movies with more influence than that of the local
preacher. [4] And, it can be pointed out, "Middletown" or Mun-
cie, Indiana was in the heart of Republic's distribution strong-
hold--the Midwest. Frederick Lewis Allen, the journalist and
popular historian, also comments on the popularity of the movies in the thirties and attributed it to their escapist themes:
"The movies took one to a never-never land of adventure and
romance uncomplicated by thought. The capital invested in
the movies preferred to steer clear of awkward issues, not
to run the risk of offending theatregoers abroad or at home". [5]
He feels that these escapist themes represented the desires of
the moviegoing public and that the movies actually neutralized
the immediate goals of social reformers. He points out that,
after all, there were eighty-five million moviegoers a week.
Hollywood advanced the Horatio Alger myth of individual success
and this dream helped these same moviegoers accept the economic hardships of the thirties. [6] As will be seen, Republic Pictures contributed regularly to the Alger myth as well as related positive myths. However, regardless of which myth or
myths Hollywood provided, its presence was felt in the Depression era.

With the gathering war clouds in Europe, the nation
began an economic recovery but the influence of Hollywood
did not slacken although attendance declined temporarily. The
new uncertainties of potential involvement increased the interest in diversions and Hollywood, always sensitive to the
mood of the times, began to move away from pacifism toward preparedness. Senator Champ Clark of Missouri, ever
wary of foreign influences, feared that the 17,000 movie
houses were nightly becoming "17,000 nightly mass meetings
for war". [7] Clark's fears were not totally unjustified. During wartime the need for entertainment did not abate and Hollywood's importance increased. Geoffrey Perrett, journalist/
historian, in his book on the home front, emphasized both
the popularity of the movies and emotionalism of the audiences.
"In 1942 it [the movie industry] fell heir to sudden riches.
Movie attendance jumped 50 percent over the 1940 level,
reaching 80,000,000 paying customers a week. Boomtown
movie theaters stayed open twenty-four hours a day to ac-
commodate the swing shifts. No more free dishes, bingo,

breakfasts, and other gimmicks. The customers packed in
regardless of what was being shown. But these were also
the rowdiest audiences in memory, booing, hissing, cheering
and leaving demolished seats and tattered draperies in their
wake. "[8] True, the emotionalism was perhaps more due to
the period than to the immediate experience of the film being
shown but the reactions were there in any case.

Moviegoing, especially among the young, became a cas-
ual but persistent habit.[9] The war mood undoubtedly contributed. It was "a curious atmosphere that wartime is to some
extent vacation time, a time in which life is not quite the
same as it has been before".[10]

The movie industry prospered as the movie theatre
became a social experience. More than 90,000,000 people
went to the movies every week and grosses were over a bil-
lion dollars per year even though admissions increased 33
percent on the average.[11] War pictures seemed to predom-
inate although most films were profitable. During the war,
the emotional effects on segments of the audience remained
high. "Morale was the excuse for Hollywood's wartime prod-
uct--an elusive word if there ever was one. Probably, the
morale most frequently energized was that of small boys and
teen-age girls who sat in darkened theaters, their hearts
quickening to the phony war on the silver screen."[12] The
point is that in a great many films morale and patriotism did
continue to have a place for the youthful audiences.

After the war, during the late forties came the decline
of the movie industry. Nonetheless, the movies were indeed
a major force in American popular culture from the Depression until after World War II. The historian, while usually
acknowledging that the movie medium had some influence on
American society and the American "way of life" during this
period, has not really delved into what this influence was to
any great extent. In order to analyze the influence of the
medium or to place it in the broader aspects of American
historical studies it is necessary to consider film not as art
or as history but as a part of American life.

Michael T. Isenberg, historian at the University of
Colorado, has recognized and summarized the historian's dilemma. He points out that popular art, in this case the film,
should not be considered only for artistic values, especially
by the professional historian, since it also reflects society.[13]
Instead of recognizing the film's contributions, historians have

used the movies as a whipping boy because of their commercialism. [14] Isenberg feels that the film industry has been criticized unfairly because elitists faulted its business/commercial orientation because it addressed itself primarily to "puerile audiences", and finally, it was seen as an intrinsic leveller, even degrader, of the national culture. [15]

In his conclusion, Isenberg makes a strong point which is particularly applicable to the historical study of the B movie and its influential role in the lives of its audience.

Historians who have become comfortable with the concepts of "symbol" and "myth" within the last quarter century have balked at extending these concepts from the literary to the visual media. History has been slower than most of the other social sciences in realizing the social dynamism hidden in such concepts. The movies operate on both symbolic and mythic levels. One ardent proponent of the film even claimed that this situation was ideal for the historian. "It is not the man who describes what actually happens who best tells history," wrote Harry C. Carr in 1918. "It is the genius who symbolizes it for us, who puts it into doses we can take without mentally choking. "[16]

While some film historians such as Michael Wood and Robert Sklar have indeed emphasized the mythic proportions of Hollywood's product, none have seriously considered the contributions of the B genres such as the Western and the serial to the American attitude over a long period of exposure. While the historian has indeed had an anxiety concerning the role of the film in history, the relationship of the two is being recognized.

Perhaps Garth Jowett, whose Film: The Democratic Art, stresses that motion pictures are a major social phenomenon which continually interrelates with the changing mores and attitudes of American society, best sums up what the historian faces. "It is my contention that we historians must see the movies as commercial products--but products that had a tremendous and unknown influence on American Society as a whole. It was because of the 'unknown quality' that the movies were subject to forms of social pressure and censorship never before seen in the U. S...."[17] To the historians then, the influence of the film, while recognized, remains an "unknown quality."

    If the historian has been hesitant about this influence
and how to approach it, other disciplines have been less so.
The well known and articulate anthropologist Hortense Powdermaker readily accepts the significant role of Hollywood in
American culture--that the movies reflect the audience and
the audience is influenced by the film.   She states, "Through
the study of American movies we [the anthropologists] should
likewise contribute to the understanding of American society ...
we assume that movies will reflect values and goals, as folklore, the theater, and literature (both 'fine' and 'popular')
have always reflected them.   In a period of rapid change and
conflict within the value system it will be of interest to note
which values are most stressed by the movies."[18]   In other
words, the movies emphasize selected values over others
based upon audience preferences as a major factor and these
emphases change with the historical situation.   Since we live
in a rapidly changing world there is some time lag involved
but the movies still provide a gauge by which to observe the
changing social patterns.

    In recognizing the influence of the movies on the popu-
lace, Powdermaker specifies that the movies are often examined for their effects on the abnormal audience but that
they also impress the general viewer.   "As anthropologists,
we are more interested in the normal than in the pathologi-
cal.   What is the effect of the movies on the vast audience
who are not criminals, delinquents, or drunkards?   How do
movies influence their concepts of human relations, their value systems, their notions of reality?"[19]   In the long run the
more subtle long range effect on the general multitude is
more significant than any aberrant reaction on select unstable
members of the viewing group.

    Powdermaker sums up her viewpoint on the relation-
ship of movies and society: "There is almost no important
American pattern that is not reflected in Hollywood.   Frequently it is exaggerated, sometimes to the point of carica-
ture."[20]

    Psychologists and sociologists tend to agree with an-
thropologist Powdermaker that the cinema is influential although the interpretation sometimes varies.   Psychologist
Hugo Münsterberg was convinced that the movies influenced
the minds of the audience and, unaware of the future commercialism and profit motivation of the medium, he projected
a highly idealized picture of the good effects movies would
have.[21]   He enthused, "No wonder that temples for the new

goddess are built in every little hamlet. "22 Later students
of the film were not so positive although they too recognized
the motion picture as influential.

In the early thirties, the potential influence of the movies was of concern to many, and a series of scientific studies, predominantly psychological and sociological, were undertaken. These were the famous Payne Study and Experimental
Fund studies, eleven volumes of which were published, and
while the techniques used and the social perspective from
which the researchers operated have caused the entire body
of work to be viewed cautiously, the Payne Fund volumes do
include some interesting material and do recognize the influence of Hollywood on society. 23   This project and others of
the period tended to find that the film product of the times
was undermining or even destroying American society without recognizing that the movies were in reality reflecting and
reinforcing the culture. They were in effect propaganda a-
gainst the movies but they did increase our awareness of the
import of the screen.

Herbert Blumer and Philip M. Hauser, authors of one
of the clinical studies and one of the most critical of the series, summarize the approach of the Payne Fund volumes.
"While primarily a form of recreation, they [motion pictures]
play an appreciably important role in developing conceptions
of life and transmitting patterns of conduct. They may direct the behavior of persons along socially acceptable lines
or they may lead, as has been indicated, to misconduct.
They may be, therefore, an agency of social value or of social harm. "24 Both authors at least admit that the movies
can contribute to acceptable behavior and can have value. It
was just that, given the slant of their beliefs and approach
to the subject, these psychologists failed to realize that there
was more to the films than sex and crime.

The summary volume for the series was undertaken
by Henry James Forman, a journalist whose role it was to
popularize the scientific studies. He acknowledges the pervasiveness of the movies. "A good motion picture, briefly,
with its peculiar and inherent capacity to circulate throughout the globe, to penetrate into the smallest town and even
into rural areas, represents a social force which may be described as nothing short of a godsend. "25 Forman also comments that the results of the Payne Fund project has indicated
that the young are the most subject to the messages of the
film.

The screen is the most open of all books. And
when the young see pictures presented in a certain
way, it is small wonder that the vividness of the
reception of those scenes, owing to the youth and
freshness of the spectators, makes of the movies
a peculiarly incisive and important factor in schemes
of conduct. The less experience the spectators
have, the less selective they naturally are. Coming
to the young, as pictures do, in the most impressionable years of their life, the effect becomes of
extraordinary weight and potentiality, and amounts
often to a shaping and molding of their character. [26]

Based on this finding, Forman pleads for the guidance and
presence of adults in order to counteract the potential negative influence of the movies on children. [27] Despite their ap-
prehensions, the Payne Fund studies did provide evidence
and arguments that the film, including that fare which would
become known as the B film, was indeed a social force with
which to reckon. The Payne Fund volumes were a tentative
attempt to identify how the influence of film might work specifically.

Later film studies stressing the psychological viewpoint were not as critical as those in the early thirties and
were more objective in their approach. For example, a later study of the Hollywood movies of the forties credited them
with reflecting the daydreams of the culture in which they
are produced. "The common day-dreams of a culture are in
part the sources, in part the products of its popular myths,
stories, plays and films. Where these productions gain the
sympathetic response of a wide audience, it is likely that
their producers have tapped within themselves the reservoir
of common day-dreams. "[28] It is the power of these dreams
which give the movies their influence.

Dore Schary, who was a major writer-producer at
RKO, then headed Metro Goldwyn Mayer, and later became
an independent producer sums up the truism of the influence
of motion pictures in his introductory remarks to a sociological study. "Of course, the fact is that you simply can't
make a picture without content or, more candidly, without a
message. "[29] Every film then carries some message. The
entire film industry was unavoidably intertwined with society.
Fritz Lang, famed German and American film director who
worked once at Republic asked, "Do you realize, by the way,
what really made propaganda for the American way of life?

American motion pictures. Goebbels understood the enormous power of film as propaganda, and I'm afraid that even
today people don't know what a tremendous means of propaganda motion pictures can be. "30

Thus, traditional historians, anthropologists, psychologists, and sociologists, working from slightly different approaches, serve to concentrate the arguments for the film
as an influential factor in American society. However, perhaps Robert Sklar of the University of Michigan best summarizes the dilemma of attempting to isolate the influence.
"This is perhaps the most vexing and murky area of all for
social historians of the movies. We know movies have a
profound impact on cultural life. But it's hard to provide
specific evidence to support broad generalizations. "31

And to add to the perplexities, most of these academic treatments of the film including those from scholars trained
in university film departments are predominantly concerned
with the role of the A film. Although most gave some credit
to the B film as a part of the general motion picture scene,
they normally studied and cited specific A productions on a
regular basis. However, much of what authorities from various disciplines say about the A picture or the motion picture
in general also can be applied to the B field. Some of their
conclusions are particularly appropriate to B pictures.

Powdermaker, the anthropologist, comments on the
importance of formulas to successful film making, "The movies have some resemblance to it [folk art] in their repetitive
use of well-known themes or formulas which is so characteristic of primitive folklore.... Many times the latest 'scoop'
is set within a well-known formula used in the past. "32 As
will be seen, Republic specifically and the B film in general
made good use of formulas with slight updatings and variations to meet the tastes of their audiences for something different. Republic writer Sloan Nibley has illustrated this
point in commenting on the fact that in the Roy Rogers pictures he wrote, the character of the hero and his supporters
as well as the formula were fixed factors. Therefore, Nibley and other B writers always turned to the villains' char-
acterizations and the different devices upon which the standard plots hinged for their variations.

The psychologists, Wolfenstein and Leites, also consider the formula picture important and, at the same time,
strengthen Nibley's point. "Within the limits of a code and

a general plot formula there remains a choice of a considerable range of possibilities. "[34] They feel that the use to
which the formula is put reflects the desires of the American people, that the themes are drawn out of society.

The acknowledgment that Hollywood, and especially
the B productions, relied on formulas brings up the fact that
the B's emphasized melodrama and violence. Wolfenstein
and Leites put this in perspective. "Violence in American
films may be fast moving and noisy or technically intricate;
it is less apt to be emotionally involved.... Death is not very
real in American films.... A murder is the starting point of
furious activities (setting off the process of investigation), or
marks the end of such activities (when the murder is elimin-
ated), thus leaving the hero free to take a holiday. "[35] While
aimed at the general Hollywood movie, this statement is very
descriptive of many B movies in general and is particularly
related to both the intricate stuntwork and special effects and
the typical plot of most Republic serials and Westerns as
shall be seen.

Melodrama also served a useful function in the motion picture by providing an external danger as opposed to
inner conflict. [36] But melodrama, a staple of the B's, has
its place. As sociologists White and Averson admit, "Whether melodrama per se is necessarily inferior art begs the question ... the movies very often have used the melodrama
form to sustain audience interest. The moving picture has
generally stressed physical action, sudden plot reversals,
and unexpected outcomes--a kind of instinctive bow to the op-
eration of chance in human life. "[37] The B films frequently
used this same violence and melodrama to reflect and en-
hance the value system of their audiences.

Still, many film analysts from all disciplines are critical of the Hollywood value system. Powdermaker, for example, feels that the movie industry should stress certain
cultural patterns. "There are, of course, other patterns in
the U. S. A. which Hollywood could elaborate. They are
the democratic ones of the dignity of man, the concept of
freedom, a belief in man's capacity to think, create, and to
exercise some control over his life--a belief that man is
more important than property--all part of our cultural heritage. "[38] This latter set of values is essentially what the B's
in general and Republic specifically did emphasize, although
frequently in an action format and often with a blatancy of
which Powdermaker might not approve. But the fact remains

that a B film studio was indeed providing material for the
audience representing the values which this anthropologist
advocates. Hollywood could emphasize positive values and
the B's produced by Republic often did just that.

As an example of positive values, White and Averson
emphasize a major theme in the message film as being one
of the individual's fight against the conformity of the system.
"The struggle of the individual to preserve his integrity a-
gainst those forces in society which would diminish him--
whether tyrant kings, political demagogues, or labor racket-
eers--has been a continuing dramatic subject of the American message film. "39 This was the message, sometimes
obvious, usually subtle, of countless B films and was a con-
tinuously employed theme in many Westerns as well as some
serials produced by Republic. In fact, Republic and the other
B producers without conscious intentions gave us many "con-
traband-message" films. "The critical comment in the con-
traband-message film is incidental; in the message film the
social viewpoint is overt and dominant. "40

The important factor is that a film need not be specifically aimed at topical social issues to serve as an index to
popular thought--the B films and serials in general and the
Republic product specifically also reflected mass beliefs and
even dealt with social issues both directly and indirectly although the topical aspect of the subject matter was often disguised or at least secondary to the action/adventure motif so
popular in escapist entertainment. But both the message of
the particular issue at hand in any given film and the relationship of the film to popular social thought was still there
in a great many Republic B's.

Thus, film analysts, utilizing various disciplinary approaches, agree that the motion picture industry in general
was influential, but their conclusions often bear direct rela-
tionships to the B film as well as the higher quality production.

Other film scholars of course have specifically concentrated upon the B field. Some of these writers are de-
fensive, noting only the merits and influences of the B productions. But perhaps Professor Russel B. Nye of Michigan
State University is typical of those who hold a negative point
of view. He dismisses the B's as routine, cheap, melodramatic, transitory, and utilizing minor players. He admits
they formed a greater body of films than the major produc-

tions but claims, "their titles and the people who played in
them are long forgotten, and appear in none of the many his-
tories of the movies. "[41] Nye admits that by their very quantity and playing time, B's did have extensive audience exposure.   And it has been shown that even cheaply made, simplified melodramas do carry messages.   Moreover, sleeper
B's and occasionally less remarkable B movies illustrating a
particular point have shown up with regularity in film histo-
ries and cults have grown up around certain B actors and
series.

        Other writers viewing the B phenomenon put it in con-
text and acknowledge the merits of B's.   Don Miller feels
that the coming of the double bill was the signal for the B
picture to become an important factor in the motion picture
industry.   In 1935, the structure of exhibiting films gave way
to "the second feature" and in the process Miller states that
B's came to stand, "not for budget, or Class B, or bad, but
in many ways signifying 'better'. "[42]

        Miller is not alone in acknowledging a debt to the B's.
Peter John Dyer, film critic for the journal Films and Filming, considered B's as "Those first rate second features"
even prior to the demise of the B film and pointed out, "They
can sharpen our critical senses.   Many of them [have] good
story telling and direction, ingenious plotting, expert photography and more than competent acting. "[43]   The director of
the film program at the Los Angeles County Museum of Art
provides the major clue to their potential influence.   They
filled needs inexpensively.   "These films fulfilled an emotional need for American audiences; that of sheer entertainment
and total escape, all for the price of a quarter. "[44]

        These films developed imagination in the moviegoer
which was coupled with a receptive mind.   "The B movie ...
was a known quantity....   These were uniquely American stories, and audiences of the Bs didn't want to be stirred but
entertained, perhaps stimulated, and certainly, comforted.
They knew that in the formula films of the Bs they could relax
and feel at home. "[45]   Because they were so dependable and so
comfortable, these films were accepted wholeheartedly by viewers and that included a life pattern and a moral, ethical framework.   "They [the B's] were plucky, predictable and often
pedestrian, yet they touched a chord in American life.... "[46]
The B films successfully reached their audience not only because they were comfortable and dependable but also because
they were often energetic, well paced, and exciting.   "[D]e-

spite the insane working conditions, the output of the best B directors had a raw crude energy and viscerally powerful quality that remained unnoticed by most critics until recently," says one critic. [47] This seeming contradiction is explainable. While the B picture was formula and normally predictable, it also had room for improvisation within the form, the budget, and the schedule. Creative men worked on these pictures--sometimes on their way up, sometimes down, and often just working to do the job as best they could--and these pictures did have some variation in plot and techniques. Moreover, since they lacked big stars and massive sets, they had to rely on movement or gimmicks. They were efficiently produced but they could have imagination and challenge. The best were fast paced, good story telling with an impact--even if it was predictable. When various authorities refer to the films or the B's striking a chord, it need not be the same reaction. The B movies could thrill, could have an immediate impact, as well as lull and be comforting to their audience. Either way, they had an influence.

In essence then the B movie was the most prolific form of movie making in Hollywood's most successful period. It provided a training ground for professionals, be they stars, directors, writers, editors, or cameramen. The B's occasionally resulted in a product superior to the A film due to the fact that their creators were given more artistic freedom as long as they brought in a marketable film on schedule and within the budget. [48] These films could alternately excite and comfort their audiences and as a result could be an extremely significant part of the moviegoer's life style. With the coming of television as a major entertainment force, the B film with its philosophies, formats, and impact was absorbed by that medium. The personnel and the formats transferred often intact over to the television screen where the B film as television series and movies maintains a continuing existence. [49] And, as most critics and authorities agree, these television products are also a major influence on American society.

Republic was the largest and best of the B studios. The styles, techniques, and messages of the Republic product led the B field. Chapter I on the history of the studio provided the basic philosophy behind Republic Pictures as represented by the studio and its head, Herbert Yates. In respect to this point, Hortense Powdermaker singled out as significant, the importance of the studio leader and pointed out how his values might affect the end product and ultimately the audience. She noted that the personalities of the mov-

ie people who are in positions of power and have the responsibility of making decisions have a continuous and cumulative
effect on millions of people. [50] The values of Herbert Yates
were the basic values of the time in which he lived.

Albert S. Rogell, pioneer director who spent several
years at Republic, noted these values when he stated that in
his Republic films "when we could wave the flag we did. "
He remembers that Yates was a proud American who frequently asked his moviemakers to get the American flag on
screen even when there was no reason. [51] The actress and
wife of Yates, Vera H. Ralston, confirms that Yates was
consciously patriotic and very moral where Republic pictures
were concerned. "We specialized in B pictures and their
message was leading the good life, the clean life. This was
consciously put into every picture. Mr. Yates ... was
very strict on this. "[52] The significant factor here is that
the studio head did have control over his company and thus
did influence the audience.

If Yates considered Republic's espousal of the good
moral life important, how then did contemporary sources
view the role of Republic and its methods of reaching its
audience? To begin with, The Film Daily Cavalcade in 1939
credited Republic with successfully reviving the action drama
and thus gaining an important place in the Hollywood studio
structure. While admitting that Republic's four year rise in
a depression period had not been expected, the Cavalcade
acknowledged that the studio had "fulfilled its promises of
reviving and revivifying the forsaken field of outdoor and action films" and had gained "the respectful attention and good
will of [the] industry.... "[53] The article went on to point
out that Republic created Gene Autry and the successful image of the singing cowboy. Autry was praised as "America's
Number One Singing Cowboy, emulated by many, rivalled by
no one". [54]

Republic was also credited with giving new life to the
serial genre. "In giving new life to the serial picture, a
phase of production that had lost its identity in Hollywood's
rush toward more sophisticated film fare, Republic's purchase of radio's popular 'Lone Ranger' proved to be another
'coup de theater'.... Republic, as it fully intended, found itself with a pre-sold, pre-publicized episodical production that
became so popular and important as to find bookings in Class
A theaters throughout the nation. "[55] All of these successes
went to prove that Republic knew "the pulse of the film-going
public. "[56]

What is the significance of all this obviously public
relations oriented copy? Seemingly, Republic knew its market, picked its area, and handled the product well. The studio was of course interested in profits but in creating generally acknowledged, documented successes in their fields of
specialization, they were also creating products which influenced their audiences. And they were trying to do just this,
not for the power of influence but because they understood
the importance of understanding and reaching the audience to
insure continued profit.

That Republic fully understood the import of audience
contact and acceptance is also shown in its insistence that its
stars tour the country. Major stars from the big studios
toured rarely but the B film stars at Republic were frequently on the road. Comedienne Judy Canova, Western stars Gene
Autry, Roy Rogers, and Don Barry, hillbilly performers the
Weaver Brothers and Elviry, all were big attractions for Republic and all made frequent audience contact. Republic's
strength was in grassroots audiences so its stars went to the
grassroots level with regularity. And the approach proved
effective. In order to stay in business, Republic needed to
produce good pictures and make them cheaply enough to earn
profits within the organization's sphere of influence. Republic's effective formula for making itself and its stars
known to audiences--the personal appearance tour--encouraged
its stars to keep up the good work and Republic never shared
in the proceeds from their outside engagements. [57]

Republic also utilized local radio talent for guest appearances in pictures whenever possible. Here again the
motive was profit but the results were to make the films
more effective in influencing their audiences. "Republic's
faith in these acts is based on the premise that they add
box office value to pictures in particular localities at a price
far less than ... ranking specialty performers.... [B]ack
home they plug Republic and their forthcoming pictures. "[58]

Regardless of the reason, Republic recognized its audience and consciously catered to the market for which the
studio was most qualified. With the coming of the Second
World War, Republic's patriotic escapist entertainment
strengthened its position with the moviegoing public. A feature on the studio announced that "Republic Aims Its Films
at Heart of America". [59] The Republic audience and its
tastes were well suited for films with a wartime emphasis.
Because the product of the studio had always aimed at the

American masses, its themes needed little alteration. [60] In
other words, the Republic product already reinforced the
traditional values of patriotism, conservatism, self-reliance,
and justice.

The war also effected a temporary broadening of the
Republic market. By shifting the population from the Republic small town strongholds to industrial centers, wartime increased the demand for Republic films in the cities. The
Republic audience physically moved and enlarged to some degree while remaining the same in their entertainment habits. [61]

As illustration of this point, it was noted at the height
of the war that Republic and its audience were still in har-
mony. "One reason why the company stands on such a firm
basis is because ... Republic always has stressed the adventure type of story, and for this reason it had a ready-
made audience awaiting every picture it turned out in this
field. ... Even had it not participated in the inflated box-office,
due to war conditions, Republic then would have continued
enjoying the best of box-office health with the same type of
pictures it has made for years. "[62] Republic was to continue to meet the demand for this type of entertainment, to
fulfill the needs of its large and identifiable audience, and
to influence them in the process throughout the forties.

In a discussion of influence, the impact of the Republic
stars must also be recognized. The three best examples are
John Wayne, who soon left the B's, Gene Autry, and Roy
Rogers. The audience reaction and the influence which these
three stars had as B actors at Republic will be included in
Chapter V. Another good example of the Republic actor is
Don Barry who was rated as number four or five in the list
of Republic top Western stars for many years. His success
was noted by a Hollywood columnist who compared him with
James Cagney as a moody violent hero and noted that in one
year he rose from an unknown to become one of the top ten
Western stars in the movie industry. [63] Well known newsman
Lee Mortimer admitted in a review of Remember Pearl Harbor, a patriotic piece rapidly rushed out by Republic, "This
quickie will have a better box-office potential in the sticks
and suburbs than on Broadway. To much of the hinterland
population, the hero of this film--"Red" Barry--is as well
known as Clark Gable. "[64] Barry's pictures followed the
clean cut formula to the hilt; Barry was tougher than most
of his Western rivals, he killed off 7 to 15 villains per picture, and fans preferred him as a bad man who reforms.

He followed the Western formula of abstinence from tobacco and sex. [65] Barry is quite proud of his career as a cowboy hero and feels that he did influence the audience positively. While he denies any deep meanings in Republic films--"they were made to entertain and to get people away from their problems"--he feels that the audiences "loved Republic and loved its stars" and that he and other Western series stars therefore did provide an effective positive behavior model for the audiences. [66]

Other Republic personnel view the question of the studio's influence on the moviegoing public in much the same way. Among the interviews conducted for this study, there was near unanimity that Republic did not set out to influence the citizenry, either positively or negatively, for any goal beyond profit. Nonetheless, upon reflection many Republic workers did comment upon the studio's role in this area, identifying its contribution to the American scene as either secondary to the entertainment factor or recognizable mainly in hindsight. But they do grant that the influence existed.

Sol Siegel, Republic producer who went on to bigger efforts at major studios and as an independent producer, feels that Republic "produced the best or worst of the B's depending upon your viewpoint". He maintains that Republic was the best of the independents but that B's produced by the majors were better. However, Siegel also commented that everyone at Republic did his best and that "every writer set out to write the best story possible within his limits." In this regard he concedes a possible influence and observes that while "we were very commercial, Republic did preach traditional morality, the American success story, the Horatio Alger story". [67]

Albert S. Rogell is more adamant and feels that the impact on youth was intended. He states that the Republic product was aimed at "John Q. Public and family" and that, while he and others were just "doing a job", he always knew that "films are education". Because of this, he and his co-workers "didn't have the dollar but did have the dream of doing something better". As a result, in his opinion, "to concentrate on the big A pictures is to miss the quality of the B's. They were the heartbeat of the industry. "[68]

Bruce Bennett, successful character actor who was known as Herman Brix in his leading man days at Republic, indicates that most Republic personnel did not think in terms

of influence. "No, absolutely not, they were bread-and-butter jobs for everyone involved--no thought of anything but
entertainment to please the Saturday matinee crowd. However, with the increased interest, nostalgia, and request for
interviews and appearances, I can see that they were more
influential than we realized. They included and reinforced
American values. "[69]

Robert Livingston, Republic leading actor best known
for his role in the Three Mesquiteer series and as the second filmic Lone Ranger, responded forcefully to the question
of nostalgia versus academic interest and in the process expressed the opinion that the Republic influence was simple
and direct. "The nostalgic interest is phenomenal and has
a lot of reasons. I don't think the academic interest is real.
Perhaps it is.... Freudian complexity in these films is bull-
shit.... It was good guys versus bad guys. Simplicity [of in-
terpretation] is fine and they [the academics] should stick
with it. It [the influence] worked, it was there, but it wasn't
deep. "[70]

Vera H. Ralston's belief in the quality and influence
of Republic has been previously noted in relationship to her
husband's position of power. She feels Republic's influence
was a real one and a good one. While not all Republic films
were good and "some were very bad," she notes the increased
quality of the pictures which made them both attractive and
helped account for the renewed interest in them. She concludes, "Our pictures were aimed at the youth and we were
very aware of it ... we tried hard, did a good job, and made
pictures we could be proud of. I'm sorry that it didn't end
better. "[71]

Barry Shipman, Republic writer still active in educational films, is of the opinion that Republic movies did indeed
have an impact and that the influence was sometimes consciously intended by the writers. However, generally speaking the influence and any symbolism was unconscious but
positive. As he puts it, "Does the apple know it's nutri-
tious?" He also commented that his writing at Republic was
deliberately juvenile and that he had to work to overcome
this upon leaving the action field. [72]

Rowland "Dick" Hills, head of the Republic script
(reproduction) department and office manager, while not involved in the creative end of the business, proved very perceptive on the subject of impact. He feels that the recog-

nized Republic morality reflected the times more than the wishes of either Yates or the Hays Office. The end product was also reflective of the times and the writers simply wrote the way they felt. They intended no symbolism because they were journeyman pragmatic writers. It is Hills' contention that Republic's "class appeal was to the common man" and that whatever influence the studio had was on that level. [73]

Morris R. Abrams, Republic script supervisor and assistant director, responded more thoughtfully to the questions on Republic's role. In regard to influence, he states that he "is unable to say since he was concerned with survival and not Republic's philosophy". This statement in itself is valuable as an accurate indicator of the realities of working within the Hollywood system. Nonetheless, Abrams does make some interesting observations. He feels that the "good guy philosophy was basic in films" and that the concept of "virtue triumphant was taken for granted" in the era of Republic and was not unique to the studio. However, "the industry and Republic did better than it [sic] knew in affecting Society ... [they] tried to study audiences and to meet expectations but did not consciously try to provide a mythology or symbolic approach. "[74]

Perhaps Peggy Stewart, Republic actress, makes the most telling point. She attends many Western movie conventions and states that when the products of Republic, Columbia, and Monogram are compared in showings, "Republic's Class A stands out". She feels the interest and the market are still there, pointing out that Republic was the "Master of B's" and that people raised on these films were influenced and have a continuing interest. She claims that private Saturday matinees are still being set up on a family basis in the South utilizing the Republic product and that she is frequently told of these projects at nostalgia conventions. She feels that the current interest is indicative of the lasting Republic influence. [75]

The significance of Republic in relationship to its contributions to the B film was perhaps best summed up on the occasion of the studio's tenth anniversary: "It can take credit for the introduction of a new type of screen entertainment in the singing western; the use of popular song titles as film titles; the invasion of the comic strip field for serial background; the policy of using radio and record talent in musical entertainment; and showmanship in both the selection of exploitation screen material and in national promotion to sell both its pictures and its stars. "[76]

These contributions to the world of the B's also apply to Republic's influence on the American scene and the Zeit-geist. Just as Republic revitalized the Western, the serial, and the country musical and aggressively sold these products, so too by the same means did it make an impact upon its chosen audience. In the case of the movies, the B film and Republic, three factors are logically and irretrievably inter-twined--entertainment, marketing/profits, and influence. Re-public was predominantly interested in the first two but out of these the third followed.

It appears that Republic's B films were more influen-tial on regular movie audiences than film scholars have here-tofore acknowledged. In various works they have analyzed many films in depth concerning their influence on the Ameri-can public. In almost all cases, the movies analyzed were top grade major productions or sleeper artistic cult films. However, a great many of these films were never seen by a major segment of the moviegoing public or were seen only once. These films were also a minority of the total output. On the other hand, the B film was legion. It was mass pro-duced in six days to three weeks usually by a dozen poverty row and independent companies and played and replayed the neighborhood and small town theatres during the week, on Saturdays and sometimes even on Sundays. These were the films that the impressionable youth, the young adults, and the mass adult audience saw and re-saw on a regular weekly basis.

For every Grapes of Wrath (Twentieth Century Fox, 1940) or Citizen Kane, (RKO Radio Pictures, 1941) that came along and may or may not have made an impression, most children and even their adult counterparts saw a dozen Judy Canova, Higgins family or Three Mesquiteers films. The same was true of the serials which by their very construction came to the audience in twelve and fifteen week doses. And these films made an impression--perhaps even greater than the A productions as a group. Even when there was no mes-sage, these films had a long term, subtle and unconscious effect. To today's audiences they are transparent, wide-eyed, unrealistic, and naive. To the immature, defenseless, and more innocent audience in those darkened theaters waiting to be entertained, a total life style or at least ethical system was often pieced together from countless B films which, un-realized by them, influenced the way they conducted the rest of their lives. If film is truly significant as an effective force on society, it was achieved both directly and indirectly through the pervasiveness of the B as well as the A film.

Notes

1. McCarthy and Flynn, Kings of the Bs, p. 12.
2. "When the Movies Really Counted", Show: Magazine of the Arts (April, 1963), p. 77
3. Schlesinger, p. 125.
4. Robert S. Lynd and Helen Merrell Lynd, Middletown, A Study in Modern American Culture (New York: Harcourt, Brace and World, Inc. , 1929), p. 381, n. 6.
5. Since Yesterday: The 1930's in America (New York: Harper and Row, 1939), p. 222.
6. Allen, p. 224.
7. Geoffrey Perrett, Days of Sadness, Years of Triumph: The American People 1939-1945 (New York: Coward-McCann-Geoghegan, 1973), p. 162.
8. Perrett, p. 239.
9. Sklar, Movie Made America, p. 269.
10. Manny Farber, "Movies in Wartime", New Republic, CX (January 3, 1944), p. 19.
11. Film Daily Yearbook of Motion Pictures: 1944 (New York: Film Daily, Inc. , 1944), p. 44
12. Richard R. Lingeman, Don't You Know There's a War On? The American Home Front, 1941-1945 (New York: G. P. Putnam's Sons, 1970), p. 206. Lingeman goes on to cite a Republic production The Fighting Seabees, as illustrative of the Hollywood patriotic film of the period and its effect on youth.
13. "A Relationship of Constrained Anxiety: Historians and Film", The History Teacher, VI (1973), p. 553.
14. Isenberg, p. 557.
15. Isenberg, p. 561.
16. Isenberg, p. 568. A book length treatment, Paul Smith, ed. , The Historian and Film (New York: Cambridge University Press, 1976), covers much of the same ground, comes to many of the same conclusions and includes historical and geographical surveys of the subject as well as a look at resources. Most contributors conclude that the import of a film, "the film fact," is more than just the factual material in a film and what it is about. It is the sum of the film, where it was made, how it was made, how the audience perceived it and accepted it, and what it can add to an understanding of the society out of which it came. Film as a reflection of and an influence of society is where the importance of film to the his-

74   Republic Studios

torian lies, seems to be the general conclusion of
the book.
17. Letter from Garth Jowett, to author, December 22,
    1975.
18. "An Anthropologist Looks at the Movies", The Annals
    of the American Academy of Political and Social
    Sciences, CCLIV (November, 1947), p. 80.
19. Powdermaker, p. 81.
20. Powdermaker, p. 87.
21. The Film: A Psychological Study: The Silent Photoplay
    in 1916 (New York: Dover Publications, 1970), p. 100
22. Münsterberg, p. 95.
23. Sklar, pp. 135-139.
24. Movies, Delinquency, and Crime (New York: Macmillan
    Company, 1933, reprint, ed., New York: Arno Press,
    1970), p. 202.
25. Our Movie Made Children (New York: Macmillan Company,
    1935, reprint, ed., New York: Arno Press, 1970, p. 2.
26. Forman, p. 177.
27. Forman, p. 277.
28. Martha Wolfenstein and Nathan Leites, Movies: A Psy-
    chological Study (New York: Free Press, 1950, re-
    printed, New York: Hafner Publishing Company,
    1971), p. 13.
29. David Manning White and Richard Averson, The Cellu-
    loid Weapon: Social Comment in the American Film
    (Boston: Beacon Press, 1972), p. x.
30. Peter Bogdanovich, Fritz Lang in America (New York:
    Frederick A. Praeger, Inc., 1967), p. 16.
31. "A Broad Mosaic on the Social Screen," American Film
    I (June, 1976), p. 73.
32. Powdermaker, p. 80.
33. Interview with Sloan Nibley, Republic writer, Los Ange-
    les, California, May 4, 1976.
34. Wolfenstein and Leites, p. 14.
35. Wolfenstein and Leites, p. 178.
36. Wolfenstein and Leites, pp. 304-05.
37. White and Averson, p. 107.
38. "Hollywood and the U. S. A. " in Bernard Rosenberg
    and David Manning White, ed., Mass Culture: The
    Popular Arts in America (New York: Free Press,
    1964), p. 292.
39. White and Averson, p. 207.
40. White and Averson, p. 25.
41. The Unembarrassed Muse: The Popular Arts in Amer-
    ica (New York: Dial Press, 1970), p. 387.
42. Miller, B Movies, p. 34.

43. "Those First Rate Second Features", Films and Film-
    making, II (September, 1956), p. 17.
44. Joan Cohen, "The Second Feature: The Rise and Fall
    of the B Movies", Mankind, V (June, 1976), p. 26.
45. Cohen, "Second Feature", p. 29.
46. Cohen, "Second Feature", p. 35.
47. Francis Nevins, Review of Kings of the Bs, Films in
    Review, XXVI (October, 1975), p. 499.
48. William Everson, Review of B Movies, Films in Re-
    view, XXV (November, 1974), p. 564.
49. Sklar, p. 282.
50. Powdermaker, "An Anthropologist Looks at the Film",
    p. 86.
51. Interview with Albert S. Rogell, Republic director, Los
    Angeles, California, May 5, 1976.
52. Telephone interview with Vera H. Ralston, Santa Bar-
    bara, California, May 10, 1976.
53. David B. Whalen, "Republic Pictures", The Film Daily
    Cavalcade (1939), p. 176 in the Republic clipping file
    of the Margaret Herrick Library of the Academy of
    Motion Picture Arts and Sciences, Los Angeles, Cali-
    fornia.
54. Whalen, "Republic", p. 179.
55. Whalen, "Republic", p. 179.
56. Whalen, "Republic", p. 181.
57. David Hanna in the New York Times, February 2, 1941.
58. New York Times, February 2, 1941.
59. Variety, Ninth Anniversary Edision, October 29, 1942,
    p. 271.
60. Variety, October 29, 1942, p. 271.
61. Variety, October 29, 1942, p. 271.
62. Variety, Tenth Anniversary Edition, October 29, 1943,
    p. 455.
63. Vern Haugland, "Don Barry Is Western Star No. 5 af-
    ter Short, Swift Rise in Films", November 8 [1942].
    Unidentified newspaper clipping in the Donald Barry
    clipping file of the Theatrical Division of the New
    York Public Library at Lincoln Center.
64. New York Daily Mirror, June 4, 1942.
65. Haugland, "Don Barry", November 8, [1942].
66. Interview with Donald Barry, Hollywood, California,
    May 6, 1976.
67. Telephone interview with Sol C. Siegel, Los Angeles,
    California, May 5, 1976.
68. Interview with Albert S. Rogell, Los Angeles, Califor-
    nia, May 5, 1976.

69. Telephone interview with Bruce Bennett, Los Angeles,
     California, May 7, 1976.
70. Telephone interview with Robert Livingston, Los Ange-
     les, California, May 8, 1976.
71. Telephone interview with Vera H. Ralston, Santa Bar-
     bara, California, May 10, 1976.
72. Interview with Barry Shipman, San Bernardino, Califor-
     nia, May 11, 1976.
73. Interview with Rowland "Dick" Hills, Los Angeles, Cali-
     fornia, May 13, 1976.
74. Interview with Morris R. Abrams, Los Angeles, Cali-
     fornia, May 17, 1976.
75. Interview with Peggy Stewart, North Hollywood, Califor-
     nia, May 18, 1976.
76. "Republic Pictures Celebrates Its Tenth Anniversary,"
     The Independent, CXXXVIII (June 23, 1945), p. 30.

Chapter IV

THE SOUND SERIAL AT REPUBLIC

Republic did not invent the serial format--the company simply developed it to its highest form in the sound era
through judicious application of talent, care, and technical
knowledge. Early in the silent period, the serial was locked
into the "cliffhanger" format. In some respects this was a
mixed blessing in that it proved detrimental to plot and character development, but because the development necessitated
a "thrill" ending to each chapter, it did result in an emphasis on action and violence. By the time that the first tentative completely sound serial, The Indians Are Coming (Universal, 1930), was produced, the action-escapist entertainment format was assured.

Thomas Wood, entertainment feature writer for the
New York Times, summarized the basic approach. "The
first episode establishes the characters and the goal that is
to be achieved. The rest of the chapters try to keep the
audience in a state of nervous exhaustion until the star ac-
complishes the appointed task. The goal, of course, is of
earthshaking importance, like a new formula for cracking the
atom. "[1] This rigid formula based on physical conflict meant
that there was a minimum of dialogue. This fact was unchanged with the coming of sound. One columnist noted,
"[T]he essence of good serial-making is action. Ron Davidson [Republic director, writer] sets his writers a standard
of no more than 700 words per episode, which makes for a
pretty tight-lipped 15 minutes. "[2] All of which meant that
the serial genre is dependent upon getting its entertainment
values, minimum plot, and message to the audience by the
simple technique of pacing and action. As a result the genre
proved a good training ground for directors and writers concerning the maintenance of suspense and good pacing. [3] In
any case, the action-oriented "cliffhanging" trademark to
grasp and hold on to the audience was irreversibly linked to
the sound serial.

*Notes to Chapter IV begin on page 115.

Prior to the end of the motion picture serial in 1956,
231 sound productions were released.   Universal produced
69; Republic, 66; Columbia, 57; Mascot, 24; and 15 came
from independents.   Universal depended mainly upon relatively more plot with adequate action, effects and sets; Republic,
and its predecessor Mascot to a degree, relied heavily on
outstanding action, special effects, and pacing with secondary
consideration upon plot; and Columbia with a few notable exceptions was concerned with short-cut production to maximize
profits after the first few years so that the plot and the action, which was usually frenetic if nothing else, suffered accordingly. 4   The quality and value of the independent productions varied greatly.

The serials tended to fall conveniently into several
categories.   There were, of course, some productions such
as Phantom Empire (Mascot, 1934) which defied classification,
which is to say that it had elements of science fiction, the
Western, and even musical comedy.   Nonetheless, the following are the important categories with an outstanding example
from each:

(1) Mad Scientists - Mysterious Doctor Satan (Republic,
    1940);
(2) The Western - The Lone Ranger (Republic, 1938);
(3) Aviation - Tailspin Tommy in the Great Air Mys-
    tery (Universal, 1935);
(4) Jungle Adventures - Jungle Girl (Republic, 1941);
(5) Detectives - Dick Tracy (Republic, 1937);
(6) Costumed Heroes - Adventures of Captain Marvel
    (Republic, 1941);
(7) Outer Space Science Fiction - Flash Gordon (Uni-
    versal, 1936);
(8) Straight Adventure - Daredevils of the Red Circle
    (Republic, 1939).

The sound serials were generally considered to be in their
Golden Age, due mainly to the Republic contributions, from
approximately 1938 to 1944 and after the war began to decline. 5   Possibly the last really unique serial in terms of
imagination and story concept was King of the Rocket Men
(Republic, 1949) and that production, although worthy, was
flawed because of the pressures of grim economic reality.
Movie serial production ceased in 1956 due predominantly to
the competiton of television and to an increasing sophistication in the audience.   Their last years were quite abysmal
with increasing reliance on stock footage and routine action
sequences. 6

In order to understand the serials, their potential influence, and the reaction of their audience to them, it is important to be familiar with the basic value system upon which they were predicated and a simple requirement for absorbing them. The importance of conflict has been established but, more importantly, it was always virtuous conflict. The basic value system of the serial is represented in a plot formula which is a simplistic representation of good versus evil in black and white terms with evil temporarily winning each round but with good ultimately triumphing. The major audience, comprised of children, the uneducated, and those desiring a temporary escape into a more simple approach to life, accepted and understood this basic rule. The concept of good ultimately triumphant over evil resulted in a firm moral and ethical basis for all sound serial production, the foundation of which was a naive idealism.

The requirement for absorbing and enjoying the serial was also a simple one--easily understood by the generations of the thirties and forties but a bit more difficult for the later sophisticated television era. The requirement was simply that the viewer accept a willing suspension of disbelief. No serial would stand up under stern, critical, realistic analysis. It was necessary to accept the spirit of the concept-- that villains were maniacal with no redeeming social qualities, that they could have vast networks of henchmen, that heroes were dedicated, compulsive, and believed in direct action, and finally that both sides would clash violently on a regular basis until good won out. These confrontations rarely involved anyone outside the combatants except abstractly in that society as a whole was theoretically a gigantic pawn which represented the final prize in the contest. Also, either side was frequently conveniently identified by a costumed mystery leader. The element of the unknown, the outlandish situations, and the basic physical conflict of good and evil kept the audience coming back.

The concept of a willing suspension of disbelief is not only basic, it is perhaps the most important aspect of the serial form's success and the key to whatever influence the genre may have had. Jon Tuska touches on this point in commenting on the significance of Nat Levine who, as it has been pointed out, headed Mascot and supervised the early Republic serials. "As a producer, Nat Levine sought neither prestige nor profundity. He loved the serial as a very special medium. ... The serials were mostly intended for youngsters and so stressed images and settings and situations that

appealed instinctively and indelibly to youthful imaginations.
In fact, one of the strongest and most notable aspects of the
Mascot serials is this importance of make-believe. "[7] Because Levine was such a master of make-believe and utilized
the suspension of disbelief so well even with inexpensive budgets and extremely limited schedules, Tuska attributes an influence to Levine's serials, particularly the Mascots, which
he finds almost mystical.   While this interpretation diverges
sharply with the hypothesis of a simple straightforward message of good versus evil, Tuska's viewpoint does indicate
that the serial form had an influence and, by implication,
that it supported the traditional morality.   "The viewer be-
lieves because the characters themselves believe, so caught
up in the basic premises of the farfetched and imaginative
plot that ... all critical faculties are suspended before the
somewhat awesome spectacle.   The overwhelming visual impact of Levine's images ... generate ... a dream-like quality which is vivid and unassailable. "[8] Tuska is speaking of
a specific serial but the generalization is that with serials
the audience accepted the premise wholeheartedly, and were
extremely receptive because they were so involved.   As a
result, the serials became a learning process for a value
system.

    The genre might also contribute to learning in yet an-
other way. P. E. Emery, an Australian behavioral psychologist, has studied the potential learning processes in the Western film and discusses the relationship of the learning effect
to the completion of the goals of the story or, to put it another way, the attention of the audience and thus its receptivity to learning is held to the climax.   Moreover, a climax
filled with tension increases attention.   As an illustration, he
concludes that with serials and their multiple tension filled
climaxes, the receptivity to learning is similarly multiplied. [9]
To make profits and to entertain, the serials continually
ended in tension to keep the viewer coming back.   This fact
also results in holding that same viewer's attention which
leads to a potential learning effect.   So, while the serial
was not created as a learning device, it did so function.

    Even the Payne Fund studies acknowledge this fact by
using as an example the illogical fears of an adult woman
based upon movie serials she had seen as a receptive child.
"[W]e wish to point to the fact that ... her attitude, notwith-
standing her greater knowledge, is permanently qualified by
the ideas of the movies she had seen in childhood.... "[10]

Hollywood accepted both the idea that the serials were influential and that, without proper controls, they would be a negative force. "Probably nowhere else in the world does Crime pay less than in the moving picture serial. Because its sub-teen admirers are felt to be in the 'impressionable' state, the serial is considered as harmless as a time bomb. Every episode, before its public release, is subjected to a scrutiny that could do credit to the Gestapo. Not only must the chapter pass the officious Hays organization, but it must also satisfy the delegates of a dozen women's clubs in the vicinity."[11] Actually the Hays office and various private and public censorship groups were much harder on serials than on adult-oriented features. The writers were aware of this but in order to make the serials acceptable to the theaters, the double standard was tolerated.[12]

All of this of course contributed to the moral emphasis of the serials--action, conflict, and the denunciation of evil. As already noted, the Zeitgeist and the attitude of Herbert Yates were also prime Republic motivations. As a result, the serials were blatantly patriotic. During the Second World War period, for example, the locales remained unchanged but the plots concerned espionage and sabotage by Nazi and Japanese villains.[13] Actually, there were even several serials at Republic prior to the war which were either service oriented or, as the war approached, had the home front fending off nefarious schemes by thinly disguised Axis agents. Then, after the war, the serial frequently began to shift to anticommunism as a theme with varying degrees of success.[14] Despite their patriotism, the simplicity and action orientation of the serials also made them popular world wide.[15]

Thus, the serial genre in the sound era did indeed exert an influence, sometimes political in tone but always basically moral. Despite strenuous efforts to control and modify the content, the serial remained a popular international commodity until its demise and even continues in limited distribution on television and in overseas markets to the present.[16]

With its attention to detail and spirit of teamwork, Republic quickly evolved their serial production work into a science. The studio decided what serials it would schedule each year from the suggestions of their exhibitors and the studio's own ideas of what would be profitable. In the spring of each year, four titles for the next season would be announced,

the first to be released in the fall and the last the following
summer. The four projected serials were then budgeted and
divided into two groups--twelve chapter "streamline" serials
or fifteen chapter "super" serials. [17]

The producer then met with the writers who worked
on schedules of three months for each serial. The writers,
varying from one to seven, then developed the plot to go
with the title, always considering the use of possible stock
footage from other films, the use of existing sets, and de-
termining possible location sites available for their use. Each
writer then developed several individual chapters and finally
as a group they integrated their efforts into a complete
script. [18] The first chapter developed the plot, the ingenious
devices and schemes, and laid out the basic cast of characters. Each following chapter began with a brief synopsis of
plot, an "overlap" of previous footage reviewing the cliffhanger, and the actual escape. The plot then moved along including an obligatory action sequence midchapter. The tension
climax was then set up and abruptly upon its occurrence, usually with a great deal of action and/or suspense, the chapter concluded.

Upon approval of the preliminary submission the writers wrote an "estimating" script which was used to determine probable shooting costs. This same "estimating" script
was used to check any legal problems, was submitted to the
review board for censorship, and was the basis for the pressbook publicity campaign. A polished rewrite became the
shooting script which occasionally underwent some alteration
during the actual production.

Preproduction was the next step and included casting
of leads, costume design, set construction, location contracts,
and the lining up of props and equipment. A daily breakdown
of set-ups was normally created to permit all scenes on one
location or set to be filmed together and re-edited into plot
sequence later. Serials had shorter shooting schedules,
eighteen to forty-eight days at Republic, and more separate
scenes than most features. Shooting all scenes for one location together saved time and money.

Production began normally on location with interiors
shot later and two crews were often used--the first shooting
dialogue and plot and the second unit crew shooting chases
and stunt action. The special effects were shot last because
they took more time and care and because the miniatures

(models of buildings, cars, planes, etc. carefully designed by the well known Lydecker brothers) had to match the previously shot footage utilizing full size action. At Republic, separate music was also composed for the serials in the early years which undoubtedly contributed to their slickness.

The completed serials of Republic ran from 166 minutes and 40 seconds to 289 minutes and 54 seconds and the final negative costs ranged from $87,655 to $222,906 without distribution and print costs which were extra.[19] It generally took between a year and eighteen months to complete each serial's run in original release.

Because of the combination of good people and fine facilities, Republic serials gained recognition from the beginning. According to one historian, of all the serial companies, including those of the silent era, only Republic succeeded in making their product "socially acceptable."[20] The serials of Republic emphasized in varying degrees and in order of importance the virtues of patriotism, law and order, fair play, individualism, leadership, upright living, and other middle American values. While it is not possible to discuss each of the sixty-six Republic serials in detail here, a chronological survey of some outstanding examples will give both an overview of the rise and fall of the studio's serials and the messages which they so effectively carried to their viewers.

The first serial made under the Republic banner was Darkest Africa, released in February, 1936, and directed by B. Reeves Eason, noted action director and film second unit man, and Joseph Kane, who graduated to Republic feature director. A jungle adventure with fantasy overtones, the story centered on the Lost City of Joba hidden in the African jungle where a white girl named Valerie was kept prisoner and worshiped as a goddess. After fifteen chapters of confrontations, Clyde Beatty, the white hunter hero, eventually rescued Valerie. His rugged individualism and fairness as contrasted with the greed and cheating of a variety of villains was a prominent motif but the message was subdued.

Since the Republic staff was feeling its way, the serial suffered from padding--a result of Republic's well intentioned decision to make first chapters of their serials a hefty one-half hour and subsequent chapters approximately twenty minutes.[21] However, the special effects were well done, especially those of the flying Bat-men who guard the Lost City.

They were a worthy predecessor to the flying figures in
Captain Marvel (1941) and King of the Rocket Men (1949),
and were an early indication of the studio's striving for quality. All in all the serial was a good, if not outstanding, beginning.

Since the element of fantasy had worked in their first
serial, Republic continued it in its second effort, Undersea
Kingdom, again directed by Eason and Kane and released the
same year. This was the first of the service-oriented serials, but since the Navy was in prominence only in Chapters
One and Twelve, its patriotic theme was limited. The plot
concerned a young Naval officer and his friends who dove to
the ocean floor in a rocket propelled submarine and found the
Lost City of Atlantis where two factions were in constant
combat, with the villains intent upon world conquest. Obviously, the newcomers soon found themselves allied with the
forces of good.[22] Battle scenes between the two factions
were considered superb and were directed by Eason who also
specialized in doing massive second unit direction for the majors, including the burning of Atlanta in Gone with the Wind
and the crowd sequences in Duel in the Sun,[23] again showing
the expertise of Republic personnel.

The message to the audience was fairly clear. The
hero was a clean-cut, handsome, athletic American youth
and a pride of Annapolis. His heroism and leadership abilities were heavily stressed although the heroics sometimes
approached the foolhardy. For example, at the end of Chapter Eight, he was captured and bound to the front of the futuristic tank utilized by the villains. When the action heavy
threatened to run the tank through the fortress gates using
Corrigan as a battering ram unless he cooperated, the hero's
brave reply was a snarling bravado, "Go ahead and ram!"
It was a moment of hero-worship for the youth in the audience and led to an exciting chapter ending but one which is
known as a "cheat". In Chapter Eight, the tank obviously
smashed with great force into the recessed fortress gates.
In Chapter Nine, however, the gates were opened at the last
second and the tank stopped quietly in the courtyard. Incidently, such "cheat" endings were relatively infrequent at
Republic.

Republic began 1937 by producing the first of their
comic strip heroes in serial format. Dick Tracy as portrayed by Ralph Byrd was an unqualified success and eventually
led to three sequels. In the first Tracy outing, he was di-

rected by Ray Taylor and Alan James, and was opposing a
gang of criminals headed by a mastermind known alternately
as the Spider and the Lame One. This serial included an
economy or retrospect chapter which was a money-saving device that Republic and other studios utilized in order to save
money. In Chapter Thirteen of Dick Tracy, various members
of the cast sat around and discussed what had happened up
to that point using flashbacks from earlier episodes before
bringing the episode to a conclusion with a new cliffhanger
ending. [24]

Since Republic was in only its second year of serial
production, the serial unit was still finding its way but was
convinced that the use of comic characters and specifically
Dick Tracy would be a successful venture. To this end, Republic was extremely competitive with both Universal and Columbia to obtain rights to this property. [25] Of course, the
success of not one but four Tracy serials was to vindicate
Nat Levine's confidence. However, he and others at Republic did have one reservation about Tracy and it was concerned
with influence and censorship. Tracy symbolized hard line
law and order but with massive doses of explicit violence.
"This violent means of self-preservation and approach to
eradicating crime--upon which both [Chester] Gould [Tracy's
creator] and [Joseph Medill] Patterson [Chicago Tribune-New
York Times syndicate] bestowed their blessing--evinced Republic's only cause for concern. . . . Levine, although admitting
the strip's 'blood and thunder' would have to be toned down
to circumvent unfavorable reaction from women's clubs and
churches . . . contacted . . . [the syndicate] which represented
Gould. "26

The Los Angeles office of the Federal Bureau of Investigation cooperated in the production of this serial and the
result was an action coated paean to the forces of law and
order. So effective was the figure of Dick Tracy as the
archetypal representation of law enforcement that the identity
of the lead actor was submerged to that of the hero which he
played. At the time of Tracy's greatest popularity, Ralph
Byrd was identified as the detective in the popular mind. "On
a recent personal appearance tour Ralph Byrd, who plays
'Dick Tracy,' was billed as 'Dick Tracy in person.' The
name Ralph Byrd wouldn't have meant a thing,' one theater
exhibitor said. "27

Republic's next release in 1937 was The Painted Stallion, and it was directed by Ray Taylor, Alan James, and

William Witney--the third of whom took over this production
in progress and went on to become one of the greatest of the
Republic action directors. The straightforward Western plot
was set in the early nineteenth century when Mexico had just
broken ties with Spain and wished to establish trade relations
with the United States. Clark Stewart, portrayed by Ray Corrigan, represented the United States and was traveling with
a wagon train to Santa Fe to sign a pact with the new Mexican governor. Opposing the wagon train was the about-to-be-
ousted Lieutenant Governor of Santa Fe who moonlighted as
the head of a gang of outlaws which preyed on wagon trains.

Despite the fact that it was bogus history, this serial
did maintain an historical flavor and somewhat paralleled the
Westward movement in the 1820's. The prologue set the tone.
"Westward! The Trail to Empire! From Independence, Missouri to Santa Fe, New Mexico, dogged pioneers fought to
penetrate a wilderness of savage Indians ... massacres and
death. To the heroes of yesterday!--Those pioneers who
braved the perilous trek westward, defeated a hostile wilderness, and blazed a glorious trail across the pages of American history."28 Stirring words which in emphasizing our historical heritage perhaps made history classes a little more
palatable and maybe even interesting to the Saturday matinee
audiences.

Republic's third serial of 1937 was SOS Coast Guard
and had Ralph Byrd as Terry Kent of the Coast Guard opposing a mad inventor portrayed by horror star Bela Lugosi.
William Witney and Alan James directed this serial which
was Republic's annual honor to a branch of the military service complete with patriotic prologue. The preceding year,
it was the Navy. The next year it was to be the Marines.
After the third year the policy was dropped. 29 The patriotism of the war years was to more than make up for the
omission.

For the last serial of 1937, Republic turned to the
pulp character Zorro. Zorro Rides Again concerned the exploits of the great-grandson of the original Zorro, James
Vega, as portrayed by John Carroll, in his fight to save the
California Yucatan railroad from a crooked American entre-
preneur trying to seize it with the help of an outlaw gang
headed by El Lobo. This serial is a landmark in that it was
directed by William Witney and John English. With this serial the Witney-English team was formed. Together, they
proved to be perhaps the best sound serial directors of all

time. Their professionalism, pacing, and technical knowledge was evident in Zorro Rides Again and in sixteen serials
that followed. It was this directorial team which was responsible for a large portion of the serials characteristic of
the "Golden age".

There have been many tributes to the Witney-English
team but one of the most interesting appeared in the French
movie journal Positif. A liberal translation includes the
statement, "The serials directed by William Witney and John
English ... are as a group among the most lively and intense
expression of art from the American cinema of the period.
These films present the spectator with a sense of suspense
and danger ... of camaraderie.... In these films Witney and
English are mirroring present life ... frontiers of violence,
cooperation, destiny, scientific inquiry ... this is the purpose of the cinema. "30

Consciously or unconsciously, Republic Studios had
utilized its first eight serials as a continuing experiment to
determine the best format for this type of production. As
Ed Connor stated in Screen Facts: "At the end of their first
eight serials, Republic had 'found' themselves. Having ironed
out the kinks in their serial armor, they now set out to apply
a high polish, and in the next six years they would produce
the finest talking serials ever made. "31

William Witney, one of the men who brought the Republic serial to near perfection in its golden years (1938-1944),
analyzed the role of action in these productions. Just as Republic conceivably had a positive effect upon their audience
with their action ladened serials and B movies, so might
these same films be criticized for their potential negative influence of the violent aspects of such action sequences. Witney recounted that there was a sign on the wall at Republic,
which read "A pair of wet panties for every little kiddie". 32
Although the story of the sign might be apocryphal, it illus-
trates that the goal of the sound serials was to excite, to
thrill, and sometimes to slightly frighten (although through
apprehension and excitement rather than shock) the children
at which they were aimed.

The first serial in 1938 was The Lone Ranger based
on the well known radio show and directed by the Witney-English team. Set in Texas in the Reconstruction era, the story
dealt with the conflict between an outlaw attempting to become
dictator of the state and a mysterious masked Ranger who was

the sole survivor of a group of Texas Rangers killed by the
outlaw's gang.

It was determined by the heavy that one of five men
in the town which he used as headquarters was indeed the
Lone Ranger. In the course of fifteen chapters the quintette
of Ranger suspects was gradually lessened, one after the other
being killed off every three or four chapters, until in Chapter Fifteen only two remained. One was shot and killed, but his
identity was not yet disclosed to the audience. After a service
for the four dead Rangers in the last chapter, the Lone Ranger,
portrayed by Lee Powell, identified himself to the heroine and
a few others before making the traditional exit so familiar to
the radio audience. The Lone Ranger is considered by many
experts to be the best Western serial ever made although it is
rarely seen today. [33] The mystery hero motif first utilized by
Republic in this serial proved highly effective.

And the serial was quite successful at the time of its
initial circulation and gave the genre in general and especially
the Republic product a noticeable boost. Thomas Wood summarized it.

> The best record hung up in recent years is that of
> the 'Lone Ranger,' a serial which cost $285,000
> [somewhat inflated estimate] and eventually grossed
> $1,250,000 [also inflated]. Based on a radio pro-
> gram emanating from Station WXYZ in Detroit, the
> film played 7,500 houses in Canada and this coun-
> try, including some of the swank Loew's theaters
> in New York City, and was ultimately translated
> into ten different languages: French, Dutch, Bel-
> gian, German, Spanish, Italian, Swedish, Turkish,
> Portuguese and Chinese. The only country which
> didn't go for it was Great Britain, which has al-
> ways been a blind spot for serials. In 1940, how-
> ever, the "Lone Ranger" was telescoped into a fea-
> ture picture and re-released under the title, "Hi-Yo
> Silver." The British liked it fine in the abridged
> form.
> The popularity of the "Lone Ranger" reversed a
> serial trend. It inspired King Features, the news-
> paper syndicate, to release a cartoon strip based
> upon his activities. [34]

The Lone Ranger as presented by Republic was a
classic good guy. This was partially due to contractual de-

mands by the character's co-creator, George Trendle. "Trendle envisioned his creation in real-life form as following the
mold of such contemporary western stars as Tom Mix, William S. Hart, and Richard Dix. Specified to be a clean-shav-
en, rugged outdoors type of a height not less than 5-foot-11
and a weight of approximately 170 pounds, the white-stetsoned,
boot-shod, but chap-less Lone Ranger was not to swear or
drink and could only smoke if the plot demanded...."[35]

Not only did the Ranger behave with heroic selfless
qualities, his four helpers emulated him admirably, each
eventually dying heroically. For example, in Chapter One
all five suspects were imprisoned in jail whereupon the real
Lone Ranger identified himself and stated, "I didn't tell Jefferies [the villain] because I wanted to speak with you men
first. There is a lot to be accomplished. Texas needs loyal
fighters." One of the heroes replied, "Jefferies won't keep
his word anyway. We're in this thing together and we'll
stick together." The Lone Ranger pointed out, "I can't let
you die on my account." To which a spokesman for all the
heroes replied, "If we die, it will be together and for Texas."
The Ranger concluded, "You men have the spirit of Rangers.
I am glad."[36] The ideals of loyalty, honor, and dedication
to a just cause were thus impressed on a youthful audience.

Republic utilized two of the stars of The Lone Ranger,
Lee Powell and Herman Brix, in its next serial, The Fighting
Devil Dogs, which was the last officially service oriented
chapterplay with the Marines spotlighted accordingly. It included a traditional patriotic credit in the prologue--"To the
United States Marines--vigilant guardians of our flag at home
and abroad,"[37] and military heroism was neatly interwoven
with a science fiction plot.

Republic's third serial for 1938, a sequel to the successful Dick Tracy, was entitled Dick Tracy Returns and
starred Ralph Byrd again in the title role. The story centered around Tracy's battles against a notorious West Coast
criminal, Pa Stark, and his five sons in their imaginative
criminal activities. The resemblance to Ma Barker was in-
tentional and the serial lacked the science fiction elements of
the first and later Tracy entries. This straightforward crime
drama approach possibly strengthened the law and order message of the serial.

That both Republic and the censors were aware of the
impact that serials might have is shown in this case. Dick

Tracy Returns received some sixteen separate cuts in the
first chapter following its initial release. These were cate-
gorized as "details of crime" and "scenes of gruesomeness"
and included a brutal killing of a wounded FBI man and the
graphic suffering of a victim writhing in an iron lung. [38] Republic of course made the required cuts in the questionable
scenes which in no way detracted from Tracy's image as the
guardian of the law.

The Lone Ranger Rides Again was Republic's first release of 1939. This time the Lone Ranger was portrayed by
Robert Livingston and was identified as Bill Andrews, a completely different character from that of the Lone Ranger in
the original serial. He was a scout for a wagon train of
homesteaders and went into action as the Lone Ranger when
the homesteaders were threatened by villainous ranchers. It
was a standard Western plot of ranchers versus settlers,
showed little imagination, and is often felt to be a lesser
Witney-English effort. [39]

These facts in no way detract from the continuing popularity of the main character and the serial was still a success, only relatively less so than its almost archetypal predecessor. Based partially on the widespread popularity of the
first serial, the Lone Ranger radio program had increased
circulation fourfold, a comic strip version had been created,
and various merchandising products had been authorized. The
figure was truly an influential force for American youth. And
the serial counterpart retained his heroic proportions and
virtuous image.

Perhaps the most obvious example of the Lone Ranger's
power as a force for good came in the concluding scenes of
the final episode when one of the antagonists, now at peace
with a treaty signed and the plot resolved, eulogized, "Lone
Ranger ... New Mexico, as well as your mother state of
Texas, owes you an overwhelming debt of gratitude. Owing
to your efforts, this is now a peaceful territory. Law and
order prevail. This document guarantees that now a man can
live with safety, work in the fields, ride the range, or otherwise indulge in the pursuit of happiness."[40] A more succinct
statement of the hero's goal and therefore of the message
found in this, and many other Republic serials, would be hard
to locate.

While the Lone Ranger sequel is not among the top
rated serials, Witney and English came up with an outstanding

serial in the next release, Daredevils of the Red Circle. An
escaped convict sets out to revenge himself upon the indus-
trialist responsible for his imprisonment. Three athletic
circus performers, billed as the "Daredevils of the red circle," were determined to stop the attacks upon the industri-
alist's enterprises.

It was an excellent serial and is often rated as the
best single example of the adventure serial in the sound era.[41]
It was in this serial that the Witney technique of choreogra-
phing fight sequences, famous among fans, first appeared--
which is to say that the sequences were laid out in advance,
filmed in short segments with rest periods or less strenuous
shots in between, and expertly edited into a finished flowing
action shot later. While this development may not have been
directly influential upon the audience since fight sequences,
good and bad, were an integral part of the serial genre, it
was certainly a contribution to the technique of stunting and
made the final product all the more polished and exciting.
Perhaps this fact--i. e. , the slickness of production--in-
creased the audience acceptance of the story and therefore
did contribute to potential impact upon the viewer by enlarg-
ing his receptivity.

Dick Tracy's G-Men (1939) portrayed the master detective in opposition to Zarnoff, the head of a vast spy organization. Here again, Tracy obviously represented the theme
of law and order. However, there was a slight variation,
one which would become dominant over the next few years.
Instead of fighting a science fiction criminal mastermind or
the fictional counterparts to a real life criminal family, Tracy was in conflict with an international spy ring. With this
type of plot, the themes of patriotism, the FBI as guardian,
preparedness, and protection of democracy were prevalent
throughout.

In the opening sequence, a pseudo news reel report
showed Tracy capturing Zarnoff and concluded with Tracy's
ringing words, "Nicholas Zarnoff was like a rat, gnawing at
the foundations of democracy. Like any other rat carrying
germs of plague and disease, he had to be exterminated. I
sincerely hope his execution ... will serve as a warning to
any other spies or troublemakers who might think America
is easy pickings."[42] The effect upon the Saturday matinee
crowd, while predictable, was significant.

Zorro's Fighting Legion was Republic's final 1939 se-

rial and was the only one of the five Zorro titles and two
imitations in which the original Zorro character actually appeared. Zorro/Vega as portrayed by Reed Hadley was opposed to an activated Indian idol, Don Del Oro, who was in
reality a white man attempting to take over Mexico by using
the Indians for his own end in 1824.

    At least one critic feels that Zorro's Fighting Legion
surpassed The Lone Ranger as the best Western sound serial.
Francis Nevins states: "A sense of exhilaration, good humor, joy in life, and in fighting the good fight and in making
movies, permeates every frame. From Zorro's Fighting Legion we learn what the serial at its best can be."43

    Censorship came in to play once again although the
end results were a bit different. Concern was expressed
over the fact that Zorro lightly carved his initial on his op-
ponent's forehead during sword play in Chapter One. However, it was allowed to stay and with a minimum of blood.
It gave the appearance of a surface scratch. "Exactly one
year later the Hays office refused to pass such a scene for
the Tyrone Power feature Mark of Zorro [Twentieth Century-
Fox, 1940]. So what was okay for the kiddies was too much
for their parents.44 This amusing anecdote was an exception
to the reverse rule in an environment where the effects of
serials on the younger audience was a continuing concern.

    By 1940 the Golden Age of Republic serials had really
dawned. Drums of Fu Manchu bore little relationship to the
book and was unique in that it relied more on plot than any
other Republic serial while still retaining a great amount of
action for the fans. The basic conflict concerned the imple-
mentation of a plan by Fu Manchu to have himself declared
the messiah who would appear bearing the sceptre of Genghis
Khan to unite the Orientals of the world and conquer Asia.
Fu and his minions were opposed by six whites including Fu's
old adversary Nayland Smith, Doctor Petrie, and the action
hero Allan Parker portrayed by Robert Kellard. Although Fu
was defeated in the final chapter, he escaped with his life
and swore vengeance.45

    This serial is considered one of Republic's finest chap-
ter plays predominantly due to its emphasis on mood and
Henry Brandon's performance in the title role. A sequel,
originally planned, was never made because of complaints
from the Chinese government due to the touchy international
situation in 1940 (apparently the yellow peril motif, blatant

as it was, was not appreciated universally), and because of complaints from various parent groups that the serial actually frightened children due to its excellent use of suspense.[46] This second point is ironic indeed because steps had been taken prior to production to remove the fearful aspects of Fu's dacoits, action heavies derived from historical Burmese or Indian killer thieves who actually existed. "The writers decided to make him [the chief dacoit] a real terrifier and described him in their original script as not having a mouth. Obviously the censor felt this was a little too much, so Loki remained mute, and had a mouth, with two vampire-like fangs protruding from under his upper lip."[47] Even with the visual menace toned down, the suspense element remained.

The second serial of 1940 was the straightforward Western, Adventures of Red Ryder, adapted from the popular comic strip by Fred Harman. It centered on the villainous activities of a banker and his outlaw allies in trying to gain control of the territory needed as a right-of-way by the Santa Fe Railroad.

Red Ryder, while perhaps not in the same category as the godlike Lone Ranger, also was quite a popular figure and great care was taken that his upstanding "good guy" image remained untarnished. In Chapter Eleven he was to kill a major villain in a showdown and it was originally planned to have him shoot this unfortunate four times. Joseph Breen of the Motion Picture Producers and Distributors of America cut this down to one shot as the additional three would seem both brutal and revenge motivated--not appropriate reactions on the part of the hero.[48]

The third 1940 serial was King of the Royal Mounted and again was taken from a comic strip character. However, this character had also previously appeared in a book by Zane Gray. Since the United States was not yet at war with Germany, the villains were not identified as Germans but the implication was obvious. The writers concocted a plot concerning discovery of a "Compound X" at a Canadian mining spot. The mysterious "Compound X" had both the power to cure infantile paralysis (good) as well as being important in the manufacture of magnetic mines (evil). A villainous mine owner attempted to deliver the compound to a "foreign power" with the assistance of enemy agents. They were opposed by the Canadian Mounties led by Sergeant King, portrayed by Allan Lane. During the course of the serial, Sergeant King's father and best friend, both Mounties, gave their lives to save his, and he was ultimately triumphant over powers of

evil as represented by Germany. The entry had the usual
Witney-English polish and served to introduce Allan Lane to
the Republic stable of serial stars.

This serial was the second to emphasize patriotism in
relation to contemporary international affairs (the first was
Dick Tracy's G-Men) and, by setting the action in Canada,
the plot was able to get across a message concerning a situation in the offing but not yet upon the United States. "In the
character of Sergeant Dave King, the studio had the perfect
hero for a well-made 'preparedness' chapter-play at a time
when our country had not entered World War II, but was feeling the tensions the Axis powers were causing."[49]

The theme of self sacrifice was logically interwoven
with the patriotic message. In the final chapter, King's best
friend, fellow mountie and secondary hero, sacrificed himself
and saved King by knocking King out, ejecting him from a
submarine through a torpedo tube, and destroying the sub, the
villains, and himself--an act which King had planned to per-
sonally perform before his friend intervened. Later King
told his friend's sister, "Orders are orders Linda. Tom
obeyed his, that's why the King presented him with the Vic-
toria Cross. You must be awfully proud of him." She replied, "I am. I don't even think of him as dead. I'll always see him riding as he used to ride ... happy, free,
proud of the uniform he wore ... proud to serve Canada.
I'll see him riding like that as long as I live."[50] A super-
imposure of the mountie riding appeared over this dialogue.
This theme and similar dialogue, appropriately rewritten, was
to reoccur in other Republic serials and was undoubtedly an
effective influence in promoting the romantic concept that submission to the cause of right even to the ultimate sacrifice
is worthwhile. It must be remembered too that such scenes
did not have to overcome the sophistication and cynicism of
the modern audience. Its acceptance was assisted by the prevailing ideals of the time and by a more receptive audience.

Republic's final serial in 1940 was not based on a
book or comic strip character unlike the preceding five entries. Entitled Mysterious Doctor Satan, it was strong in the
basic dichotomy of good versus evil. A superscientist criminal, named appropriately Doctor Satan, portrayed by the
well known character actor Eduardo Ciannelli, invented a ro-
bot which he intended to be the first of an army of mechani-
cal men to take over the wealth and power of the world.
Throughout the serial, Doctor Satan was opposed by a color-

ful masked hero, the Copperhead who wore only a chainmail
hood as a disguise in order to vindicate the memory of his
father who had used the same indentity in the Old West but
was identified as a criminal unjustly.

Emphasis was placed upon the hero as an agent of
justice. For example, the Copperhead was originally motivated by a desire for vengeance--a favorite motif but always
a touchy problem. Joseph Breen once again interceded, re-
sulting in this theme being toned down in the dialogue and
legitimatized by having the hero legally deputized to fight a-
gainst the evil Satan. [51]

Republic turned to Captain Marvel, comic book hero
from Fawcett Publishers, for its first serial in 1941. The
story centered around a scientific expedition in Siam which
discovered in a sealed tomb a Golden Scorpion idol with five
lenses in its claws and a scroll with instructions for how the
lenses can be arranged to either turn base material into gold
or, rearranged into another position, to become a powerful
disintegrating ray. The scientists agreed to divide the five
lenses among themselves as a safety precaution against greed
and to give the scroll with directions and the scorpion idol
to reporter Billy Batson for safekeeping. The serial then
centered around the conflict between Captain Marvel, a nearly
invulnerable mortal with powers of flight, and the mysterious
Scorpion who was actually a member of the expedition. [52]
Given the superhero motif, the special effects of the Lydeckers were even more numerous than usual. They were outstanding and have been recognized throughout the film industry. [53] Although the superman aspects of the hero decreased
the traditional fight and chase action motifs, the serial was
indeed a tour de force. Captain Marvel was unquestionably
a force for good as shown in his last statement and his long-
est speech. The character was not given to words where action would suffice. Upon destroying the Golden Scorpion, he
delivered a stirring plea for decency, "This scorpion is a
symbol of power that could have helped build a world beyond
man's greatest hopes ... a world of freedom, equality, and
justice for all men. But in the hands of men like Bentley it
would have become a symbol of death and destruction. Then,
until such time when there's a better understanding among
men, may the fiery lava of Scorpio burn the memory of this
from their minds." [54]

Another 1941 release was to have not only the required message of good prevailing over evil, but as expected

liberal doses of patriotism, preparedness, sacrifice, fair
play, and Americanism. It also included an explicit vengeance theme until this aspect was overridden. Why Republic writers continually introduced this plot device knowing
full well that it was verboten and would be watered down or
removed is an unresolved mystery.

The serial was entitled King of the Texas Rangers
and starred "Slinging" Sammy Baugh, former All-American
quarterback and professional football player with the Washington Redskins. Tom King as portrayed by Baugh left college
football and thus sacrificed a brilliant career to join the
Texas Rangers to avenge, through legal means, the death of
his Texas Ranger father. He and a Mexican aide battled
espionage activities on the border. The fifth column menace
was a timely and, in this period, an obvious theme.

The vengeance motive did not fit into the traditional
idealism of a fairminded, justice-oriented hero and brought
about some detailed and severe comments from the censors.
The Hays office in a lengthy letter to Republic cautioned
that: 1) killings should be held to a minimum, 2) gruesomeness and horror should be avoided, 3) the hero must be motivated by a desire for justice rather than revenge, 4) killings
by the hero should be altered so that the heavies' deaths are
caused by their own actions, and 5) gun battles be limited to
two or three shots with the criminals using only legal wea-
pons. An illegal weapon, the Hays office pointed out, was
one firing two or more shots without the trigger being released. But the censors weren't finished yet. They went
on to specific criticism of scenes involving: a) gun muzzles
looking straight into the camera, b) the heavies having machine guns and zeppelins, c) references to "nitro" (the censors suggested "soup" be substituted), d) scenes with characters being hit on the head with furniture, and e) a sound
track emphasis when the hero knocks out a heavy off screen.[55]

The details of the Hays office letter seem excessive in
retrospect but give an insight into both censorship of the period
and the role of serials. It is true that the Hays office was
somewhat inconsistent in that scenes such as (4), (5), (a), (d)
and (e) were periodically included in both Republic productions and in films at other studios. Still, the incident shows
the concern and care which the serials received and speaks
indirectly as a strong argument in favor of their significance.

The final production for 1941 was the fourth of the

Dick Tracy quartet and again stressed law and order, honesty,
fair play, and other basic values. Entitled <u>Dick Tracy vs.
Crime, Inc.</u> it again starred Ralph Byrd as Tracy, and concerned his continuing battle against a mysterious masked
crime king called The Ghost, who through an ingenious inven-
tion, was capable of making himself invisible. The final
chapter has a concluding confrontation which is invariably
commented upon. [56] Tracy had a lamp equipped with an infra-
red ray which makes the invisible Ghost visible. A violent,
surrealistic fight between Tracy and The Ghost followed his
discovery and was photographed entirely in negative.

This entry unfortunately was the last of the seventeen
Witney-English serials for Republic although each director
went on to do some very good work on his own. Together
they had been responsible for over half the total output of the
Golden Age of Republic serials. Had this team continued,
perhaps the quality of Republic serials would have extended
indefinitely. Nonetheless, it still had two to three years to
run before the luster wore off and routine set in.

For their first production of 1942, Republic turned to
<u>Spy Smasher</u>, another Fawcett publisher's comic book char-
acter. Alan Armstrong alias Spy Smasher, portrayed by Kane
Richmond, was doing battle in a wartime situation against
his Nazi enemy, the Mask--a carry over from the comics.
This chapter play was solo directed by William Witney and,
since he specialized in action rather than dialogue sequences,
was non-stop action whenever conceivable.

If the themes of patriotism, sacrifice, and a glorification of Americanism were noticeable in previous serial efforts
as they obviously were, then it might be said that in <u>Spy
Smasher</u> these themes became all pervasive. <u>Spy Smasher</u>
was especially rich in high moral, middle class American
values. In addition to being a fine action serial, it was a
primary example of the serial with a message--and it worked.
Since it was the first Republic serial production released during the war, any flimsy pretense of neutrality which might
have watered down the message was unnecessary and so it
went all out. As a result, "'Spy Smasher' is still considered
to be one of the best comic-strip based spy fighter serials."[57]

Prior to our actual entry into the war, a prologue to
<u>Spy Smasher</u> was written to be delivered on film by none other
than FBI head J. Edgar Hoover. He accepted the offer and
was to pontificate:

>Unlike almost every other country in the world, the
United States has never resorted to the use of spies
except for purely military purposes when we are
not actually at war. Unfortunately for the peace of
the world there are nations that do not hesitate to
use not only spies but their more sinister compan-
ions, the propagandist and the saboteur. Today is
a time of crisis; a period during which all Americans must be alert to these enemies within our
borders as well as the dangers from without. Only
by the utmost vigilance can we safeguard our liberty
and maintain our national unity. While this picture
you are about to see is entirely fictional, its hero
Spy Smasher symbolizes American patriotism in action against those subversive forces which may be
far from imaginary. 58

When war was actually declared prior to Spy Smasher's filming, this prologue was dropped as no longer being relevant.
But its existence and original acceptance shows the tone of
the serial.

There were of course related themes dear to American audiences. Pierre Durand, the hero's French ally, sacrificed himself for Spy Smasher in a submarine encounter
bridging Chapters Two and Three which was very similar to
the previous confrontation in King of the Royal Mounted. Spy
Smasher's brother later commented, "This must have been
his way of saying 'Go on and win for freedom and democracy.'"59 Then, the same theme was even more forcefully
brought forth when Alan's twin brother Jack substituted himself for Spy Smasher in Chapter Eleven, walked into a trap,
was shot several times, and fell from a high building, thus
making the ultimate sacrifice for the American way of life
as represented by the godlike hero.

In another vein, Spy Smasher in the comic book had
the use of a futuristic aircraft called the gyrosub. In the
name of fairness, this was transposed into the Bat plane in
the serial and was at the service of the villains, though only
for one chapter. The reasoning behind this reversal was
that should Spy Smasher have had this weapon it would have
given him an edge. In the interest of justice and fair play
it was considered inadmissable for the hero to have the advantage over the villains. 60

In commenting on Spy Smasher, William Witney claimed,

" 'It was an era of ruggedness in America.   My generation
won a war with them (serials). '   Although he knows that the
serial is gone today, he thinks that the audience for which
they were made is still the same.   'Anyone under 13 today
still has the same dreams and hopes that you and I did when
we were under 13,' he said. "[61]

Republic's second entry in 1942, again directed by
Witney alone, was Perils of Nyoka.   This pseudo-sequel to
an earlier effort Jungle Girl (1941) pitted Nyoka, portrayed
by Kay Aldridge assisted by hero Larry portrayed by Clayton Moore against Vultura portrayed by Lorna Gray (Adrian
Booth) and her minions in search of lost mystical tablets
called the Golden Tablets of Hypocrites.   While the secrets
of these tablets were invaluable to medical science, they unfortunately also were the key to lost treasures and therein
lay the conflict between good and evil.

While Nyoka lacked the patriotism and obvious Americanism of those serials of this era directly related to topical
events, it nonetheless included many of the standard values
of the traditional morality play.   And it had something extra.
It was ammunition for the women's liberation movement served
up in an action package.   William Everson notes, "Another
interesting wartime development was a momentary return of
the serial queen.   Republic, which has been responsible for
some of the best quality serials, tried to build Frances Gif-
ford and Kay Aldridge into modern Pearl Whites and Ruth
Rolands. "[62]

The aspect of equal rights and justice for women as
represented in the self-reliant serial queen was also commented on more directly by the contemporary columnist, Hedda Hopper.

> Back in the dear, dead days when woman's place
> was in the home and she was plenty burned up about
> it, we had quite a sizable escape literature in the
> form of the serial queen....
> Last year Republic again decided to take a crack
> at the serial queen.   "Perils of Nyoka" was readied
> and the hunt was on....   [T]he winner emerged in
> the shape of Kay Aldridge ... [Much] more impor-
> tant than her beauty was her ability to take it on
> the chin and elsewhere!   These flowers of the Old
> South may look as if a breath would blow them
> away but underneath their fragile exteriors, they're

as tough as whipcord and will tackle their weight
in wildcats once their dander's up--as many a man
has discovered to his sorrow....[63]

Allowing for Hopper's chatty "Hollywoodese," the point is
still valid. How effectual the message of the emancipated,
self sufficient woman was is open to debate. For example,
Linda Stirling, who portrayed similar roles upon several occasions, feels that female serial fans were and are a rare
breed--something like "one out of ten".[64] However, Peggy
Stewart, also a serial heroine, says that not only has she
been complimented on her toughness by fans (she often played
the "tough no nonsense Ella Raines type of heroine") but that
she finds female fans quite numerous especially at Western
and serial conventions.[65] Whether the viewer accepted the
message or not, it was present.

King of the Mounties, a direct sequel to the 1940 King
of the Royal Mounted, with Allan Lane again portraying Sergeant Dave King, was the final entry in 1942 and was directed
by Witney. This time, King's adversaries were clearly identified and their goals clearly specified. The plot was basically a wartime espionage story with some science fiction
themes included to increase the excitement. Sergeant King
not only opposed the Nazis but also Japan and Italy. Large
ads for Chapter One proclaimed the message in capital letters: "UNSCRUPULOUS PLANS FOR WESTERN WORLD
CONQUEST ARE SHATTERED TO BITS WHEN THE HORDES
OF YELLOW-BELLIED RATS COME TO GRIPS WITH THE
COURAGE AND CUNNING OF CANADA'S MOUNTED PO-
LICE! ..."[66] Patriotism was again emphasized with United
States-Canadian cooperation a strong secondary theme brought
home by a stirring speech delivered in Chapter Twelve by the
heroine beneath pictures of Franklin Delano Roosevelt and
Winston Churchill with appropriate background music.[67]

The first entry for 1943 kept with America's wartime
awareness, as did the majority of appropriate contemporary
Republic releases in this period. Entitled G-Men vs. the
Black Dragon, it starred Rod Cameron in the first of two
serials which he would do for Republic portraying secret a-
gent, Rex Bennett, Republic's only non-media originated continuing hero. In this particular serial he was fighting the
Oriental Axis secret society, the Black Dragon. Bennett had
assistance from both a British and a Chinese Secret Service

agent reflecting allied cooperation upon every possible occasion.[68]   As Eric Hoffman, movie archivist and serial buff, puts it, "Crammed with action, 'Black Dragon' was one of the many 40's adventures that moved like a runaway express train, with fights, chases and cliff-hangers popping up at the drop of a hat.... Here the villains were truly hissable with none of them above shooting, killing, strangling and stabbing anyone in their way."[69]

Specifically, arch villain Haruchi stated his goals in Chapter One. "Keep in mind that our aim is to spread terror and confusion ... to attack industry and leaders of industry ... to cripple America's war effort and undermine her morale. So we shall speed the day when Japan will completely rule the Pacific and all the lands bordering on the Pacific."[70]   Later Haruchi sent an American traitor to his death and told his henchmen that, as he betrayed his own people, so he would eventually betray the Black Dragon--thus providing a vivid object lesson in the value of loyalty. By Chapter Fifteen after several dialogue (as well as the expected physical) confrontations spelling out the good versus evil theme, the villains were defeated.

Recalling Albert S. Rogell's claim that, according to Yates' instructions, Republic films would be flag waving whenever possible, this serial took that suggestion literally. "One bit of amusing patriotism was that a villainous organ grinder used a raven in helping Haruchi.... At the fade-out of the last chapter, Rex asks the raven to show his colors and the bird waves a miniature American flag."[71]

The second of the Rex Bennett serials was the third Republic release of 1943, again starring Rod Cameron. Entitled Secret Service in Darkest Africa the chapter play basically had the federal agent doing battle against the Nazi and Arabs in Northern Africa. The ads set the tone, "Secret service agents battle a sinister peril on a land of mystery--intrigue!"[72]

The hero, now in the military, was opposed by Nazi villain Baron Von Rommler who had a hideout in Casablanca. Almost every chapter had several physical confrontations while the screenplay provided audiences "additional ideas as to what kind of s.o.b.'s the Nazi spies were."[73]   The serial of course once again concludes on a patriotic note. The hero freed the imprisoned leader of the African sheiks who was friendly to the allied cause and this sultan addressed his

peers, "Ours is the cause of freedom, of justice, and of truth.
The mission of the United States is a crusade against tyranny,
intolerance, and oppression. Our banners will never be low-
ered until the light of freedom shines not only over the peo-
ples of North Africa but the entire world."[74]

Secret Service was directed by Spencer Gordon Bennet who had a lifetime of experience in the action field and
was in a category with William Witney although his later Columbia serials were hurt by that studio's poor quality. Bennet started in serials in 1912 and directed the last one made--
Blazing the Overland Trail (Columbia, 1956). He received
training under George B. Seitz, an important silent serial
director, and took over as a leading director when Seitz re-
tired in 1925. "In the 31 years since then Bennet directed
52 serials, and 54 features which contained the same kind of
action and melodrama serials did. Physical action is natural
to Bennet. He has been an athlete all his life."[75]

Bennet was quite appreciative of the quality he found
in the Republic serial unit. "Spence thoroughly enjoyed his
period with Republic and states that Republic was extremely
well organized and the budgets ... were always adequate to
make a good picture."[76] He felt that "Republic was geared to
the action picture." They had "better equipment", the "technical know how," and a group of workers "who knew their jobs."
As an example he relates how Republic had rheostats on
their cameras which enabled him to shoot chase sequences
without interruption and increased his efficiency. "We didn't
have those things at Columbia. Republic gave us what we
needed to do a good job."[77]

Bennet's second Republic serial also had a patriotic
motif and proved to be a favorite. The Masked Marvel was
the last entry in 1943 and utilized the same theme of the
earlier Lone Ranger serial transposed to modern World War
II espionage backgrounds. The Masked Marvel was one of
four insurance investigators who have joined ranks to fight
the espionage activities of Japanese villain Sakima, portrayed
by Johnny Arthur. In the closing scenes of Chapter Twelve
the true Masked Marvel revealed himself to the heroine and
to the audience, but requested that his identity remain unknown in case he was needed to fight America's enemies in
the future.[78] The Masked Marvel, dressed in a nondescript
gray business suit, wide brimmed white hat, and a black
mask molded to tightly cover the entire upper portion of his
face, was indeed an awe inspiring, if somewhat simply garbed
hero.

The Masked Marvel proved to be the last Republic entry with a wartime patriotic background. Nonetheless, the
advertising campaign made extensive use of the theme. "Who
is this fearless man who risks his life at every turn to thwart
Jap attempts at sabotage?" asked the newspaper ads. Another proclaimed, "SENSATIONAL SABOTAGE UNCOVERED!
... A fast, exciting surprise-studded serial showing the Jap
menace crawling underground in an attempt to destroy the
American war effort!"[79] And wartime activities, events, and
paraphernalia--air raid alerts, posters, ration stamps--were
liberally scattered throughout the serial and sometimes used
in the plot development.

The serial included large doses of dialogue illustrating
the baseness of the villains as opposed to the essential honesty, decency and justice of the heroes as was normal for
this type of product. However, the concluding confrontation
was somewhat different, slightly more realistic, and subtlely
amusing, although still obvious propaganda. "In the last
chapter Sakima and the Marvel engage in a gunfight in the
former's hideout. After the Marvel fires six bullets, Sakima
emerges from his hiding place to announce: 'Your bullets
are gone, but I still have one left.' He is felled by another
bullet, then the Marvel asks: 'Didn't it occur to your Oriental mind that I might reload.' "[80] In other words, yellow
peril deviousness was no match for American pragmatism!

Thus, it is obvious that the Republic serials reinforced
middle American values and that in so doing they influenced
predominantly the youthful audience and inculcated these virtues into their life style. Patriotism was a basic among
these values, and the serials of the late thirties and early
forties which emphasize this theme were among the most
successful examples of the serial's impact. When Republic
dropped this theme in relation to the war it lost one of its
most effective forms. The message of patriotism continued
although in a diluted form but the war effort serials were
discontinued following The Masked Marvel. Possibly, Republic felt that the public was tiring of war themes or felt that
they had done all they could with the subject.[81] But it is
interesting that they were dropped so early. Also coinciden-
tally and ironically the Golden Age began to taper off at approximately the same time and drew to a close within a year
or two at the outside. "With the end of the war, B-pictures
and serials lost probably the best real-life heavies they could
ever hope to find in the Axis forces. The next batch of spy-
villains would come when everyone was seeing Red under their

bedsheets. Their villainy was fairly nasty as well on the
screen, but somehow, it was a pale shadow compared to the
all-out ruthlessness of the World War II heavies."[82]

Captain America, the first Republic serial of 1944,
oddly enough was a natural for a patriotic wartime plot.
However, the seven writers chose to use a straight hero versus villain approach thus weakening the obvious patriotism of
the character. Nonetheless, Captain America is a good sample of the Republic serial product. Directed by John English
and Elmer Clifton and produced at the turning point in Republic's serial history when the Golden Age was gradually coming
to an end, it bears examination as a representative Republic
chapter play. It was better than the serials of the declining
years but its flaws remove it from the ranks of the classic
sound serial.

Captain America as a character is an excellent example of a popular culture hero who has withstood the test of
time. Created in 1941 as a comic book hero by artist Jack
Kirby and writer Joe Simon in response to the growing concern of the American people with the possibility of involvement
in the European war, the figure immediately gained popularity
and the hero's battle for the American way of life became
representative of the good of democracy against the evil of
totalitarianism. At his height of popularity during the Second World War, the figure was purchased by Republic Studios.
As an adaption of a comic book character to film the production was not accurate; nonetheless, the serial stands in its
own right as a legitimate addition to the development of the
figure's popularity. In many respects it contributed to the
reputation of Captain America and certainly broadened his
audience. After the war, the attempt was made to convert
the comic book figure to a standard crime fighter, a move
which proved to be less than wise at that time. In 1949 the
comic book was allowed to die a natural death only to be revived in 1961 by publisher Stan Lee for Marvel Comics where
the character is still quite popular.

Republic's version relied on Captain America's fame
as a comic strip figure of heroic proportions fighting for the
case of right and justice. [83] The Republic newspaper ads set
the tone. One proclaimed: "HE'S HERE! CAPTAIN AMER-
ICA HERO OF MILLIONS! Now on the screen! Adventurous
and death-defying, as he pursues a desperate and crafty criminal bent on world destruction!" Another emphasized his comic
strip background: "THE NUMBER ONE CHOICE OF YOUNG AND

OLD - CAPTAIN AMERICA! ... The thrilling exploits which
have spellbound a nation of comic fans--now catapulted to the
screen in a serial packed with action--adventure and excitement!" A third enthused: "NOW - ON THE SCREEN ... The
country's favorite ... bold, daring, fearless ... in a serial
packed with action entertainment!"[84] Patriotism and other
wartime virtues might be played down but good versus evil
was nonetheless in the forefront.

    The plot, as usual, was relatively simple. The Repub-
lic story department actually summarized the story in one
line. "Because he feels he has been cheated of the wealth
and fame accruing from an expedition he headed, Dr. Maldor
secretly starts a campaign to kill and rob every member of
the expedition."[85] The strong modern vengeance theme was
acceptable to the censors since it involved the villain and his
forces of evil. While the Republic story synopsis develops
the plot somewhat further, the vengeance theme and the attempts by Captain America to discover and block the related
crimes were basically all there was to the story.

    This serial, as several others before it, opens itself
to conjecture by the very fact that it was an adaptation of a
fictional character from one medium to another. The Republic film version offered Captain America's alter-ego as Grant
Gardner, a crusading District Attorney possessing brains and
brawn only somewhat above average. The original Captain
of the comics was United States Army Private Steve Rogers
who secretly was a scientifically created near superman, although mortal, who was pledged to defeat America's enemies.

    The reaction to the Captain America serial over the
years by serial fan writers has been generally favorable.
They agree that the serial was not the same as the comic
strip but that on its own it stands as a fine example of the
genre. For example, an article on "The Return of Captain
America" as a comic book hero includes extensive coverage
of the movie serial. The basic reaction was: "Captain America's fights however were the pièce de résistance! The amaz-
ing talents of Dale Van Sickel (doubling for Purcell), Tom
Steele, Ken Terrell, Fred Graham [all top stuntmen who remained active following Republic's demise] and their cohorts
were combined to make the fight 'choreography' some of the
most frantic ever fashioned for film and all this took place
among some of the most imaginative settings ever seen in a
chapter play; including a wonderful 'power house' set!"[86]

In fact, the consensus seems to be that the stunt work
and Republic production values make this an excellent serial.
"Those fight scenes, though repetitious and often predictable
as to when they would appear, were the highlights of the
film.   Directed by John English and Elmer Clifton, but large-
ly staged by the stuntmen themselves, these celluloid battles
were equal to those in any action film.... Captain America
represented the apex of the traditional action film fight, in
the opinion of many cliffhanger enthusiasts, but followed the
long-dictated formula."[87] Perhaps Alan Barbour's reaction
to the liberal changes in both the hero's identity and his
cause summarizes the reaction of most movie fans. "Captain America was Republic's final entry in the comic-strip
sweepstakes, and it was superb in all aspects of production.
... All three studios took liberties in the scripting of their
films based on comic strips.... But no one really cared."[88]

Most fans, however, did comment on the identity
change from super-strong patriot in a wartime setting to
masked law officer fighting master criminals. And, aside
from the considerations that the change in identity was perhaps inconvenient, unnecessary, or even untrue to the original character, this particular alteration also has additional
implications.

Movie historian Chris Steinbrenner rather astutely
points out the basic problem. "There is no attempt to explain Captain America's origin and Grant Gardner's stopping
to change into costume seemed at times only to impede the
action.... The real mystery was left unexplained; why should
a crusading district attorney, the one person in our society
fully capable of running the machinery of justice, step well
outside the Law for jungle combat with evil forces? It just
didn't make sense. Not that Captain America wasn't a fast-
moving, adventuresome serial, it was."[89] In other words,
the decision to have Captain America fighting a master criminal rather than the enemies of his country results in an unconscious hint of fascism. Here is a district attorney, sworn
to uphold the law, donning a masked outfit and, with the blessing of the authorities, using violent extra-legal means including murder to overcome the criminal element which the district attorney and the legal system cannot control through
normal channels. This "escapism" is a basic element of attraction in serials and youth-oriented entertainment of the
period.   However, in Captain America the incongruity becomes blatant. By making the character a major representative of the legal system fighting domestic criminals with

the cover of an unknown identity, the aspect of vigilante violence with the tacit approval of the system is undeniable.

The change and any implications therein remained and
the decision by Republic not to conform to the original characterization can basically be traced back to the profit motive.
"Chaos struck when the heads of Timely Comics learned of
the changes in their character that would burst on the screen
in the 1944 release of the serial.... Republic coldly informed
Timely that the sample comic book pages sent them by the
publishers in no way indicated that Captain America was a
soldier named Steve Rogers and that he did not carry a re-
volver. Furthermore, since the serial was well into production they could not and would not return it to the original
concept through costly retakes.... Since Republic was under
no contractual obligations to do any of these things, the matter was closed."[90]

What then is the status of this chapter play both as a
serial and as a representation of a popular culture hero from
another medium? As an adaptation of the original comic book
character, the serial was admittedly less than successful and
relatively dishonest. However, this was not a great drawback in the overview since many in the serial audience were
not that familiar with the comic book, and most of those who
were Captain America readers were able to accept even the
unnecessary changes readily. And, as a representative of
the serial genre Captain America was indeed a success, again
when considered as a whole. To the audiences in 1944 and
even in 1953 when the serial was re-released, the American
faith in basic good winning out over evil with justice (questionable only upon reflection) and honesty rewarded stood out
as the message in Captain America. The subtleties of analytical criticism were not for serial audiences.

Republic's final serial of 1944 was Zorro's Black
Whip, directed by Spencer G. Bennet. This twelve chapter
effort is unique in that Zorro was never mentioned by name
aside from the title and the black-masked mysterious Zorro-
like figure was a female--none other than the heroine portrayed by Linda Stirling.

The serial was quite strong in its espousal of law and
order as the prologue shows: "IDAHO--1889. Law abiding
citizens call for a vote to bring their territory into the Union.
But sinister forces, opposed to the coming of law and order,
instigated a reign of terror against the lives and property of

all who favored statehood."[91] Secondary themes included
freedom of the press--the heroine's murdered brother was
an editor and she took over for him both as editor and as
masked hero with appropriate dialogue--and patriotism--a
patriotic speech by the heroine in Chapter Five was interrup-
ted by the villain with, "Never mind the Fourth 'uh Jooly
Speech."[92]

It is generally conceded that, although the action, special effects, and pacing in chapter plays continued unabated
at Republic through at least 1949, the plots and the general
care which were lavished upon earlier productions gradually
fell off after 1944.[93] Also, with the exception of some anti-
communist themes, the messages and morals of the later
productions remained fairly consistent. From 1945 on, a
gradual decline set in which is not to say that good serials
were not released but rather indicates that the general average and overall quality lessened noticeably for reasons which
will be seen.

An example of what was to come was The Purple Monster Strikes (1945) directed by Bennet and Fred Brannon.
While routine because of standard stunts and cliffhanger situations, it nonetheless utilized a villain which, while from
outerspace, foretold of Republic's coming emphasis on anti-
communist themes. "The Purple Monster, a man from
Mars, murders scientist Dr. Layton, inventor of a plane capable of interplanetary travels. The Monster assumed Layton's identity, stealing plans, and prepared for an invasion
of this planet by the Martian Army."[94] He was of course
defeated and destroyed by a special detective/attorney hero
and Layton's niece.

During an early confrontation between the Monster and
Dr. Layton, the former warned, "My people have planned for
a long time to invade the earth and enslave its inhabitants,
destroying all those who resist us ..." and the good doctor
replied, "Then you landed in the wrong country, my friend.
Do you think the American people will sit by doing nothing
while you build a jet plane for the purpose of bringing in an
army of conquest?"[95] The patriotism as well as the Cold
War fear of the United States over a communist take-over
in the late forties and early fifties is clear and the advertising campaign played on this theme: "Invasion of America
from 50,000,000 miles away!" "America Meets Unknown in
War of Worlds! Secret Agent from Mars in first war movie!"[96]

Jesse James Rides Again, a 1947 release, marks the
point at which Republic shifted from four original productions
per season to three with one re-release, [97] illustrating the economic problems which the serial genre and the movie industry
were facing. Directed by Fred Brannon and Thomas Carr, the
plot had Jesse, in an attempt to redeem himself, aiding frontier
settlers against vicious oil interests who want their land and
who conduct a reign of terror to get it. [98] Jesse blocked the
evildoers and saved the day. Republic seemed self-conscious
that an acknowledged outlaw famous in American history was
representing the side of law and order and significantly the ad
campaign stressed Jesse's reformed role. "JESSE JAMES....
The dreaded name that haunted a thousand lawmen ... NOW ...
strikes terror into the hearts of the lawless!" The Fabulous
Pirate of the Prairies Turns Lawman! Thrill to Jesse James
pitting his wits and bullets against a ruthless band ... The
HOODED BLACK RAIDERS."[99] The serial was a success and
was to lead to sequels. [100]

The last entry for the 1949 season was King of the Rocket
Men directed by Brannon as were the next eleven serials. Despite the fact that most Republic serials had declined in original-
ity, it was considered to be an exception and was the last of the
really original serial heroes. [101] The flavor of this last important serial innovation is caught in highlights from the synopsis
in the Republic Story Department inventory. "Jeff King, ideal-
istic young member of Science Associates ... in the guise of
the Rocket Man, frustrates countless attempts of the cruel Dr.
Vulcan to get control of the project's devices, which ... could
easily wreak world disaster."[102] Vulcan was another mystery
villain and in their final verbal confrontation, the position of
the protagonists was further illuminated. His identity discovered, Vulcan said, "A bizarre name, but it's what I stand
for: power! The power of steel forged into what I believe
is right!" To which the Rocket Man replied, "Sure ... the
right of a criminal to steal ... the right of a criminal to
betray his country ... the right of a warped mind that works
toward the destruction of peace."[103]

The implied presence of an outside hostile nation and
the concern for national security are prevalent in the story
line. The studio even proclaimed: "Top Secret! The brains
and brawn of America combine to hold off the madmen who
would rock the world in disaster!" and "See what America
has up her sleeve to save the peace of the world!"[104]

King of the Rocket Men benefited from the expected

high quality stunt work and special effects which recalled the
Golden Age. In fact Theodore Lydecker pointed out that the
Rocket Man flying sequences used the same techniques and
identical model in a different costume that were used in creating Captain Marvel. [105] The success of this serial was to
result in two pseudo-sequel chapter plays and a spin off television series, none of which came close to the original in
terms of either excitement or basic undisguised morality.

By the 1952 season, Republic produced only two productions and both were quite derivative imitations of King of
the Rocket Men. Rocket Man became Commando Cody in
Radar Men from the Moon and Larry Martin super scientist
in Zombies from the Stratosphere. Zombies proved to be
Republic's last space science fiction serial. Interestingly
enough, Spencer G. Bennet who had by this time moved to
Columbia posited: "Heroes follow the trend of the times but
the plot remains the same in serials ... only two studios
make them now, and there are only five serial directors left.
We seem to be dying out as a breed."[106] He might have
been speaking of the genre.

By 1953, Republic was stressing anti-communism.
Canadian Mounties Versus Atomic Invaders, directed by
Franklin Adreon as were all the remaining Republic efforts,
portrayed an agent of totalitarian government who was attempting to build missile launching bases in Canada to invade
both Canada and the United States. But the plan was aborted
by the ever vigilant Royal Canadian Mounted Police. The ads
trumpeted, "SPIES AT WORK IN THE FROZEN WILDERNESS! !
What Secrets are they after? What diabolic plot are they
hatching? The Mounties know ... and they're ready! ! !"[107]
Despite the return of a patriotic motif with appropriate dialogue and the topical subject matter, the serial used more
stock footage in the action sequences than new footage and
was a pale copy of earlier Mountie efforts.

Republic's final serial released in 1955 was yet another
anti-communist effort. Given a circus background, King of
the Carnival had a group of counterfeiters using the big top
as a front to ruin the credit of the United States. [108] Their
avowed aim was verbalized by one villain when he stated,
"Then the countries of the world will do business with my
country."[109] The villains were brought to justice by Treas-
ury men represented by the trapeze artist/veteran undercover
agent.

The later Republic serials frequently had topical references by tying in with the fifties news stories but, in usual serial technique, they were always presented as absolutes. As had been discussed, the anti-fascist serial propaganda of the Second World War worked and even had a positive effect on the audience but the anti-communist propaganda seemed relatively ineffectual at best.[110] Perhaps the solution partially lies in the approach taken in each era. The major difference between the propaganda films of the Second World War and of the Cold War era seem often to be that the "former was more interested in exploiting the potential menace of Communism itself."[111] The former was concrete and opposition was exciting. The latter was nebulous and vaguely disconcerting. Perhaps it was because of the feeling of unity and therefore heroism was greater against the enemies in a world war and exciting conflicts fit the mood and needs of the mass audience. In the Cold War era with recriminations on the home front, divided allies, and an enemy which was often hard to identify, confusion and uncertainty on the part of the audience made the villains less exciting and the conflict more sinister.

Regardless of the reason for changing attitudes and the success of the serials in either second guessing or influencing them, the fact remains that there was a relationship. It may have been represented by patriotism, anti-totalitarism, or simple good versus evil. As Robert Malcomson astutely pointed out: "Production of new serials ceased almost twenty years ago. When they were popular during the '30's, '40's and early '50's, no doubt they did reflect the general public's attitudes of the day. Today ... we (as adults) laugh at the exaggerated stereotyped images. We may think that this is all a thing of the past. But is it?"[112]

Beginning with the end of the Second World War, the rising production costs, the problem of diminished market, and the failure of the studio to adapt to changing times and tastes all contributed to the decline of the serials. Serial production had to be inexpensive with a minimum of frills. A serial averaged three to four hours in length, far longer than the most expensive epics, yet the serial budgets were perhaps five to ten percent of the blockbuster's budget and when costs were inflated in the post war period, Republic opted for more economy in a system already based on economical production methods.

Scriptwriters dropped from a high of seven to one in

the final thirteen Republic serial efforts. As we have seen,
plots became listless and repetitive. Whereas first chapters
ran to thirty minutes for plot development in the Golden Age,
they ran less than twenty minutes after the war. Later chapters dropped from near twenty minutes to under fifteen. The
plot resumé and footage overlap so important in keeping
things straight were cut mercilessly. Location shots and ingenious sets were gradually phased out except through stock
footage. Moreover, stock shots from earlier serials and
feature films became prevalent and, even worse, were often
the best section of the "new" releases. Re-issues became
standard in the late forties and equaled new releases the last
four years. When Republic ceased serial production in 1955,
it was a different time and a sorry product which bore little
relationship to the genre and the era which had flourished in
the late thirties and well into the forties. [113]

    There is no denying that the sound serial, even in its
most highly developed phase at Republic, eventually came to
its final chapter, ended by the competition of television and
grim economic pressures. However, the serial did have its
heyday and indeed experienced periodic revivals prior to its
actual demise in 1956. The first revitalization came in 1936
with the phenomenal success of Universal's Flash Gordon.
Then came the Golden Age of Republic and one writer could
note in 1941, "It's the life blood of the matinee business.
Ordinarily, theater operators go out of their minds trying to
lure people up to the box office.... It's a different story on
Saturday afternoon. No problem then in filling the house.
Tough part is getting the kids to get out."[114] William Saal,
Republic's head of public relations, was quoted as saying
there were 5000 theatres in the country which would always
play Westerns and serials. He pointed out that many theaters ran two serials at a time and that even first run houses
in the south ran them but small town theaters in the South
and Midwest remained the greatest area of strength. [115]

    Five years later as a result of a reorganization, Uni-
versal Studios withdrew from the serial field and the importance of the genre was again acknowledged. "Unless something happens pretty soon to correct it, theatres will be
showing fewer serial pictures than ever before in history....
[S]erials are the life-blood of nearly half this country's ...
theatres. Quality films ... may be fine for the big cities,
but it's the serials, like 'Hop Harrigan,' 'G-Men Never Forget' and 'Jesse James Rides Again' that keep the small town
operators in business."[116]

In fact, 1946 was the movie industry's best year and although the quality of serials was beginning to go down, the product was still much in demand. In that year it is interesting to note that Film Daily Yearbook reported that out of the 18,765 theaters operating, approximately 8,000 houses regularly showed serials, not including 2,000 more which utilized serials periodically but not fifty-two weeks out of the year. Furthermore, the average serial played to an estimated audience of four to five million people according to the Yearbook.[117] One source even stated that serials were used in the rural areas to sell A pictures which were less desirable to the unsophisticated, action-oriented audiences.[118]

By 1950, while serials were on the decline they were still considered to be a potential antidote to the competition of television. "Video's boxoffice inroads are providing a modest upbeat for film serials, as an increasing number of exhibs are starting to book cliffhangers as a means of again attracting the moppet trade--which has been particularly attentive to tele and consequently frequenting theatres less often.... Serials are a source of modest income to Columbia and Republic at this time."[119] The preceding sentence is the kernel of true prophecy in the hopeful report. The economics of the serial was against it in an era of declining box office income. Variety noted that the average serial rental was approximately $5 per chapter in 1950.[120] Three years later rates had increased to $50 per episode in first runs but decreased to "a few dollars' at the end of their circulation.[121] Even with the inflationary rentals, income was down in the fifties due to declining bookings after 1950. The economic pinch could not be ignored.

Television delivered the death blow. It literally absorbed the serials. Television action series were the equivalent of the serials even though they lacked the melodramatic climaxes requiring a week's wait. Television series were even built around serial heroes--Dick Tracy, the Lone Ranger, Wild Bill Hickok, Kit Carson, and others. At the same time, television revived most of the top serials of the sound serial's peak period, the late thirties to the mid-forties. Said one critic in the early fifties of the classic serials: "These elaborate mounted affairs, and TV's own expensive series-films, put the contemporary cheaply made movie serials very much to shame."[122]

Even after the official dismissal of the serial genre from the ranks of the moviemaker's options, it continued to be a popular seller in retrospect on television, overseas, and in areas of the United States. Variety headlined in 1964, "Theatrical Cliffhanger Serials of Yesteryear Still Sell 'Far Out' " and reported that Republic serials were favorites in the Far East, internationally and on military bases in the Southwestern United States. [123]

As late as 1968, a major entertainment publication was calling on the motion picture industry to consider the serial format to revitalize the moviegoing habit. "One of these exhibitors suggested, 'We need something like the serials that, certainly, pleased the kids--and a fair portion of the adults--such as we had back in the old days. Don't magazines and newspapers still run serials? And what about the series programs on TV?' "[124]

At the same time, Detroit attorney and author Raymond J. Meurer appeared before the 1968 annual convention of the National Association of Theatre Owners as a featured speaker and recommended a revival of the serial. He pointed out that American youth was not entranced by "sex, sadism and lust on the screen", and insisted that they were seeking out the traditional values. Meurer felt that one technique to reach the younger patrons was through the basic film serial, "the same format that brought children by the millions into theatres and established viewing patterns that lasted for ten years or more". [125]

Even though Republic had produced the best and most technically proficient sound serials, in the long run, they failed due to economic factors and changing public tastes. But in their day, they were effective and accounted for much of the studio's significance. Jack Mathis summarized the Republic serial product:

> Considered the best sound serials ever made, the
> Republic cliffhanger exhibited that intangible asset
> of production values which combined with a genius
> for organization to produce polished products which
> belied their cost. The array of film-making talent
> assembled by Republic was unduplicated anywhere in
> the industry, and the imagination expressed in their
> writing, direction, regular and process photography,
> original musical scores, miniature and special effects,
> and daredevil stunt work rivaled that of any major studio. [126]

Although the movie serial is a thing of the past, the fact remains that Republic did well and that it was a factor in the lives of its viewers--sometimes a force for patriotism, sometimes for heroics, and escape, but always a reinforcement of traditional morality and the American value system.

Notes

1. New York Times, December 22, 1946.
2. Los Angeles Times, November 20, 1946.
3. Los Angeles Times, November 20, 1946.
4. Robert Malcomson, "The Sound Serials of Yesteryear", Yesteryear (1971), No. 1, pp. 2-5.
5. Malcomson, "Yesteryear", p. 2.
6. Raymond W. Stedman, The Serials: Suspense and Drama by Installment, pp. 138-142.
7. Jon Tuska, "From the 100 Finest Westerns: The Lightning Warrior", Views and Reviews, II (Spring, 1971), p. 50. See pp. 2, 4 for Levine's relation to Republic.
8. Tuska, "Warrior", p. 55.
9. P. E. Emery, "Psychological Effects of the Western Film: A Study in Television Viewing", Human Relations, XII (1959), p. 201.
10. Henry James Forman, Our Movie Made Children, p. 162. The Oriental villains in the Pearl White serials made her fearful of all Orientals.
11. Thomas Wood, "Corn in the Can", unpublished manuscript, dated 1941, in the Serials clipping file of the Margaret Herrick Library of the Academy of Motion Picture Arts and Sciences, pp. 4-5. Wood was a frequent feature writer for the New York Times.
12. Wood, "Corn", p. 5.
13. William K. Everson, "Serials with Sound", Films in Review, IV (June-July, 1953), p. 271.
14. Everson, "Serials", p. 273.
15. Los Angeles Times, November 20, 1946.
16. Interview with Rex Waggoner, National Telefilm Associates, Publicity Director, and Ernest Kirkpatrick, National Telefilm Associates, Technical Services, Los Angeles, May 12, 1976.
17. Mathis, Valley of the Cliffhangers, p. vii.
18. Interview with Barry Shipman, Republic writer, San Bernardino, California, May 11, 1976.
19. Mathis, p. viii.
20. Kalton C. Lahue, Bound and Gagged, p. 23.

21. Edward Connor, "The First Eight Serials of Republic",
    Screen Facts, II (1964), p. 52.
22. A list of the appropriate films viewed especially for
    this dissertation appears in the bibliography. Addi-
    tional information was obtained from Eric Hoffman,
    "Undersea Kingdom", Those Enduring Matinee Idols, I
    (December 1970-January 1971), p. 90.
23. Rudy Behlmer, ed., Memo from David O. Selznick
    (New York: Viking Press, 1972), p. 369.
24. Interview with Barry Shipman, Republic writer, San
    Bernardino, California, May 11, 1976.
25. Mathis, p. 35.
26. Mathis, p. 36.
27. Wood, "Corn", p. 20.
28. "The Painted Stallion", Those Enduring Matinee Idols, I
    (April-May, 1971), p. 122.
29. Mathis, p. 79.
30. Charles Jameux, "William Witney and John English",
    Positif (October, 1967), No. 88
31. Connor, "First Eight", p. 60.
32. "Serial Panel Discussion", Those Enduring Matinee
    Idols, III (n.d.) p. 351. In the transcript of the
    Serial Panel Discussion at the Houstoncon '73, Wit-
    ney elaborates: "I'll tell you something about the
    violence in serials. We felt that it was all play act-
    ing. You never saw any blood; you never saw a bul-
    let go into a man and blood spurt out fourteen feet.
    You never saw anybody's teeth get kicked out, and
    never in any serial saw a man get hit over the head
    with actual contact. You never saw a man get physi-
    cally beat up, where somebody holds him and just
    beats him to death as we see now. Sure, it was play
    acting violence. The Hays Office had certain codes
    and they would look at these things. Sometimes there
    were arguments and you'd have to cut something out,
    but you'd ALWAYS argue about them. They had a lot
    of backup--they could ban your pictures. We weren't
    as afraid of the Hays Office on the serials as we were
    of the Church groups--the Catholic League. We never
    had a serial put on the list, as far as I know. They
    were made for children and we always had in the back
    of our mind that while the slogan on the wall said, 'A
    pair of wet panties for every little kiddie,' we really
    didn't mean it."
33. Edward Connor, "The Golden Age of Republic Serials,
    Part I", Screen Facts, III (1968), pp. 48-49.
34. Wood, "Corn", p. 18.

35. Mathis, p. 68.
36. Mathis, p. 73.
37. Continuity (estimating) script (No. 1740, April, 1939), in the Republic Studios Collection #979 of the Special Collections Library of the University of California at Los Angeles Library.   A thinly disguised actual marine assignment in China in 1937 was included in order to use actual news reel film in the first chapter. Flag waving and patriotism were obvious but worked well in the context of the story's action themes.
38. Mathis, p. 90.
39. C. M. "Parky" Parkhurst, "The Lone Ranger Rides Again", Those Enduring Matinee Idols, II (April-May, 1972), p. 218.
40. Shooting script (No. 1009, January, 1939) in the Duncan Renaldo collection (Accession number 5189) of the University of Wyoming Library.
41. Daredevils of the Red Circle, Cliffhanger Ending and Escape Pictorials (Chicago: Jack Mathis Advertising, n. d.).   This series of privately published brochures includes chapter-by-chapter synopses and frame blow ups from the actual film.   Next to having the film, these are perhaps the best research tools available concerning film content.   Unfortunately, only nine titles were issued before the series was discontinued.
42. Continuity (estimating) script (No. 896, August, 1939) in the Republic Studios Collection #979 of the Special Collections Library of the University of California at Los Angeles Library.
43. Francis M. Nevins, Jr., "Ballet of Violence: The Films of William Witney", Films in Review, XXV (November, 1974), p. 531.
44. Earl Michaels, "The Serials of Republic", Screen Facts, I (1963), p. 56.
45. Drums of Fu Manchu, Cliffhanger Ending and Escape Pictorial Series (Chicago: Jack Mathis Advertising, n. d.).
46. Earl Blair, Jr., "Reminiscing with Henry Brandon", Those Enduring Matinee Idols, II (December 1972-January, 1973), p. 291.   Published transcript of interview.
47. Eric Hoffman and Bob Malcomson, "Drums of Fu Manchu", Those Enduring Matinee Idols, II (December, 1972-January, 1973), p. 284.
48. Mathis, p. 149.
49. Bob Malcomson and Eric Hoffman, "King of the Royal Mounted," Those Enduring Matinee Idols, III (n. d.), p. 338.
50. Mathis, p. 161.

51. Mysterious Doctor Satan, Cliffhanger Ending and Escape Pictorial Series (Chicago: Jack Mathis Advertising, n. d.).
52. The Adventures of Captain Marvel, Cliffhanger Ending and Escape Pictorial Series (Chicago: Jack Mathis Advertising, (n. d.).
53. Interview with Theodore Lydecker, Republic special effects expert, Los Angeles, May 17, 1976.
54. Taped transcription of complete sound track in possession of author.
55. The Hays Office letter is quoted in Wood, "Corn," pp. 5-6.
56. Connor, "Golden Age, Part II", p. 33, as well as every critical commentary that covers this production of which the author is aware. The use of negative photography is quite striking.
57. Eric Hoffman, "Saturday Matinee Spy Hunters of World War Two", Serial World (1974), p. 8.
58. Mathis, p. 200.
59. Taped transcription of complete sound track in possession of author.
60. Mathis, p. 207.
61. Edwardsville [Indiana] Intelligencer, November 29, 1973.
62. Everson, "Serials", p. 271.
63. Los Angeles Times, May 31, 1942.
64. Interview with Linda Stirling, Republic actress, Los Angeles, May 13, 1976.
65. Interview with Peggy Stewart, Republic actress, Los Angeles, May 18, 1976.
66. Kokomo [Indiana] Tribune, June 10, 1943. Kokomo, a small city in northern Indiana, had a population of about 40,000 during the forties, six theaters and is representive of a major segment of the Republic market.
67. King of the Mounties. Still Manual. (Hollywood: Republic Pictures, 1942). Still manuals were a series of photographs from the film accompanied by publicity information for use by the theaters. They were created and released by the picture companies themselves, and, in the case of the serials, were the most extensively used promotional material (along with pressbooks) provided to the theaters. Advertisement copy from pressbooks was also extensively used in small towns but studio written "reviews" which were from pressbooks also were rarely run by the local presses.
68. G-Men vs. the Black Dragon. Still Manual. (Hollywood: Republic Pictures, 1943). Also Kokomo [Indiana] Tribune, May 4, 1944.

69. Hoffman, "Spy Hunters", p. 9.
70. Taped transcription of the sound track in the author's
     possession.
71. Ron Stephenson, "Concerning Serials and Trends",
     Those Enduring Matinee Idols, III (n. d.), p. 445.
72. Kokomo [Indiana] Tribune, December 16, 1943.
73. Hoffman, "Spy Hunters", p. 9.
74. Shooting script (No. 1295, June 1943) in the Duncan
     Renaldo Collection (Accession number 5189) at the
     University of Wyoming Library.
75. George Geltzer, "Forty Years of Cliffhanging", Films
     in Review, VIII (February, 1957), p. 60.
76. Glenn Shipley, "King of the Serial Directors: Spencer
     Gordon Bennet", Views and Reviews, I (Fall, 1969),
     p. 21.
77. Interview with Spencer G. Bennet, Republic director,
     Los Angeles, May 10, 1976.
78. The Masked Marvel. Still Manual. (Hollywood: Repub-
     lic Pictures, 1943).
79. Kokomo [Indiana] Tribune, March 30, 1944 and March 31,
     1944.
80. Stephenson, "Serials and Trends", p. 445.
81. Interview with Spencer G. Bennet, Republic director,
     Los Angeles, May 10, 1976.
82. Hoffman, "Spy Hunters", p. 9.
83. "It's Ingenious! Captain America Versus the Arch-Crim-
     inal of Them All. It's Suspenseful!" emphasized
     the Captain America. Still Manual. (Hollywood: Re-
     public Pictures, 1944).
84. Kokomo [Indiana] Tribune, June 22, 1944; June 23, 1944;
     and June 24, 1944.
85. "Republic Productions, Inc. Produced Properties,
     1935-1951", unpublished manuscript from the Repub-
     lic Studios Story Department, January 1, 1951, in
     the Theatre Arts Library of the University of Cali-
     fornia at Los Angeles, p. 21. Prepared by the Re-
     public staff for industry purposes, this exhaustive
     listing of all Republic films is an invaluable primary
     source.
86. "The Return of Captain America", Screen Thrills Illus-
     trated, II (February, 1964), p. 24. The same opin-
     ion is echoed, practically verbatim in Alan Hewtson,
     "Comics in Cinema", Cinema, V (1969), p. 7.
87. Harmon and Glut, The Great Serial Heroes, p. 263.
88. Days of Thrills and Adventure, pp. 28-29.
89. "The Four-Paneled, Sock-Bang-Powie Saturday Afternoon
     Screen", in Dick Lupoff and Don Thompson, ed., All
     in Color for a Dime, (New Rochelle, New York: Ar-
     lington House, 1970), pp. 211-12.

120   Republic Studios

90. Harmon and Glut, pp. 259-60.
91. Elwood [Indiana] Call-Leader, November 21, 1946.
     Elwood, a medium-sized town in central Indiana,
     had a population of 8,000 in the forties, two
     and later three theaters, and is representative of
     the other important segment of Republic's market.
92. Mathis, p. 281.
93. Earl Michaels, "The Serials of Republic", Screen Facts,
     I (1963), p. 54. Most students of the genre concur.
94. Republic Productions, Inc. Produced Properties," p. 129.
95. Tape transcription in possession of author of sound
     track excerpts from D Day on Mars (feature ver-
     sion).
96. Elwood [Indiana] Call-Leader, February 14, 1947, and
     Kokomo [Indiana] Tribune, February 12, 1948.
97. Mathis, p. 336.
98. Jesse James Rides Again. Still Manual. (Hollywood:
     Republic Pictures, 1947).
99. Kokomo [Indiana] Tribune, October 9, 1947. The still
     manual also emphasizes that Jesse is "trying to re-
     form and go straight" and that his new adventure
     results from his attempts "to prove his innocence".
100. The two sequels caused equal difficulties in whitewash-
     ing the James Brothers and the studio discontinued
     the concept upon the recommendation of its legal
     department. Mathis, p. 381.
101. Greg Jackson, Jr., "Serial World Interviews Rocket-
     man Tris Coffin", Serial World, No. 10 (Spring,
     1977), pp. 8-9.
102. "Republic Productions, Inc. Produced Properties,"
     p. 87.
103. Tape transcription in possession of author of sound
     track excerpts from Lost Planet Airmen (feature
     version).
104. Kokomo [Indiana] Tribune, January 19, 1952.
105. Interview with Theodore Lydecker, Republic special ef-
     fects man, West Hollywood, California, May 17,
     1976.
106. New York Herald-Tribune, October 31, 1952.
107. Alan G. Barbour, ed., Great Serial Ads (Kew Gardens,
     New York: Screen Facts Press, 1965), unpaged.
108. King of the Carnival. Still Manual. (Hollywood: Re-
     public Pictures, 1955).
109. Stephenson, "Serials and Trends", p. 446.
110. For a comparison of attitudes between the patriotism
     of the World War II period and the paranoia of the
     Cold War era see William Manchester, The Glory

and the Dream: A Narrative History of America
1932-1972 (Boston: Little, Brown and Company,
1973), pp. 289-328 "The Home Front" and pp. 555-99
"House Divided". Hollywood, including Republic
serials, reflected the times.
111. Stephenson, "Serials and Trends", p. 446.
112. "Editor's Notes", Those Enduring Matinee Idols, III
     (n.d.), p. 446.
113. Michaels, "Serials," pp. 58-60.
114. Wood, "Corn", p. 18.
115. Wood, "Corn", p. 17.
116. New York Times, December 22, 1946.
117. Film Daily Yearbook of Motion Pictures" 1946 (New
     York: Film Daily, Inc., 1947), p. 206.
118. Los Angeles Times, November 20, 1946.
119. Variety, November 9, 1950.
120. Variety, November 9, 1950.
121. Everson, "Serials", p. 276.
122. Everson, "Serials", p. 269.
123. February 12, 1964.
124. Ben Shlyen, "Editorial", Box Office, January 15, 1968.
125. Box Office, January 15, 1968.
126. Mathis, p. viii.

Chapter V

REPUBLIC'S COWBOYS--THE THREE MESQUITEERS,
GENE AUTRY AND ROY ROGERS

Although Republic prestige among action fans and
scholars of the B cinema rested with the serial, it was actually the Republic Westerns, the B "cowboy pictures," made
in series of six to eight entries, which were the reliable
breadwinners for the studio. While many theaters played
serials either on a regular schedule or only occasionally,
most neighborhood theaters and even the first-run theaters
in small towns featured at least one or two Westerns regularly to satisfy the requirements of the Saturday matinee
crowd. And the B Western feature frequently came from Republic, since this studio was acknowledged to make the best
of that type of product.

As film scholar William K. Everson pointed out,
"From the beginning, Republic got more excitement into their
chases, more pep into their stunts, and more punch into their
fights, than any other studio. Camerawork was always clean,
sharp and crystal clear, and locations first-class.... Their
musical scores were among the best in the business. Few
'B' Westerns could long escape the taint of standardization,
and since the key requirement of the 'B' was action, it hardly mattered that Republic's machinery showed. It was exceptionally well-oiled machinery and operated flawlessly."[1*] Republic Westerns also stood out from the young audience's
point of view. "Republic Pictures was the King of the Cowboy Hero studios. There would not be a single Front Row
Kid from 1935 to television whose heart did not beat faster,
whose imagination did not catch fire, and whose Saturday af-
ternoons were not made infinitely richer in Cowboy-Hero fantasies by the mere sight of the Republic Pictures Eagle....
The Front Row Kids pledged their allegiance to that bold Eagle and to the Republic Pictures for which it stood."[2] On
the strength of such a reputation, the studio remained a leader in the genre until the passing of time and changing audi-

*Notes to Chapter V begin on page 157.

ence habits spelled an end to the Saturday matinee. In fact,
as Republic began to venture into A productions, the program
series were actually strong enough to carry the burden of
these A ventures which were not always successful until the
late forties when the market for B's also began to slip. [3]

What was the message inherent in the B Western?
Like all things complex, it cannot be satisfactorily simplified
without encountering some contradictions. Even within individual series among the several hundred such films put out
by Republic alone, there are many exceptions to the standard
concept of what the program Western was about. But, as a
starting point, the general themes of the majority of the
genre produced from the early thirties until the mid fifties
was in the form of the traditional morality play or sermon.
The standard Western plot even with its variations was much
like the Sunday School sermon and the traditional values of
the American Bible Belt. Thus, the B Western emphasized
again and again the importance of decency, justice, and law
and order in the early United States as well as the search
for a fundamental dignity for all good people. The genre
thereby formed a basic restatement of American idealism
and the general optimism which has pervaded the American
way of life. [4]

As was indicated in Chapter II, both the significance
and entertainment aspects of the Western film have made it
the subject of several studies, dating almost exclusively from
the early sixties. Most of these works have been popular in
concept and, until recently, none have given more than a passing mention to the pervasiveness of the B format and formula. Among those books which dwell on the importance of the
relatively scarce A productions but do nonetheless acknowledge the contributions of the B's, one must include the volumes by William K. Everson. The first was an original
pioneering work with George N. Fenin and devoted three separate sections to the B form while his second was solo authored. [5] Jon Tuska, editor of Views and Reviews and stu-
dent of the B Western, has recently published a major work
aimed at the entire spectrum of the Western film but which
devotes a great deal of space to the program Western. [6]
Tuska sees the Western as more of an art form than most
scholars acknowledge it to be. And there are a few works
which emphasize the B Western film; both Alan Barbour's
The Thrill of It All[7] and Don Miller's Hollywood Corral[8]
are unabashedly nostalgic.

Just as the message of the "cowboy picture" can be
summarized, so too can it be acknowledged that this message
had an effect. Specific reactions, of course, varied with the
audience, but the broad effect of such films was that the message set in a period piece could be generalized to the realities of everyday living. As one psychological study states:

> In the film world one may in identifying with the
> hero strongly wish to draw a gun on and kill the
> villain, but in the real world there is no such vil-
> lain, no gun, and an absence of the concerns im-
> pelling that film hero to violence. It is in the la-
> tent content of the film that one finds a certain
> congruence and hence the greatest chance of carry-
> ing over into real life. Although the actions and
> concrete circumstances of the Western film are
> markedly different from those of everyday life they
> still involve basic features such as the general re-
> lations of men in their own actions and desires, to
> other men, and to the social environment at large.
> It is very likely that it is because of the manifest
> differences that the film can work out these basic
> problems and yet retain and entertain its audiences. [9]

In other words, the B Western entertained with its action/fan-
tasy themes set in a prior time period but also affected the
viewer's ability to solve basic problems in the real environment.

Since the behavioral patterns presented in the fantasy
Westerns can be related to the real world, it is well to examine the message of the B Western film in a little more
detail. The Western film in its long history from The Great
Train Robbery (1903) to the seventies anti-hero, downbeat
film, such as the Missouri Breaks (1976), has advanced
many viewpoints on man interrelating with man. Will Wright
in his recent structural study of the genre classifies the multitude of Western plots into four basic approaches: 1) the
classical plot of the thirties to the fifties, 2) a transitional
period in the fifties, 3) a vengeance variation into the sixties,
and 4) a professional emphasis on the present. [10]

In the classical plot, there is a strong hero defending
a weak society with its values of family, school, church,
and civilization against the selfish villains who wish to control power for themselves. The hero successfully defends
society's basic values, gains its respect and honor, and either

joins society or rides off voluntarily at the conclusion. In
the transitional period, society becomes a threat to the hero
and rejects him as in the classic movie High Noon (1932)
where the sheriff is not supported by the cowardly citizenry
when killers seek vengeance against him. Villains become
secondary. The vengeance variation has the hero rejecting
society to revenge himself on the villains as in The Searchers
(1956), where the heroes search for a white girl kidnaped
by Indians against advice. He does, however, normally return to society. In the last of Wright's classifications, the
theme is on the professional hero fighting the villains who
are much the same as the hero but with slightly different
goals. The emphasis is on the struggle. Society and the
traditional values become secondary and even irrelevant to
the theme of doing a job. An example is The Wild Bunch
(1969) with professional gunmen fighting Mexican military
men because they refuse to back down. Wright sees these
four approaches as a reflection of the prevalent American
values and the economic institutions accepted at the time
when each approach was the major format used in most Western films. The traditional B Western fits Wright's classical
mold closely because it showed Americans that rugged individualism could successfully combine with society's goals of
community and equality to defend law and order and to achieve
success over the selfish forces of evil.

What do these theories mean in relationship to the
specific themes of the B Westerns? An analysis by Frederick Elkin concerned with the program Westerns summarized
the many implications in the typical Republic series Western.[11] A lecturer at the Cinema Department of the University of Southern California who was previously a member of
the Research Staff of the Motion Picture Association of America, Elkin was familiar with the Hollywood Western from both
the viewpoint of the scholar and the industry. In this pioneering study, he analyzed this genre and its specific themes
while the format was still an active force in the entertainment world. He stressed the positive aspects of the B Western and included potential educational influences. At the
same time, he avoided the symbolic or deeply subconscious
aspects and emphasized effects which are either conscious or
easily understood unconscious reactions.

Elkin pointed out that the B Western, with few exceptions, was set in the American West in the late nineteenth
century. The action often centered around a small town in
which law and order was just coming into its own. The char-

acters were ordinary ranchers, miners and a few town-folk.
The basic characteristics of these films were action and
simplicity. The standard B Western became a continual
series of chases, rescues, gun battles, and fist fights to appeal to the basic unsophisticated audience. Moral values
were those of a Judeo-Christian society, and in the conflict
between good and evil good was invariably held up as right.
Those on the side of good were honest, loyal, sympathetic
to the oppressed, and had a respect for just law. On the
other side, the evil were treacherous, callous, ruthless and
had a contempt for the underdog. It was implied without
subtlety that justice and morality were worthy of great risk,
and those who fight to achieve the worthy goals were honored
and respected. [12]

     The B Western had additional positive themes. It
emphasized the rich and exciting heritage of America. Rugged individualism, frontier equality, and other popularly accepted characteristics of the Western way of life were focused
upon. Whether these concepts were based in fact or folklore
was immaterial to the viewer of the program Western. Similarly, the B Western also stressed the value of integrity and
character in that the particular participants were usually
judged by their surface personalities and abilities. [13] Although the action content was usually emphasized in these
program pictures, with the coming of the Western musical,
leisure time was shown in which men played and sang Western songs. This little examined emphasis reinforced the
American musical heritage and suggested that life in the open
spaces of the West could be a peaceful rewarding one. [14] A
positive emphasis on these values, however, implied a de-
valuation of some others. For example, the stress on rugged
individualism devalued strong family themes. The emphasis
on action and accomplishment played down intellectuality and
contemplation. Finally, the primary emphasis on the struggle between good and evil de-emphasized any aspect of romance. [15]

     The heroes of B Westerns invariably had what some
feel to be respectable Anglo-Saxon qualities. They were attractive, rarely lost their tempers, and did not smoke, drink
or gamble except when role playing. Normally, they did not
express deep emotion. In a fight, they battled fairly. The
coming of the Western musical brought a slight change in the
hero's qualities. He had the above qualities but, in addition,
he sang and was somewhat more friendly and charming. He
wore theatrical costumes and became involved more frequently

with the heroine, but not on a romantic plane. For their
part, the heroines tended to fall into two types. The first
was the traditional female who played a secondary role and
was normally in a subsidiary position. The second type was
a later development and was much more of an independent
heroine. She was more likely to have an important job and
to participate in an open camaraderie with the hero in bringing the plot to a conclusion. On the other side of the conflict was the villain with obvious disreputable characteristics.
The gang leader was frequently a white collar villain and although dishonest, sinister, and ruthless, appeared to be a
respectable citizen within the plot. He utilized the services
of the "dog heavy" (action heavy) or the brute villain who
was crude, menacing, and almost sadistic.[16] The fourth set
of characters who were standard in the B Western and who
had some degree of importance were the comic sidekicks.
They were rarely held up as ideals worthy of emulation, but
were sympathetic, basically good, and provided aid to the
hero.

    Elkin was aware that B Westerns appealed predomi-
nantly to children. Although he stated that children comprise
less than half of the audience, he felt that they did not just
see a Western, but "vividly and emotionally participate[d] in
it".[17] The "cowboy picture" thus filled a void in the children's world. In the B Western the child could imagine himself to be in a well ordered setting. There were no unnecessary characters, no intrusions of complex personalities,
and the problems were always resolved in a satisfactory
manner. The child could identify with the competent hero in
the Western story, could be assured that no matter what the
odds he would overcome his adversaries, and could thereby
affirm his own strength and importance. At the same time,
the vigorous aggressive action in which the hero actively participated, and in which the child could vicariously take part,
was justified and condoned because he was fighting for the
forces of right. "In fighting for justice and in winning moral
victories, the child symbolically wins the love and admira-
tion of his parents, teachers, and religious leaders."[18]

    Another important segment of the audience for pro-
gram Westerns was the almost two-thirds which consisted
of adults with a rural background.[19] This group was also
gratified by the themes, characters, and general format of
the Western film. The rural audience at the time the B
Westerns were most popular frequently resented urban superiority. When the Western hero with his strong suggestion

of country origins defeated the villains who quite frequently
had a "citified" background, the rural audience bolstered
their own sense of pride by identifying with the cause of "justice". [20]

Of course, not everyone saw the classical theme of
the B cowboy films as benign. For example, during the
Second World War, the Office of War Information became
critical of the cowboy hero's activities as essentially demor-
alizing. As previously mentioned, the villain of the B film
was often cast as a supposedly responsible head of the community. The Office of War Information noted this frequent
occurrence and stated, "This plot is becoming a Hollywood
habit, the men who should be the town leaders are bandit
leaders instead, and some itinerant cowboy has to administer
justice for the people."[21] But, of course, the intention of
the writers was not that insidious demoralization which so
concerned the Office of War Information. It was to please
the audience and to identify believable villains. The audience
seemed to understand and took it all in stride.

In the category of the B Western program picture, Republic represented quantity as well as quality. The studio
released the following B Western films: sixteen with Bob
Steele, eight with Johnny Mack Brown, eight with John Wayne,
twenty-nine with Don "Red" Barry, twenty-four with Wild
Bill Elliott, (sixteen Red Ryder), fifty-one with Allan Lane,
(seven Red Ryder), fifteen Sunset Carsons, nineteen each
with Monte Hale and Rex Allen, four "John Paul Revere"
movies (two with Bob Livingston and two starring Eddie Dew),
four Michael Chapin juvenile Westerns, fifty-one Three Mesquiteers, fifty-six with Gene Autry (and one additional guest
appearance), and eighty-one featuring Roy Rogers (with twelve
additional guest or supporting appearances). A single Western entitled Laramie Trail brought Republic's total B Western output to 386. Each of these series or B Western stars
had its fans and its particular attraction, but all followed the basic format of the morality play.

Of the Republic Western series listed above, the final
three were the studio's most successful. They also represented three separate subthemes of the genre, and in one
case included a major alteration which perhaps saved the
genre in a moribund period. The Three Mesquiteers emphasized cooperation, comradeship and collectivism. These
films were the most successful of all B Western "group"
series. Gene Autry was the first successful singing cowboy

and his movies stressed the theme of a common man as hero
which came to be known as the "Autry fantasy." Third, Roy
Rogers was the clean-cut, fun-loving boy-hero whose films
developed into a glamorous musical environment which Republic hoped resembled a stage play on film.

The Three Mesquiteers novels were originally created
by William Colt MacDonald, well-known Western story writer,
and were a Western takeoff on the famous literary creations
of Alexander Dumas. MacDonald named his trio Tucson
Smith, Lullaby Joslin, and Stony Brooke and featured them
in a series of Western pulp novels. Two of the novels had
been adapted to the screen in prior features before Republic
began its series based upon the three friends. A brief survey of some highlights with discussion of a few of the more
important titles will be beneficial and illustrative of what
made the series unique.

The movie series was the first of the trio Westerns--
that is Westerns with three stars--and lasted from 1936 until
1943. In spite of a dizzying chronology running from the
Civil War to the present, frequent cast changes in the major
roles, and a decline in the quality of production especially
toward the end of the series, it had a spontaneity and camaraderie which led to several imitations at other studios. The
Three Mesquiteers emphasized both friendship and a high
priority of law and order in the framework of the classical
Western plot.

Alan Eyles, Western film historian, comments on the
law and order emphasis and claims that curiously these pictures were generally set in modern times, "seeming to argue
in a naive way that traditional virtues and resources are
more than enough to cope with complex contemporary situations."[22] As will be seen, although not all entries were
modern, where there were contemporary situations the strong
theme of traditional values and law and order did occasionally result in some interesting plot dilemmas. Still, the
point is that it was the value system with its reliance on
tradition which mattered in both period and modern plot lines.
And such traditional values as friendship were indeed emphasized. Moreover, with the three main characters interreact-
ing, the significance of comradeship could be made quite
clear several times in each film. Ernest Corneau, compiler
of Western biographies, has noted, "these were the horse-
operas that placed the emphasis on three heroes, each possessing his own individual talent and skills. It was a treat

to the audience to see their exciting teamwork, providing us
with three times as many thrills. In times of danger, their
'one for all, all for one' attitude gave us the message that
true friendship was a valuable asset in life. A lesson that
too many people in the world tend to forget."[23]

     Of course, this emphasis on collectivism was in cer-
tain respects tied into the spirit of the times. Both the Depression Era and the Second World War period gave impetus
to the idea of working together, to a collective spirit as it
were. The trio Westerns consciously and sometimes unconsciously reflected this feeling. "The trio concept of Westerns ran its course and ended shortly after World War II.
It symbolized in its way the collectivism and group spirit of
the period and managed, incidently, to elevate the status of
the sidekick--in the instance of Terhune [Max, well known
ventriloquist] and Hatton [Raymond, silent film star and
sound era character actor], at least--to more than a buffoon,"
according to one critic of The Three Mesquiteers.[24] This
symbolism became so overpowering in most of The Three
Mesquiteers pictures that it even entered into the physical
aspects of the heroes' interrelationship. A review of Three
Texas Steers notes, for example, "He [George Sherman, the
director] even succeeds in imparting a poetry-in-motion effect
in his handling of The Three Mesquiteers, achieving this with
unified timing of cowboys mounting, riding, wheeling, galloping
and dismounting of steeds."[25] While all Western series upheld
the concept of cooperation, the first and most successful of
the trio Western series perhaps did it best of all.

     The theme of law and order was also inherent in all
Western films but was especially noticeable in many of the
Mesquiteer films. Robert Warshow related the law and order motif to the personal honor of the hero. "What does the
Westerner fight for? We know he is on the side of justice
and order, and of course it can be said he fights for these
things. But such broad aims never correspond exactly to
his real motives... If justice and order did not continually
demand his protection he would be without a calling... What
he defends, at bottom, is the purity of his own image--in
fact his honor."[26] Compare Warshow's statement with a review of Rocky Mountain Rangers which implied that the Mesquiteers enjoyed their roles of dispensing justice and brought
forth this comment from a contemporary reviewer. "Of
course several of the outlaws did end horribly, but that is
to be expected. They have lived horribly; let them die horribly. Hurrah for the forces of law and order!"[27] True,

the law and order theme could be brutal. Equally true, the
New York reviewers could be somewhat less than serious in
their comments on the B Western. The point remains that
the law and order theme was indeed noticeable by fan and
critic alike and that it did indeed have latent implications to
the life styles of the audiences watching these films.

There were several valid reasons for the series' popularity in addition to its heavy reliance on the values of
friendship and the importance of law and order. Max Terhune, the best known comic member of the team, provided
the following observations to author David Zinman. Terhune
told Zinman the series offered something for everybody.
"For the girls, it had a running gag of rivalry between Stony
and Tucson. . . . It had plenty of action and fights, and the
boys liked that. I like to believe the kids liked Elmer [the
ventriloquist's dummy], too. And the adults, I think, liked
the variety of plots and the scenery and beautiful horses. "[28]

The first movie in the series was entitled logically,
The Three Mesquiteers, and was released in 1936. It starred
Ray "Crash" Corrigan as Tucson Smith, Robert Livingston
as Stony Brooke, and Syd Saylor as Lullaby. The post World
War I story had the three heroes assisting veterans who have
settled on land leased to them by the government and who
are opposed by cattlemen utilizing that territory. The up-
dated "homesteaders" plot made ample use of the themes of
patriotism and veterans' rights. [29]

In the second series entry, Ghost Town Gold, Syd
Saylor was replaced by Max Terhune, the ventriloquist comic.
Terhune, Corrigan, and Livingston were the best remembered of The Three Mesquiteers. Although Tucson Smith
was the leader and stabilizing influence of the group in the
MacDonald novels, in the movies the leadership soon passed
to Stony Brooke who was portrayed as much more individual-
istic and even hot-headed, thereby leading the group into various difficulties. While Tucson was still solid and secure,
Stony became the more attractive character. Nonetheless,
a certain romantic competition normally developed between
Tucson and Stony. In spite of this theme of rivalry, both
handled the heroics with aid from Lullaby at the height of
the action. Tucson was the stronger both physically and
emotionally of the two and Stony was the more volatile, dash-
ing lead. Lullaby invariably provided the comic relief. The
formula was quickly set and the first eight Three Mesquiteers Westerns came across as unpretentious but solid B

Westerns. The fifth entry in the first eight was entitled Hit
the Saddle (1937) and had a strong law and order plot involving the protection of wild horses on a government preserve. 30 The story as developed also brought in heavy overtones of ecology and conservation long before such themes
were popular in the mass media. For example, the need
for government protection of wilderness lands and endangered
species was advocated by the heroes--although not in those
terms. 31 It was otherwise noteworthy in that Stony and
Tucson are romantic rivals for the heroine who was played
by Rita Cansino, later to become the famous star Rita Hay-
worth. 32

     In the second of the next series of eight entries en-
titled Trigger Trio, Livingston was replaced temporarily by
Ralph Byrd, better known as the serial hero Dick Tracy.
The plot was a murder mystery built around the dangers of
hoof and mouth disease. Livingston returned in the following film, Wild Horse Rodeo (1938). Wild Horse Rodeo included a plea for freedom for wild horses, had all three
heroes romantically involved, and also included a young actor by the name of Dick Weston in a musical number. Weston, of course, soon became Roy Rogers.

     One entry that same year entitled, Call the Mesquit-
eers, had a sequence which appeared many times throughout
the series and which emphasized the cooperative aspect of
the films. The plot had the heroes falsely implicated in a
silk robbery and killing. 33 They obviously had to catch the
real culprits. The villains in their attempt to escape the
heroes, took off in three different directions; the Mesquiteers
in pursuit simply divided the trails and each captured his
quarry in his own unique way before returning to the collective group and concluding the plot satisfactorily.

     At the end of the second season, Robert Livingston
was moved into non-Western Republic features and was
groomed for potential stardom. John Wayne, who had not
been with the studio for two years, returned and took over
the role of Stony Brooke for the next series of eight pictures.
The first entry in the Wayne series was entitled Pals of the
Saddle (1938) and like many of the Mesquiteer films was set
in modern times. The plot had enemy agents attempting to
gain control of a valuable chemical in order to smuggle it
into Mexico for resale to foreign interests. The Mesquiteers,
needless to say, patriotically defeated the plans of the spies
by assisting the secret agent heroine and saving the war gas/
explosive for the United States. 34

With The Night Riders (1939), the Mesquiteers took a journey back into time when they battled a villain in the 1880's by donning hoods and capes to fight for the forces of law and order, and defeated a fraudulent Spanish don with a phony ancient deed. Raymond Hatton appeared as Rusty Joslin replacing Max Terhune as Lullaby Joslin in Wyoming Outlaw released the same year. The plot revolved around a crooked political boss--a favorite villain as has been discussed.

The final entry in the Wayne series was perhaps one of the more interesting of The Three Mesquiteer Westerns. Entitled New Frontier (1939), the plot had strong currents of the rural environment versus metropolitan needs as was discussed by Elkin. The Mesquiteers' ranch, located in a valley settled fifty years before, was about to be flooded in order to make way for a reservoir to fill the needs of a nearby city. Although the plight of the settlers was presented sympathetically, the legal confrontation scene wherein the judge found for the urban interests presented the dilemma quite accurately and seemingly insoluably for the rural folk. The judge, emphasizing "the greatest good for the greatest number," decided that the settlers must be removed and the reservoir project continue. The Mesquiteers representing the rural interest accepted the necessity of change based on law and order. The reservoir builders and a crooked politician proved to be in league to cheat the settlers by removing them to alternate land which was unacceptable and which the villains did not plan to improve by irrigation. The Mesquiteers, functioning as the voice of law and order against the hot-headed settlers, discovered that the promised land had not been irrigated and led the settlers in an attack on the dam builders at the conclusion. The settlers were saved, the villains were imprisoned, and the new land was irrigated. Thus, the urban interests had their needed water reservoir while the old settlers had even better lands than they did before. It was a happy ending which neatly avoided the original questions. 35

Although it turned out to be a strawman conflict with a rather pat ending well masked by the exciting action-packed conclusion, the two messages were still there. Law and order must prevail and when people work together and communicate all can be satisfactorily accommodated.

It was during this period that John Wayne made the movie Stagecoach (RKO, 1939). The last four of his Mesquiteer series were made after he had made Stagecoach and

all were released after he had begun his successful rise to
stardom. "He hated Republic for sending out these terrible
Mesquiteer pictures, but he couldn't stop them. Wayne's
down home fans loved the Mesquiteers and were glad that
John Wayne was back in the saddle.... They loved him as a
good-guy western hero. They even loved his Mesquiteer
movies ... as much or more than they loved his high-class
fancy dude westerns directed by John Ford. Republic Pictures knew their audience."[36] Wayne's biographer, although
critical, makes some good points about Republic's contributions and Wayne's indebtedness to the studio. Although Wayne
may have resented Republic's using his B pictures after he
had finally begun to make the big breakthrough, he did remain under contract with the studio in its bigger productions
for many years thereafter. And in retrospect, Wayne has
fond words for his years at Republic. "I didn't know how
good I had it when I was makin' those quick westerns for
Republic. April to September--we worked like Hell, makin'
our quota of pictures, which were already sold in advance in
a package to the exhibitors."[37] Thus, Wayne acknowledged
that the B films had been presold and recognized that he received training and exposure in some of the best B Westerns
made at Republic.

    The Mesquiteers series now underwent some additional
cast changes. John Wayne was replaced by Bob Livingston.
Wayne was going on to greater things; Livingston had had his
chance and was being returned to the B Western field.[38]
Corrigan, who had always resented to some degree the fact
that he was not the main lead as had originally been planned,
decided to depart also. He was replaced by Duncan Renaldo
who became Rico, the second-ranked Mesquiteer. Raymond
Hatton continued on in his role as the comic relief. Livingston, Hatton, and Renaldo made seven Three Mesquiteer pictures. The first was fairly typical. It had Livingston and
Hatton going to a Caribbean Island where they assisted in-
surrectionist Renaldo in defeating the ruthless and corrupt
island dictator thus leading to a strong freedom motif in the
film. Renaldo, as Rico, then decides to stay on with the
Mesquiteers and returns to the American West with them.
The film was Kansas Terrors (1939).

    From the 1940-1941 series Tucson Smith was recalled
and was portrayed by Bob Steele, well known Western star.
The new Lullaby Joslin was comic Rufe Davis, who bore a
resemblance to Terhune. Bob Livingston continued in his
role of Stony Brooke. After seven films with this team, Tom

Tyler became Stony Brooke for the final thirteen entries while
Jimmy Dodd played Lullaby in the last six films. The Phantom Plainsmen released in 1942 is perhaps worthy of mention in that the Mesquiteers opposed the Nazis in keeping
with the wartime interest. [39] An unscrupulous American is
selling horses to the totalitarian interests and the heroes patriotically intervene. Even with the defense theme in this
particular entry, the time period in the series remained
quite loose in that some of the films were also still placed
in the Old West. In their last season the Mesquiteers once
again faced the Nazis and saved a secret rubber formula in
Valley of the Hunted Men (1942).

The fifty-one Three Mesquiteers had been a highly
satisfying B Western series. While the quality declined,
overall the series was a significant one. [40] When asked
about his career at Republic in the series and whether he
had thought of any potential impact on audiences, Robert
Livingston replied, "Not really, the studio put out a good
product until they lost interest. The enthusiasm of the people was good. Corrigan wanted to be a Western star. I
didn't care.... The Republic product was hit and miss.... I
didn't like the heroes to be too corny. Sam Sherman [the
movie historian] gave me a great compliment once. He
said, 'Bob, your Westerns did things they're doing today before anyone else.' My Mesquiteer films are good for what
they are, Westerns."[41]

Just as Republic's Three Mesquiteer series was the
best of its kind, so too did Republic lay claim to the first
successful musical Western series. Nat Levine brought
young country Western singer Gene Autry to Hollywood in
1935 directly from a Chicago radio station where his radio
program and record sales were solidly respectable. Levine's
Mascot Studio featured him as a singer in the Ken Maynard
Western In Old Santa Fe (1935), in the Maynard serial, Mystery Mountain (1935), and, based upon an acceptable if not
exciting reaction in those films, cast the young Gene Autry
as the lead in the serial Phantom Empire as a replacement
for Maynard. The serial was one of Mascot's most successful. On the basis of Autry's success in these three tryout
vehicles, Levine decided to put him in a series of musical
Westerns for the newly-formed Republic, which had absorbed
Mascot. In doing so, he changed the history of the Hollywood Western. [42]

The introduction of Gene Autry revolutionized the B

Western cinema and, according to some critics, ultimately
destroyed it. His success was to lead to the creation of his
most well known competitor, Roy Rogers, also from Republic. Both contributed significantly to the B Western movie
and influenced several generations of youthful audiences.
Their importance is tinged with a note of irony:

> It seems a bit incongruous that in a genre that
> depended primarily upon real he-man action and
> thrills from its start two guitar strumming, war-
> bling, saddle serenaders should become the reign-
> ing kings of the Western film empire in the late
> thirties and forties--but that is exactly what hap-
> pened. Gene Autry and Roy Rogers both parlayed
> pleasant singing voices and winning personalities
> into public popularity unmatched since the early
> days of Tom Mix's phenomenal mass appeal.[43]

While there were obvious similarities between the two stars
and their movie careers, each was unique and made a separate, if similar, contribution to the influence of Republic
upon its audiences.

Not all fans or scholars of the Western film consider
Autry's influence to be benevolent. In fact, many felt that
the beginning of the "singing cowboy pictures" signaled the
end of the B Western genre as a viable format because such
movies featured musical production numbers and "superfancy
clothes" which made a mockery of the true West.[44]

To his critics, Autry's appeal could not be explained.[45]
His lack of acting as well as physical ability, his bland movie personality and the fact that he did indeed change the B
Western are all brought up as adverse points especially
among hard core action purists. On the other hand, it is
generally acknowledged that the success of Autry's features
were the salvation of Republic in the early years, enabling
the studio to spend more time and money on their other B
Western films as well as improving the lot of their entire
output. Also, Autry outlasted all of his competitors and
imitators although he did not remain at Republic. Other
stars such as Roy Rogers and Tex Ritter retained their popularity and audience appeal until the end of the B Western
genre, but they were undeniably followers in the footsteps of
Gene Autry.

It is quite true that Autry had little acting ability.

However, it was rarely necessary because in most instances
he portrayed no personality other than his own. Since his
singing ability was very real as compared to his status as
an action star, his pictures became more successful as he
sang more. Added to this development was the fact that
while he started out somewhat awkwardly in physical sequences
he did improve as time went along to the point where he
could ride adequately if not skillfully and to where his fist-
fighting technique was acceptable.

Autry made a career out of playing the singing "nice
guy" and this pleased his fans. Autry and his studio realized
this and cultivated his image. As one movie analyst states:

> Gene was good and his opponents were evil, and
> to kids who were unable to handle the fine shadings
> between these two, the moral lesson was clear.
> While it might seem peculiar to the generation of
> today, most of us welcomed and accepted the Autry
> philosophy that it wasn't a bad world after all and
> could be made better if every man stood up for
> his beliefs, even if we didn't care for the singing.[46]

As far as the singing was concerned, it obviously appealed to a
segment of the audience. It remains that Autry had a workable
formula and morality was a mainstay. A critic for Harpers
conceded that his cynical son could reject Autry's music but
was captivated by the image of heroism and action.[47] A
Western film authority summarized it, "...he came along at
the right time.... Autry was new, and had something different
to offer."[48]

Autry himself was to prove to be a businessman of
note and contributed to the commodity of his image.[49] Undoubtedly his own instincts served him well in developing
his career as the foremost singing cowboy of the thirties and
early forties. While there had been a few isolated attempts
at "singing cowboys" previously,[50] Autry's Westerns emphasized the music and there is no denying that this caught the
audience's attention. But there was more than this to the
image. Autry early pushed his vehicles as good family
trade. Jon Tuska noted somewhat critically, "Autry was
primarily a singer who consistently tried to build his films
around hit songs and, almost begrudgingly, incorporated action sequences.... He appealed to parents, extolling the virtues of his clean films ... encouraging the public to believe
that Westerns were intended strictly as family pictures."[51]

This emphasis on family entertainment had an interesting corollary. Autry developed an image of himself as a clean-cut, unassuming, average young man, morally on the side of right who was able to overcome great odds with the use of a smile, a song, and a charmed mystique.[52] Again, this "Autry fantasy" has been ascribed to Nat Levine, Director Armand Schaefer, and Autry himself. Autry and his advisors consciously turned his character into a dandified hero, charming and singing his way past villains and danger. He was a hero with which the underdog and physically undeveloped could identify.[53]

Whether Autry's phenomenal fame was due to his timing, his music, his morality, his family entertainment emphasis, or because he represented a change from the usual Westerner may never be determined with certainty. However, the fact remains that he was influential within the industry and was a force with his fans. Autry himself recognized this, "I know that I owe about all I have to the devotion and support of the kids ... to youngsters, Gene Autry is not simply a human being, but a kind of Superman. They accept anything he does or says as the right thing. That's why Gene Autry has to be so careful about the way he handles himself."[54]

Republic was also aware that Autry represented pulling power for the studio and gave out frequent press releases spotlighting and emphasizing his popularity. For example, in covering the Republic program for 1939, the New York World Telegraph used Autry's rise as the lead-in headline "GENE AUTRY OF WESTERNS GOES OVER BIG WITH FANS." The article pointed out his appeal to women and his vast popularity in small towns. He headed all the polls, received more mail than superstar Robert Taylor, and outsold Bing Crosby in the record market. Outside of the large cities Autry outdrew major stars, the article concluded.[55]

The claims were not all studio press agent puffery. Statistics showed that Gene Autry was in the top ten Western stars from the first year the polls were taken in 1936 through 1942 when he entered the service and again from 1946 to 1954. Also, he was number one in popularity from 1937 to 1942. Perhaps even more significant in terms of potential influence on general audiences, he was one of the top ten movie moneymakers for the entire industry from 1938 to 1942.[56] For a B Western cowboy star to be in the same league with the Gables and Garbos was success indeed!

Although Herbert Yates probably did not analyze or even appreciate the basis of Autry's popularity, he recognized it as important to the studio. In an interview in the New York Times he spoke of the continuing success of B Westerns and in the process gave an indication of the reasons for Republic's success and a hint of why it was to eventually fail. "The public has always liked Westerns--you know, cowboys, horses and fine scenery--hillbilly comedies, and serials. The proof of the pudding is that Gene Autry is one of the best loved stars in pictures today. Sure, the story is pretty much the same. There's the hero and the girl and the heavy who is trying to gyp them out of a mortgage or land or cattle. But you change it around a little, give it new trimmings. You've got a formula that the public likes and it's as standard as granulated sugar. If you like sugar in your coffee why use salt?"[57]

If Yates was content to accept Autry's success for what it was in terms of profit, Autry was not so complacent. For whatever reasons, economic or moral, he built upon his image, molded it, aggressively propagandized it, and in the process became a major influence on his fans. The "Cowboy Code," a public image list of rules for cowboy stars, is attributed to Autry. Interestingly enough, Autry's "Ten Commandments" of the Cowboy also mirrored quite accurately what Yates considered important in films morally and what were normally featured in Republic program films, Western or otherwise. So Yates and Autry, both hard-headed businessmen, had more in common than the mere pursuit of profit. The Code as developed by Autry stated:

(1) A cowboy never takes unfair advantage--even of an enemy.
(2) A cowboy never betrays a trust.
(3) A cowboy always tells the truth.
(4) A cowboy is kind to small children, to old folks and to animals.
(5) A cowboy is free from racial and religious prejudices.
(6) A cowboy is helpful and when anyone is in trouble he lends a hand.
(7) A cowboy is a good worker.
(8) A cowboy is clean about his person and in thought, word and deed.
(9) A cowboy respects womanhood, his parents and the laws of his country.
(10) A cowboy is a patriot. [58]

Although these Commandments were not uniformly followed
during the twenty to thirty years in which the B Western
series film flourished, in general they were adhered to quite
closely, especially at Republic.

The final commandment is particularly significant for
Autry. Not only were patriotic themes utilized in Autry's
pictures extensively, but he also left a thriving career at its
height to enter the Second World War. At that time, he
gave an interview widely circulated in the newspapers in
which he espoused his philosophy:

> Everybody ought to think of winning the war ahead
> of anything else. This is the most serious time
> in our history and our country is in more peril
> than any other time.... I think the He-Men in the
> movies belong in the Army, Marine, Navy or Air
> Corps. All of these He-Men in the movies realize
> that right now is the time to get into the service.
> Every movie cowboy ought to devote time to the
> Army winning or to helping win until the war is
> won--the same as any other American citizen. The
> Army needs every young man it can get, and if I
> can set a good example for the young men I'll be
> mighty proud. Seventeen and eighteen [year olds]
> are needed, and some of those boys are my fans.
> I say to them and to all you young men, every
> young man should give everything he can for the
> war effort. If we train young pilots and the war
> continues for a long stretch, those boys of seven-
> teen or eighteen will be a protectorate over the
> whole country. I wanted to join the Air Corps
> rather than the other branches of the services be-
> cause I felt I could do more good for the war ef-
> fort there than any other place--because I have
> been interested in flying for the past ten years. [59]

Autry's beliefs, his image, and traditional American values
were strongly reflected in his films.

The first film in the Autry series was Tumbling Tumbleweeds (1935). It was also the first directorial effort for
Joseph Kane, who was to become the premier house action
director at Republic in future years. The plot had Autry join
a medicine show and then return home to uncover his father's
killer using a song as a decoy. [60] Music and action were
well balanced. Joseph Kane has stated that he was nervous

at his first major responsibility but with so much prepara-
tory experience in various assistant positions, the film was
successful and he was pleased with the results. [61]

The second in the series of Autry Westerns was entitled Melody Trail and continued experimenting with the new
formula. Whereas the first movie had tried to balance the
music and the action with a slight emphasis on the action,
the second entry relied predominantly upon the musical and
broad comedy supplied by Smiley Burnette who had come
with Autry from Chicago. The story concerned a rodeo,
rustling, and even some romance and was routine. [62] While
the studio was definitely experimenting at this point, time was
to prove this second format to be the most utilized and therefore, it is to be assumed, the most popular used in the series. While there were several good action entries, especially in the early years, the music was eventually to predomi-
nate. The Autry Westerns were, as did The Three Mesquiteers, to vary between the West of the past and contemporary
Westerns. However, in the case of the single star with his
musical background, the wide variations in time did not seem
to be as noticeable and difficult to accept. Also his period
pieces tended to group around his early phase while the contemporary backgrounds clustered around the musicals.

The Big Show made in 1936 was the eleventh in the
Autry series for Republic and was a landmark in that it
benefited from special location shooting. It was filmed at
the Texas Centennial in Dallas which gave the production
added gloss and values. Another interesting point is that
Autry played a double role, that of a cowboy star and his
double or stuntman. Since a stuntman doubled Autry in his
stuntman's role, the producers had to be all the more careful. The plot had the prima donna star walking out and his
he-man double saving the day. This film included a young
singer Leonard Slye who changed his name to Dick Weston
and finally took the movie name Roy Rogers. Rogers was at
that time singing with the Sons of the Pioneers who were featured in the film. The group also appeared in Autry's next
picture, The Old Corral, and in the course of the plot development, which has Western lawman Autry defeating New
York gangsters, Autry and Rogers have a brief fight which
Rogers loses.

Although the music was becoming more and more important as these Autry productions progressed, during this
early segment of his movie career a respectable action quota

did remain. A good example is Boots and Saddles released
in 1937. The story was a standard plot concerning rivalry
over an army contract for horses which was decided by a
horse race. Autry was of course motivated by altruism.[63]
However, it included some lively chase sequences--one of
which had Autry turning the tables on two villains by means
of unusual stunt work. As the two villains rode by, separat-
ing to avoid sagebrush behind which the hero was hidden, he
flipped a branch around throwing each of the villains to the
ground simultaneously and as smoothly as a gymnastic routine. Such a sequence is indicative that good, seemingly
spontaneous, action remained in the Autrys.[64]

By this time, Autry was securely on top of the Western field. Knowing his own worth and being a good businessman, he demanded more money. When Herbert Yates refused, Autry finished his current picture and left for an un-
scheduled personal appearance tour throughout the South and
Southwest, the areas of his greatest popularity.[65] The studio's process servers could never quite catch up with him
because Autry's fans protected him to the point of escorting
these servers directly out of town. Such was Autry's popularity.[66] Yates eventually had to give in and come to terms
since Autry was still Republic's top star and because he was
so popular in the recording field which boosted the success
of his movies. It was at this time, however that Yates began to promote Roy Rogers as the new singing cowboy star.
As a result, when Autry returned, Yates had two stars.

Joseph Kane directed the first two Autrys upon the
star's victorious return. But then he moved on to the Rogers
unit and other directors came in to handle Autry. It was at
this time that the Autry films took a more noticeable turn
away from an approximate balance of action and music to a
definite emphasis on the music. With the increasing emphasis on the latter, Autry's Westerns tended to remain
in the present time rather than in the period era of the traditional B Western film. This combination of musical fantasy and modern contemporary stories in the West was a deliberate Republic effort to make the emphasis on music more
acceptable to the Western fan. The earlier Autry historical
Westerns were abandoned and the hero became a radio, rodeo,
or movie star moving in a world of autos, planes and even
tanks.[67] Moreover, the stories hinged on modern themes
such as political corruption, big business expansion, soil
erosion, crop destruction, and various social problems.[68]

An example of the new approach was In Old Monterey
(1939). It was the last Autry feature directed by Joseph
Kane and was considered a Special. It was Republic's policy
during this era, in the case of both Autry and Rogers, to
devote average budgets to six of the eight features per year
and put extra money, stars, musical numbers, and other
special sequences into the remaining two and sell them as
Specials. 69 In Old Monterey ran seventy-three minutes,
about fifteen minutes longer than the normal B Western. To
increase the attraction and variety, some acts which had audience drawing power in the Republic strongholds such as
the Hoosier Hot Shots, a well known Midwestern radio group,
were also added. 70

The plot had an army cavalry background and gave
Autry a chance to appear in uniform thus giving a preview
of his patriotism in the coming years. In fact, at one point,
"Stirred by patriotism, Gabby [Hayes, comic character ac-
tor] springs to his feet, shouting he owes the country an
apology and breaks into the strains of 'Columbia, Gem of
the Ocean.' To a man the town hall breaks into the song."71
Autry also delivered a hard sell patriotic preparedness
speech. Not all critics accepted the message however. One
stated, "herein is some phoney flag-waving, as scripted"
and offered the opinion that the film's goal was for the "Government to preserve America for the Americans."72 The
story also enabled Republic to use some exciting tank action
footage which had appeared in a previous film. 73

Not all of Autry's films proved a proper blend of music, morality and action even in this period. For example,
in 1939 Autry made a film Rovin' Tumbleweeds that cast
him as a Washington Congressman advocating flood control.
It was perhaps inspired by Frank Capra's theme of the honest little man against the corrupt system. 74 However, while
Autry's image bore some resemblance to that idea, Autry
was no James Stewart, and Rovin' Tumbleweeds was no Mr.
Smith Goes to Washington. Nonetheless, the film is representative of the Autry format during this period and with his
personality it might have worked. But it was inappropriate
to the B Western market. It was mainly music and politics.
As one critic commented, "The picture's resemblance to the
typical western lies only in the habiliments of the stars ...
and in a scene laid at a rodeo."75

Autry's next film, however, was back in stride and
proved to be an important landmark in his career. South of

the Border gave Autry a hit song and had a plot which was
very appropriate to the period. It was released around
Christmas of 1939, and included submarine bases, counter-
spys, foreign agents, and concerned revolutionaries attempting to take over Mexican oil deposits.[76] Ironically, in keeping with the title song, the heroine enters a convent at the
movie's conclusion.[77] Confused as it may sound, the film,
its title song, and Autry as a Federal agent were a great hit
in broader markets and Republic found Autry's pictures playing first-run houses as well as attracting the usual Saturday
matinee bookings.[78]

     As Autry's general popularity increased, his films re-
ceived bigger production values and more music, but as has
been indicated the action content decreased noticeably. Variety
noted that in Gaucho Serenade (1940), concerning the hero be-
friending a small English boy whose father is in prison, there
were no horseback scenes for the first forty-four minutes, no
suggestion of fisticuffs for fifty minutes, and no gunplay for
some fifty-six minutes. In a sixty-six minute B Western film,
Variety and probably the fans felt that this was indicative
that the action content was definitely secondary--a situation
worthy of criticism.[79]

     Following a loan out to Twentieth Century-Fox to star
in the film Shooting High (1940),[80] Autry went into Melody
Ranch released the same year. Autry, as a Hollywood radio
star returning home for "frontier day", was supported by
comedian Jimmy Durante and Vera Vague as well as by tap
dancer Ann Miller.

     Obviously, this Special Premier release was definitely
more musical than Western in the traditional sense of the
word, but it was a success and Republic was pleased with its
broader markets. The New York Times even commented,
"Republic apparently intended the film for a wider audience,
weighing this super-Western with romance, radio programs,
and comedy and the varied talents of ... eminent non-West-
erners...."[81] This format continued until Bells of Capistrano, released in 1942. Then Autry joined the Air Force
and spent four years in the service of his country. With an
eye always on the profits Republic continued to re-release
the earlier films of its top Western star during his absence.
This was the time during which Roy Rogers was to meet and
surpass the popularity of Gene Autry, becoming the "King of
the Cowboys".

After the war Autry returned to Republic apparently
interested in regaining his title and crown. His first film
was Sioux City Sue directed by Frank McDonald and released
in 1946. The plot relied more on comedy and music than
on the Western formula and was a startling example of how
much the Autry success had affected the action Westerns of
the thirties. The plot synopsis from Republic's own files
shows how unlike the "blood and thunder" B Westerns of the
past the Autry vehicles had become. Autry, a rancher, has
a chance to become a movie actor but has to sing to a don-
key. He returns to his ranch disillusioned and the female
talent scout attempts to make amends. She saves him from
the villain who wants to ruin Gene. In the finale she obtains
a real starring role for him in a Hollywood musical Western. [82]

This was a far cry from the image of William S. Hart
and Tom Mix. Still, the mild self-effacing hero came through
the comedy, the music, and the media trappings a winner and
Autry's fans accepted it. Republic continued the Autry series
in this vein although Autry was restless. As a sign of the
times, Autry's black and white release played in New York
on a double bill with the first color Rogers release and significantly was somewhat overshadowed in the joint review. [83]

Autry's final film at the studio was Robin Hood of
Texas (1947), directed by Lesley Selander. Ironically enough,
it was less a musical and more of a mystery than had been true
of previous productions both before the war and upon his immediate return. Autry was blamed for a bank robbery and then
released as a decoy. Action and doublecrosses prevailed as
Autry cleared himself at a dude ranch. It was closer to a
traditional B Western than Autry had been in for years.

Because Autry was interested in setting up his own
production unit and exercising complete control, in mid 1947
he left Republic for Columbia where he continued his career
until the early fifties. Although he took with him several of
his Republic staff including Armand Schaefer, John English
and Frank MacDonald, as well as some experienced technical
people, his Columbia productions were not that much different.
The major change was a de-emphasis of the musical extravaganza and a return to the more balanced Western movie involving both action for the Western enthusiast and music for
the traditional Autry radio/recording fan. Autry sensed that
his Republic productions had become lop-sided. Moreover,
he watched his budgets at Columbia closely and musical spec-

taculars cost money. So, aside from making him richer, his
series of B Westerns at Columbia did little to alter or improve the traditional image of Gene Autry. It can even be
argued that they lacked the spontaneity and excitement of the
early Republic releases. Autry's contribution to the Western
was developed at Republic and benefited from that studio's
expertise.

Long before Autry parted company with Republic, the
studio had found and developed along the same lines the man
who in some respects surpassed him. Roy Rogers came to
the movies as Leonard Slye from Duck Run, Ohio, and appeared with the Sons of the Pioneers in a few Columbia and
Republic Westerns. As noted, he received encouragement at
Republic after Autry and the studio had financial disagree-
ments. Just as in the fifties Rex Allen, Western singer
billed as "The Arizona Cowboy", was to be groomed as a
successor to the then top-rated Roy Rogers, so too Rogers
was brought in to answer the threat of Gene Autry. [84]

Rogers, like Autry before him, developed into an image greater than the actor and the themes of his films also
paralleled Autry's to a degree. As in Autry's case, Rogers
started out with action/historical motifs, shifted into a mid-
period of glamorous musical extravaganzas, and finally developed into adventuresome outdoor dramas with a degree of
realism unusual for B musical Westerns. Autry left Republic before his third phase really developed and his Westerns
at Columbia, while having some aspects of realism, never
matched the corresponding Rogers period. In some respects,
Rogers' career was the culmination of what Autry's might
have been at Republic had the war not intervened. Only in
Rogers' case the action content was never completely submerged as it seemed to be with the Autry films when music
predominated. Rogers' third phase--the action period--was
far more stark and brutal than any of the Autry Westerns
either at Republic or Columbia.

While Rogers and Autry shared and promoted the
"good guy" image, there was a slightly different representative of the clean cut hero. Whereas Autry was the underdog, conquering through righteousness and music, Rogers
was a more convincing and virile hero. He came across as
the athletic boy next door who could take care of himself
and who would always do the right thing. As one critic said
in comparing the two, "His [Rogers] voice is 'more romantic', his smile warmer, his charm 'far more boyish' ". [85]

Pete Martin, film star interviewer, said Rogers appealed to
children, servicemen, women and even "to elderly folk, to
whom he represents the sterling qualities of a son or grand-
son they would delight to call their own".[86] And Rogers always looked more convincing in a fight. Even in his early
youthful period he never had the awkward look that Autry
did, although admittedly the hand-to-hand combat was avoided
at first since his slight build was more obvious in close
fights. However, Rogers' other physical activities such as
stunts and riding were always more impressive.

Even when Rogers' pictures shifted into the more colorful musical phase and he began to wear fancy outfits never
imagined in the pre-Hollywood real West, his image remained
untarnished to the youthful audience. The mood of his films
seemed to vary from those of Autry's made in the phase
where music surpassed the action. Not only did Rogers'
films retain relatively more action, but the music was seg-
regated and stagelike. In the Rogers' efforts, the music
took the form of reviews and deliberate interruptions in the
plot and action whereas Autry's music was frequently integrated into the plotline or at least flowed into the picture.

Rogers even told Jon Tuska that he felt Yates based
his films directly on the stage play Oklahoma. Rogers stated
that a memorandum came down to this effect after Yates had
made one of his New York trips. On the basis of this, Tuska
concludes, "There was no underlying fantasy in the Rogers pictures the way there was in Gene Autry's Westerns, but there
was glamour and a dreamlike quality, music, and magic,
beautiful men and women singing and flirting in the Golden
West."[87] The fact that the Rogers' musicals had bigger
budgets than Autry's earlier ones, as well as the conscious
attempt on the part of Yates to mimic a successful stage
effort, may account for the difference between the musical
Westerns of the two stars. The difference, while difficult
to articulate outside a movie theater, was significant.

Rogers' popularity was as unquestionable as his style
and clothing as his career progressed. He himself questioned
the gaudy outfit but came to accept the image. "His studio--
still vigorously at work creating a fictive personality ... demands that he dress as gaudily as possible in order to attract attention to himself in public. At first Roy, the shy
country boy, didn't like it....Now he is becoming more ac-
customed to his job and appears in dazzling regalia."[88] And
the ploy worked. The newspaper PM acknowledged his at-

traction and popularity in a slightly condescending article
when he entered his "colorful" period:

> A STRANGER IN PITCHMAN'S GULCH: Roy Rogers
> The Cowboy Star Gets Not a Tumble Despite Full
> Regalia.
>   The New Yorkers who saw Roy Rogers walking
> through noonday traffic one day last week, and into
> the West 57th Street office of Republic Pictures,
> turned around and stared, but not one of them
> thought enough of the apparition to ask him for his
> autograph. He was dressed in a green fitted cow-
> boy suit, bound and appliqued in brown, with a tan
> appliqued shirt, orange tie, ten-gallon Stetson and
> fancy orange boots, but blase Broadway let him
> pass like just another sandwich man. Which goes
> to show that New Yorkers above the age of twelve
> or thirteen aren't as familiar with Roy Rogers as
> by rights they should be....This a commentary on
> New York provincialism when you consider that in
> Roy's three years in pictures he's become the
> third ranking western star of the U. S. A. ... and
> that outside New York he goes over hell-for-leather
> with the fans. [89]

Like Autry before him Rogers was indeed a ranking
star. When Autry moved out of the Number One position as
top money-making Western star in the Motion Picture Herald
poll in 1942, Rogers moved in and held that position from
1943 to 1954, three years after he made his last theatrical
B Western.[90] Again like Autry, Rogers also recognized his
worth and potential influence, cultivated his image, and developed his popularity to the highest level possible. While
he did this admittedly for profit--he was for a period the
most merchandised star in the world--he always was cogni-
zant of the power of his influence over his young fans. Art
Rush, his long time manager, claims that both he and Rogers
knew for years the impact which his films were having upon
youthful audiences and this was one reason they fought Republic so hard on the release of Rogers pictures to television.[91] In any case, for commercial, moral or other reasons, Roy Rogers was concerned with the fact that he had a
strong following as shown in his frequent personal appearance tours, his top box office ratings, and general popularity.[92]

At the height of his popularity, Rogers received

74, 852 letters in one month far surpassing the previous record holder, Clara Bow. [93] At that time, he acknowledged
his influence. "That's just a part of the job.... Children
pattern themselves after you. It might be that at home a
kid's mother is trying to get him to stop smoking. If he
sees me smoking on the screen he'd say, 'Gee, Roy Rogers
does it--why can't I?' "[94]

     Rogers and his wife, Dale Evans, became very active
in religious circles in the late forties. This fact proved influential when, in the seventies, he reactivated his career
through record releases, television and county and state fair
appearances, and new movie productions. One result is that
he frequently reflected upon the potential effect of his B Westerns since they were the basis of his original popularity.
He recognized that their period of greatest impact was in the
forties and early fifties when he switched from movies to an
action-oriented Western television series. When asked about
his reputation as an All-American, he noted that he "felt like
a babysitter to two generations" and replied, "It's thrilling
that people have trust in you. It comes from many things--
the books Dale's written, the personal appearances. People
like Dale and I [sic] together; we just go good."[95]

     Rogers was also convinced that the morality of his
pictures was a positive factor. In commenting on the use of
violence in later films, he emphasized the end result. "Blood,
of course, has always been a Wild West requisite, but Roy
claims it was hardly ever gratuitous. 'Oh, you were allowed
to have a little smeared under your nose or mouth during a
fight scene... But we fought clean and what's more, the bad
guys never won.' "[96] If Rogers was thinking in terms of the
conclusion of each of his films he is absolutely right. However, in some Rogers' pictures, especially after the Second
World War, when William Witney was consistently directing
and Sloan Nibley was frequently writing them, Roy Rogers
did have some bruising battles within the films which he lost
in relatively bloody closeups. Rogers insisted that the violence and the messages in his B Western series were not
harmful compared to later Westerns "that could have an adverse effect on some of the children in the audience". [97]

     Regardless of variations in their personal beliefs,
their financial successes, and slight alterations in their approaches to the program Western, it is undeniable that Roy
Rogers followed Gene Autry in terms of studio, type of entertainment, career development, and a serious concern about

image. Rogers proved a worthy successor to Gene Autry.
He was a variant upon the image, but in terms of the message imparted by the man and his films he was basically the
same. It is also important that Roy Rogers was perhaps
more effective as an audience influence in that he was a
more believable hero.

Rogers was put under contract to Republic in October
1937 and after a few supporting roles was given the star
buildup. [98] Yates rushed the newly named Roy Rogers into
a Western series and released Under Western Stars in April,
1938. It was directed by Autry veteran Joseph Kane and produced by Sol C. Siegel who went on to better things at Republic and in a few short years into independent production
where he became a major Hollywood producer. [99]

The plot of this first entry in the new series did con-
tain music since Rogers was being molded in the Autry image. He was after all a singer and a better one than Autry
at that. However, it was a contemporary story with Rogers
as a young Congressman who attempted to obtain water for
the Dust Bowl area. The hero won the day by obtaining the
passage of a flood control bill but the Western action elements were not sacrificed to the politics. The New York
Times, after noting that Rogers was a new star, allowed
that "the dust-bowl film shown to Washington society by Roy
after his election to Congress on a free-water platform is a
darn good documentary". [100] While it cannot be said that the
film foretold the future immediately, it was a successful B
Western and Rogers' career was underway. [101]

The second Rogers entry, Billy the Kid Returns, was
a period Western in which Rogers played both the original
Billy the Kid and a look alike who takes the Kid's place after the outlaw's death in order to enforce the law in Lincoln
County, New Mexico. The film was both directed and produced by Joseph Kane. He was to handle the next forty Roy
Rogers Westerns and, as a proven action director, was to
keep the Rogers vehicles well paced.

During this phase of Rogers' career, the action was
emphasized over the music. For the next three years, he
had a series of quite successful B Western films. "As for
Rogers himself, he was more assured with each release,
and improving with experience," according to one Rogers
filmographer. [102] During this period, also, Rogers' Westerns tended more frequently to be historic rather than con-

temporary, another similarity to Autry's early development.
After Wall Street Cowboy in 1939, which dealt with Rogers
defending himself against New York gangsters on their own
ground, he appeared in such period Westerns as Days of
Jesse James (1939), Young Buffalo Bill (1940), Young Bill
Hickok (1940), and Jesse James at Bay (1941). During this
sequence, Rogers' vehicles benefited from solid supporting
casts including people not normally seen at Republic on a
regular basis, while the heroine roles were taken by such
rising actresses as Pauline Moore, Jacqueline Welles (Julie
Bishop), Marjorie Reynolds, Gale Storm and Joan Woodbury.

During this introductory phase, Rogers also was given
the opportunity to appear in vehicles other than the B Western action format--a career incentive not offered to Autry
with the exception of one loan-out. Rogers was featured in
two of the Weaver Brothers and Elviry, hillbilly musical
comedies, a formula into which he fit easily, as well as
some non-Western musical guest roles. [103]

Rogers also was given a strong supporting role in a
Republic "A" production of the period. Raoul Walsh's Dark
Command (1940) starred John Wayne, Claire Trevor, and
Walter Pidgeon with a strong supporting cast and was Repub-
lic's well received follow-up to Wayne's success in RKO's
Stagecoach. Rogers was cast as the headstrong younger
brother of Trevor in this top budgeted and quite popular pe-
riod Western based very loosely on the exploits of Quantrill's
Raiders.

While Rogers' performance was quite good and showed
promise, Republic considered him more valuable in his now
clearly successful B Western series and it was many years
before he appeared in another A film. [104]

In 1941 with Red River Valley, which concerned a
gambler's thwarted attempts to sabotage a dam, the Sons of
the Pioneers joined Rogers as a supporting musical group.
Their addition, of course, signaled more music in the Rogers
films. However, the music still remained secondary to the
action content but the second phase was gradually becoming
noticeable. The musical part of Rogers' films were noticeably increased when, in 1942, Gene Autry entered the service. Within three months Roy Rogers' B Westerns began to
receive bigger budgets, a major portion of which went into
the musical production numbers. [105]

The first entry in this phase of Roy Rogers' career
was Heart of the Golden West. It was considered to be a
Special and had Rogers defeating a greedy trucking executive
who was gouging cattle shippers--a theme near and dear to
rural interests. [106] Bigger budgets, better sets, and stronger supporting casts frequently meant more music and dialogue and correspondingly less action on such pictures but in
this case the action content remained high and the pacing was
very brisk. While the music was indeed more noticeable,
the entry was still a more than satisfying B Western with
good balance and production values. A trade review summarized, "Joseph Kane ... creates an entertaining variant
on the straight western ... and manages to collate an amaz-
ing total of standard western thrill elements [action] in with
the comedy and the music to heap up an hour's diversion." [107]

With the production of Idaho (1942) came the era when
Roy Rogers began to don grotesque and unbelievable costumes
and when his productions relied more on musical extravaganzas than standard B Western action. The change had
come gradually but this film signaled the new emphasis. But,
the action motifs did remain in segments of most of the
Rogers films and the image of Rogers as an honest hero who
saves the day for justice and the common man continued, al-
ternating with patriotic themes as the war progressed. Idaho
concerned the clearing of a framed judge who helped delin-
quent boys and while the musical emphasis was obvious, the
film was a guaranteed success. "While sophisticated moviegoers will probably stay away from 'Idaho' in droves, the
film will undoubtedly reach some 7500 theaters--a healthy
proportion of the nation's 18, 000--and will turn in a profit
of $300, 000." [108]

In King of the Cowboys (1943) Rogers was combating
saboteurs who use a tent show as a cover. This fast-paced
film concluded with a wounded Rogers disarming a bomb on
a railroad trestle to save American troops while under fire
from the spy ring. [109] Reviewers noted the patriotism in addition to the action content and the musical numbers in this
picture. [110]

It was at this time that the standard Rogers format
was developing for the Rogers films during the second part
of his career--the plot and final action sequence ended early
and the film would conclude with a musical review to appeal
to those people who were interested in the musical content
of the film. [111] Actually, this segregation seemed to work

out well and the action content was not so obviously sacrificed as had been the case in the Autry series. Both enter-
tainments could co-exist in the same picture, frequently not
intruding in any great degree upon one another. With Hands
Across the Border, the first release of 1944, the concept of
separate musical conclusions became standard in Rogers' pictures.[112]

Two important events in the Rogers series occurred
the next year. Dale Evans became Roy Rogers' leading lady
with The Cowboy and the Senorita and with the following film,
Song of Nevada, Joseph Kane left as director of the series.

Frank MacDonald directed Rogers in Bells of Rosarita
released in 1945. This film is an important one in B Western filmography in that it was the first time that Republic
used the interesting technique of introducing guest stars in
the form of other leading Western players from the studio's
various series. Rogers summarized the plot. "Republic
has got a new idea for the picture I'm working in now. In
the picture, I'm playing myself. According to the script,
I'm out on location making a picture when I run into a girl
who needs help to keep from being gypped out of a ranch
her pappy left her. I send out a call for help to Bill Elliott,
Don (Red) Barry, Allan Lane, Robert Livingston, and Sunset
Carson--all of whom work for Republic and star in Western
pictures of their own. Together, we clean up the evildoers
and get the ranch back for the girl. It's kind of Grand Hotel
on saddles....We had to ration the crooks. We were allowed one apiece."[113] These five guest heroes each had
their own action scenes when they assisted Rogers with the
Sons of the Pioneers in rounding up the villains in their
uniquely individual ways which were readily recognizable to
all Western fans. The unique ploy of major Hollywood Western stars doing good deeds and sharing the action in the same
picture was emphasized.[114] As one cinema survey states,
"Rogers and the stars appear at Dale's circus in order to
raise the money to pay off notes against her property. Perhaps Bells of Rosarita should have been Altruism Rides the
Range."[115] In any case, the guest star routine proved to
be so successful that Republic utilized it again several times
in various series.

Roy Rogers' own favorite movie was My Pal Trigger
released in 1946 and directed by MacDonald.[116] A somewhat involved episodic piece, the film had Rogers accused of
murdering a stallion whose colt he raises. He eventually

saved the ranch of Gabby Hayes and discovered the real
killer.[117] The film moved Bosley Crowther, the New York
Times reviewer, to comment, "the theme of this interloping
Western is the beautiful love that exists between kind-hearted
Mr. Rogers and his remarkably amatory horse."[118] Besides
emphasizing horses and horse raising, the film actually had
some dramatic moments and gave Rogers a chance to act.
In fact, the advertising campaign emphasized the emotional
and dramatic content of the film. "So stirring ... so exciting ... so intensely real ... My Pal Trigger. This magnificent story of man and horse will touch your heart ... will
fill you with delight!"[119]

With the conclusion of the Second World War, two
events occurred which shifted Rogers' career into its third
phase. First, Gene Autry returned to Republic and after a
brief attempt to regain his stature as the Number One Western film star left Republic for his own production company.
The Autry and Rogers vehicles were too similar. Both made
alterations in their formulas. Rogers' films received a
transfusion of new ideas as movie personnel returning from
the service joined the unit. Writer Sloan Nibley and director
William Witney were among the most noteworthy. These new
men and changing audience tastes resulted in a de-emphasis
of the musical extravaganza and more stress on the action
and plot lines.[120]

In this third phase, the Rogers' films were more interesting, rapidly paced, and were given themes which often
bordered on the brutal.[121] While Witney asserted that he
was tired of blood and killing, his experience as an action
director came to the forefront and during this period the
Rogers vehicles reached their highest quality. Witney felt
this was the happiest time of his directorial career.[122]

For his part, Sloan Nibley realized the limitations of
the B Western formula and that he had to work within a format. Therefore, he and the other writers would spend most
of their time inventing new but workable approaches to plot
development. There was also some challenge in developing
the character of the villains and supporting characters since
the characteristics of the hero, heroine and comic sidekick
were rarely allowed to change drastically. Nibley deliberately made Rogers a little more human, however, in that
Rogers would occasionally make a wrong calculation, a misjudgment, and occasionally, as a result, would be badly
beaten in mid-plot. Of course he emerged victorious at the

fadeout.[123] For example, Nibley developed the plot in Bells
of San Angelo (1947) around silver smuggling on the Mexican
border in a contemporary setting. Roy's elaborate costume
was played down and in this picture he received the first major beating of his B Western career. It occurred in the
middle of the film and Rogers triumphed in the fadeout so
that the morality message was unimpaired. Still, it was a
major change in the image.

The next production was Springtime in the Sierras also
in 1947, and this time Nibley wrote a script around wildlife
preservation. Rogers broke up an illegal game slaughtering
ring supplying a syndicate with illegal meat. The ecological
message and plea for conservation was there strong enough
to be perceived even by children and it undoubtedly had some
good effect.[124] However, the true surface appeal of the
film was in its beautiful and rousing action sequences handled
by Witney and in the alluring villainy of the female leader of
the evildoers. In this film Andy Devine became the comic
relief and Dale Evans was temporarily replaced by Jane Frazee.[125] Frazee said that, when she began to appear in
them she knew it was "the beginning of the end" of her career.[126] Actually many of the actors and actresses appearing in the Rogers Western film were distinguished and had
respectable careers before and after their appearance. The
Rogers vehicles were enhanced at various times by the presence of such well known and versatile character actors as
Jack Holt, John Carradine, Jerome Cowan, Milburn Stone,
Bob Steele, and Herbert Rawlinson. The use of the well
known faces was another testimonial to the high production
values that Republic placed in its then Number One Western
series.

In 1950 Trigger Jr. was released. It was written by
Gerald Geraghty, also a frequent Rogers contributor, and
has Rogers as a Western star running down a killer stallion
used by lawbreakers in a protection racket. Nibley felt that
this film was a particularly good example of the ability of
the Republic writers to deliver well within the standard format. The writers, he asserted, did have freedom within the
format and Trigger Jr. showed that freedom carried too far,
indicating that the movie represents an interesting failure in
that it was not as successful as most Rogers features. He
commented that it was an episodic production which did not
follow the traditional Rogers plot in any of the three phases
of his career. It was Nibley's experience that while the
writers could alter the ingenious devices and schemes within

the plots to some degree and develop the character of the
villains, the Rogers pictures were much more successful as
long as they remained within the realm which the audience
expected. 127

In Spoilers of the Plains released in 1951, Nibley had
Rogers combating international criminals who menaced the
United States through a weather prediction device. 128 The
film, while somewhat of a throwback to the patriotic pieces
of the Second World War, was appropriate to the anti-communist era and made much of national security. It was indicative that patriotism and preparedness were a continuing
part of the Rogers and the Autry images.

Although the Rogers films were maintaining their production values, and could compete easily with similar productions from other studios, the decreasing market for the
B Western film was becoming apparent. Profits were down,
theater demand was declining, reissues were more frequent,
and new productions in many series were less and less attractive. With Pals of the Golden West (1951), Rogers and
Republic parted and the B Western singing cowboy series
came to an end at Republic in so far as its two most successful proponents were concerned. Republic still had Rex
Allen and Autry lasted two years longer at Columbia, but
the decline was clear. Still, Republic did well with the
Rogers series up until the conclusion. As Don Miller said,
"It may have been consolation that even at the end, when the
Western field was swiftly descending in popularity and the
fortunes of Republic were far from sanguine, the Roy Rogers
Westerns maintained their prestige and their quality."129

Why did the era of the B Western series end? Perhaps Albert S. Rogell, who has had a long career in many
phases of Hollywood production and directorship and who
worked extensively at Republic, summarized it most succinctly
when he stated that the Rogers format was perhaps the best
and most successful for its period but that it outlived its
time. 130 Yet there are those who feel that the Rogers formula maintained its success up until the end. If anything,
Rogers quit while his films were still successful and transferred to television while Autry followed two years later.
Art Rush indicated that both he and Rogers knew that the Republic Western films, and especially his own, were saleable.
He and Rogers approached the television networks in the late
forties about taking over the old films as a major series.
They were turned down but in 1951 Rogers switched to a

standard half hour B Western television series and the Rogers name became a television standard.[131]

Perhaps the final word concerning the lasting success of the Rogers vehicles as well as many of the Republic B Western series lies in the fact that National Telefilm Associates and Telescene, Inc. in 1974 packaged a series of the best of the B Westerns mostly from Republic under the umbrella title Roy Rogers Presents the Great Movie Cowboys. These slightly edited B Western features with new introductions filmed by Rogers at his Western museum were very successful throughout the country, even being sold to educational television stations in some areas.[132]

Each of the three major Republic program Western series discussed used variations on the basic message of the morality play and each had their own coterie of fans. But regardless of these variations, the traditional plot of good versus evil in a formula development with the forces of good prevailing was the overriding theme in all three series. This was also true of the other Western series of the studio. Most were a success although perhaps not on the same level of the three which have been discussed.

Historians Arthur F. McClure and Ken D. Jones best summarized the impact of these B Westerns:

> The popularity of the "B" Western was an extension of the cowboy myth in American life. Historian Carl Becker noted that Americans are prone to cling to what he called "useful myths"... The emotional conditioning provided by these films, and the durability of that conditioning should never be dismissed by historians of American life... [I]t is entirely possible that in the midst of confusion and uncertainty created by the Depression and World War II audiences sustained many of their "faithes" by identifying with some admirable and powerful symbols of straightforward righteousness as seen in the "B" Westerns.[133]

And Republic made the most successful B Westerns.

Notes

1. A Pictorial History of the Western Film (New York: Citadel, 1969), p. 141.

2. James Horwitz, They Went Thataway (New York: E. P.
    Dutton, 1977), pp. 125-26. Horwitz's book is devoted
    to attempting to track down the heroes of his youth
    and to explaining the ideals of his generation.
3. See Chapter I, pp. 24-26.
4. An expansion on this interpretation of the message of
    the B Western can be found in Jon Tuska, "In Retro-
    spect: Tim McCoy, Last of Four Parts", Views and
    Reviews, II (Spring, 1971), p. 15.
5. The Western: From Silents to Cinerama (New York:
    Bonanza Books, 1962) and A Pictorial History of the
    Western Film (New York: Citadel, 1969).
6. The Filming of the West (New York: Doubleday, 1976).
7. (New York: Collier Books, 1971).
8. New York: The Popular Library Film Series, 1976).
9. F. E. Emery, "Psychological Effects of the Western
    Film: A Study in Television Viewing", Human Rela-
    tions, XII (1959), p. 196.
10. Six Guns and Society: A Structural Study of the West-
    ern (Berkeley, California: University of California
    Press, 1976), Chapter Three "The Structure of the
    Western Film", pp. 29-123.
11. "The Psychological Appeal of the Hollywood Western",
    The Journal of Educational Sociology, XXIV (October,
    1950), pp. 72-86.
12. Elkin, "Psychological Appeal", p. 73.
13. Elkin, "Psychological Appeal", p. 75. A similar point
    is made in James K. Folsom, "Western Themes and
    Western Films", Western American Literature, II
    (1967), pp. 195-96.
14. Morris R. Abrams, Republic script supervisor and
    assistant director thoughtfully emphasized his belief
    that Republic musicals made a contact with basic
    American chords both musically and emotionally through
    frequent use of folk music. While somewhat critical
    of the potential influence of the Republic product, this
    was one point Abrams felt significant. Interview with
    Morris Abrams, Hollywood, California, May 17, 1976.
15. Elkin, "Psychological Appeal", p. 76.
16. Elkin, "Psychological Appeal", p. 78.
17. Elkin, "Psychological Appeal", p. 79. The same point
    is registered with a clinical emphasis in Emery, "Psy-
    chological Effects", pp. 194-95.
18. Elkin, "Psychological Appeal", p. 81.
19. Elkin, "Psychological Appeal", p. 84.
20. Elkin, "Psychological Appeal", p. 85.
21. Gregory D. Black and Clayton R. Koppes, "OWI Goes to

the Movies: The Bureau of Intelligence's Criticism
of Hollywood, 1942-1943", Prologue: The Journal of
the National Archives, VI (Spring, 1974), p. 50.

22. John Wayne and the Movies (Cranbury, New Jersey:
A. S. Barnes, 1976), p. 52. Yet this was not always true. The time period in the series varied
from Post Civil War to the forties.

23. The Hall of Fame of Western Film Stars (North Quincy,
Massachusetts: Christopher Publishing House, 1969),
p. 183.

24. Tuska, Filming of the West, p. 339.

25. Variety, July 2, 1939.

26. Warshow, The Immediate Experience, p. 140.

27. New York Post, June 27, 1940.

28. Saturday Afternoon at the Bijou (New Rochelle, New
York: Arlington House, 1973), p. 179.

29. "Republic Productions, Inc. Produced Properties", p. 173.

30. Elwood [Indiana] Call-Leader, December 13, 1946. Reissue booking. Re-issue booking refers to the practice of holding a film after its first run and then re-
circulating it several years later.

31. "Republic Productions, Inc. Produced Properties", p. 72.

32. Variety, August 4, 1937. The film was also included
in the syndicated television package, Roy Rogers Presents the Great Movie Cowboys, WNED-TV Buffalo,
New York; Fall 1976 to Spring 1977.

33. New York Times, March 19, 1938.

34. "Republic Productions, Inc. Produced Properties", p. 121.

35. This film under its new title Frontier Horizon is included
in the syndicated package, Roy Rogers Presents the
Great Movie Cowboys, WNED-TV Buffalo, New York,
Fall 1976 to Spring 1977.

36. Maurice Zolotow, Shooting Star: A Biography of John
Wayne (New York: Simon and Schuster, 1974), p. 130.

37. Zolotow, p. 112.

38. Interestingly, Vera H. Ralston offers another, less
likely, interpretation. She claims that according to
her husband, Herbert Yates, the studio was still willing to advance the career of Livingston beyond the B
Western field. However, fan mail was so heavily
against Wayne in the series and for the return of Livingston that, even before Wayne made his breakthrough,
the studio had decided to remove Wayne from the series and return the popular Livingston. She cites this
"tremendous amount of fan mail" as indicative of the
popularity of the series and the Republic product as
well as the seriousness with which the fans viewed

160 Republic Studios

their Western movies. Telephone interview with Vera H. Ralston, Santa Barbara, California, May 10, 1976.

39. Elwood [Indiana] Call-Leader, December 16, 1943.
40. Miller, Hollywood Corral, p. 164.
41. Telephone interview with Robert Livingston, Republic Western and feature actor, Los Angeles, California, May 8, 1976.
42. Alva Johnston, "Tenor on Horseback", Saturday Evening Post, CCXII (September 2, 1939). pp. 19, 74.
43. Barbour, The Thrill of It All, p. 125.
44. Jack Nachbar, ed. Focus on the Western (Englewood Cliffs, New Jersey: Prentice-Hall, 1974), p. 4.
45. Jim Kitses, Horizons West (Bloomington: Indiana University Press, 1969), p. 17.
46. Kalton C. Lahue, Riders of the Range (New York: Castle, 1973), p. 35.
47. "Mr. Harper", "After Hours; Fallen Idol", Harpers, CC (January, 1950); pp. 99-100.
48. Miller, Hollywood Corral, p. 108.
49. Percy Knauth, "Gene Autry, Inc.", Life, XXIV (January 28, 1948), pp. 88-100.
50. Two of the more notable ones were Ken Maynard who did his own singing and John Wayne as Singing Sandy in Riders of Destiny (Monogram, 1933), whose singing was dubbed.
51. Filming of the West, p. 303.
52. Johnston, "Tenor on Horseback", p. 18.
53. Tuska, Filming of the West, p. 304. Tuska carried his interpretation even farther as he continued the discussion. He states, "I sincerely feel that Autry's massive appeal as a modest cowboy troubadour leading a uniquely charmed life, a musical magician who could turn darkness into light, sorrow into happiness, tarnish into splendor, a Pied Piper able to control men and alter the course of world events by means of a song, is the most tremendous single occurrence in the history of the American Western cinema. Gene Autry in his magnificent outfits, yodeling a pop tune, is an image so remote from the actual man of the frontier to rival any fairy tale," p. 305.
54. Tuska, Filming of the West, p. 309.
55. May 14, 1938.
56. Richard Gertner, ed. 1975 International Motion Picture Almanac (New York: Quigley Publishing Company, 1975), pp. 43A-44A.
57. August 4, 1940.
58. Knauth, "Gene Autry, Inc.", p. 92 and referred to in

many other primary sources. Also attributed to Autry
in secondary sources as Jenni Calder, There Must Be
A Lone Ranger: The West in Film and Reality (New
York: Taplinger Publishing Company, 1974), p. 185.

59. Article from 1942 entitled "Gene Autry's Advice to
Youth in Wartime", from the Chamberlain and Lyman
Brown Theatrical Agency Collection in the Theatrical
Section of the New York Public Library. Autry was
actually the first of the ten biggest box office stars to
be accepted into the war effort according to this article. Clark Gable's induction received a premature
announcement. Autry had already been called.

60. Johnston, "Tenor on Horseback", p. 74.

61. Harry Sanford, "Joseph Kane: A Director's Story,
Part I", Views and Reviews, V (September, 1973), p.
34.

62. Elwood [Indiana] Call Leader, August 23, 1945. Reissue booking.

63. New York Times, November 8, 1937.

64. Miller, Hollywood Corral, p. 110.

65. New York Herald-Tribune, February 4, 1938, headlined
"Studio Enjoins Gene Autry: Says 'Horse Opera' Star
Ran Away to Go on the Stage".

66. Sanford, "Kane", Views and Reviews, p. 35.

67. Everson, A Pictorial History of the Western Film,
p. 147.

68. Johnston, "Tenor on Horseback", p. 18. It should be
pointed out that these themes which had the hero dealing with modern problems undoubtedly contributed to
his influence considering his great popularity.

69. See Chapter One, pp. 9-11 for the economic guidelines
on Republic productions.

70. Elwood [Indiana] Call-Leader, February 4, 1944. Reissue booking.

71. In Old Monterey. Still Manual. (Hollywood: Republic
Pictures, 1939).

72. Variety, August 4, 1939.

73. Bob Thomas, "Hollywood's General of the Armies",
True, XXX (July, 1966), p. 87 describes how Yakima
Canutt went about staging this outstanding footage.
The fact that it was worked into a Gene Autry Western
is indicative of Republic's shrewd use of stock se-
quences.

74. Rovin' Tumbleweeds. Sales Manual. (Hollywood: Republic Pictures, 1938). Stressed the movie hero being
duped by the political machine but ultimately winning
out with the help of the masses, in this case migrants,
and even converting the main villain.

75. New York Herald, November 23, 1939.
76. South of the Border. Still Manual. (Hollywood: Republic Pictures, 1939)
77. New York Herald, December 16, 1939. The song is a story in which the girl enters a convent when the hero does not return to her as expected.
78. Elwood [Indiana] Call-Leader, April 21, 1944. Reissue booking. The film played Sunday through Tuesday at Elwood's "class" theater. These days were the week's A playdates and the theater was not a B Western outlet normally.
79. May 15, 1940.
80. Here Autry received twice his normal Republic fee ($25,000 versus $12,500). "Double Mint Ranch", Time, XXXV (January 15, 1940), p. 47.
81. December 26, 1940.
82. "Republic Productions, Inc. Produced Properties", p. 155.
83. New York Times, July 23, 1947.
84. Art Rush, Rogers' manager, claims that both he and Rogers saw Allen as a potential talent and encouraged Allen's career. Telephone interview with Art Rush, Los Angeles, California, May 6, 1976.
85. Lucy Greenbaum, "Sinatra in a Sombrero", New York Times Magazine (November 4, 1945), p. 42.
86. Pete Martin, "Cincinnati Cowboy", Saturday Evening Post, CCXVII (June 9, 1945), p. 80.
87. Tuska, Filming of the West, p. 463.
88. H. Allen Smith, "King of the Cowboys", Life, XV (July 12, 1943), p. 54.
89. Louise Levitas, May 20, 1941.
90. Gertner, International Motion Picture Almanac, p. 44A.
91. Telephone interview with Art Rush, Roy Roger's business manager, Los Angeles, California, May 6, 1976. See also Chapter I, pp. 23-24, for additional discussion of the conflict between Rogers and Republic on the use of his films.
92. New York Times, February 2, 1941. In 1943, Newsweek stated, "Rogers and his Palomino horse, Trigger, make about fifty stage bows a year. In between chores, he appears as a guest star on radio programs; stars in rodeo shows, and makes Decca records that sell at the rate of 6000 per week". "King of the Cowboys", XXI (March 8, 1943), p. 76.
93. Greenbaum, "Sinatra in a Sombrero", p. 42.
94. Greenbaum, "Sinatra in a Sombrero", p. 42.
95. Los Angeles Times, Calendar Section, April 21, 1974.

96. Leisure, The Sunday News (New York), December 28,
     1975.
97. Los Angeles Times, January 6, 1975.
98. Ashton Reid, "Hero on Horseback", Colliers, CXXII
     (July 24, 1948), p. 62.
99. Siegel commented that the Rogers Westerns were quite
     well done and something to be proud of from a stu-
     dio as small as Republic. Telephone interview with
     Sol C. Siegel, Los Angeles, California, May 5,
     1976.
100. June 25, 1938
101. Oddly enough, the film had been planned for Autry and
     in the Republic synopsis the leads are referred to
     as "Gene and his pal Frog" although it is identified
     as a Rogers release. "Republic Productions, Inc.
     Produced Properties", p. 184.
102. Miller, Hollywood Corral, p. 113.
103. Greenbaum, "Sinatra in a Sombrero", p. 42. Lake
     Placid Serenade, Hollywood Canteen, and Brazil.
104. The film was Son of Paleface (Paramount, 1952) with
     Bob Hope.
105. H. Allen Smith, "King of the Cowboys", p. 48.
106. Heart of the Golden West. Sales Manual. (Hollywood:
     Republic Pictures, 1942).
107. Variety, November 16, 1942.
108. "King of the Cowboys", Newsweek, XXI (March 8, 1943),
     p. 76.
109. King of the Cowboys. Still Manual. (Hollywood: Re-
     public Pictures, 1943).
110. Variety, April 5, 1943.
111. Miller, Hollywood Corral, p. 119.
112. Elwood [Indiana] Call-Leader, November 9, 1944.
113. Martin, "Cincinnati Cowboy", p. 80.
114. Elwood [Indiana] Call-Leader, February 14, 1946, ads
     publicized the guest stars prominently.
115. Rudy Behlmer and Tony Thomas, Hollywood's Holly-
     wood: The Movies About the Movies (Secaucus,
     New Jersey: Citadel Press, 1975), p. 223.
116. Rogers' introduction to Roy Rogers Presents the Great
     Movie Cowboys, WNED-TV, Buffalo, New York,
     Fall 1976 to Spring 1977.
117. "Republic Productions, Inc. Produced Properties", p. 109
118. New York Times, Augsut 17, 1946.
119. Kokomo [Indiana] Tribune, June 12, 1947.
120. For example Home In Oklahoma (1946) is a detective
     story with Rogers as a small town newspaper man
     who consistently outwits a big city newspaper wom-

an, played by Dale Evans, when she fails to play
fair with him in covering a local murder. The
blend of action and music was good with action and
plot returning to the forefront. An interesting side-
light was the emphasis on how the local clean-cut
hero handled, with a combination of humor and
firmness, the arrogance and slightly dishonest techniques of the city reporter. Small town and rural
audiences invariably appreciated this type of theme,
according to Sloan Nibley. Interview, Los Angeles,
May 4, 1976.

121. Everson, A Pictorial History of the Western Film,
       p. 152.
122. Nevins, "William Witney", pp. 535-36.
123. Interview with Sloan Nibley, Los Angeles, California,
       May 4, 1976.
124. Springtime in the Sierras. Still Manual. (Hollywood:
       Republic Pictures, 1947). So strong was the mes-
       sage, the advertising aid even emphasized the prob-
       lems caused by the illegal game syndicate.
125. Kokomo [Indiana] Tribune, Novmeber 13, 1947.
126. Richard Lamparski, Whatever Became Of ... ? The
       New Fifth Series (New York: Bantam Books, 1976),
       p. 49.
127. Interview with Sloan Nibley, Los Angeles, California,
       May 4, 1976.
128. Spoilers of the Plains. Still Manual. (Hollywood: Re-
       public Pictures, 1951).
129. Miller, Hollywood Corral, p. 124.
130. Interview with Albert S. Rogell, Republic director,
       Los Angeles, California, May 5, 1976.
131. Telephone interview with Art Rush, Los Angeles, Cali-
       fornia, May 6, 1976.
132. Interview with Rex Waggoner, National Telefilm Asso-
       ciates Publicity Director, Los Angeles, California,
       May 12, 1976. They ran on educational television in
       Buffalo, New York, WNED-TV, fall 1976 to spring
       1977.
133. Heroes, Heavies, and Sagebrush (Cranbury, New Jer-
       sey: A. S. Barnes, 1972), p. 11.

Chapter VI

REPUBLIC'S OTHER FILMS: SERIES AND NON-SERIES

While the serials and the B Western series were
aimed primarily at the youth and young adult audience with
a calculated strong secondary attraction to small town and
rural audiences, much of the reverse held true with the other
area of Republic series strength. The comedy series were
meant to appeal to the adult audiences in neighborhood theatres and in urban as well as rural areas. That they should
attract the youthful audience was the secondary goal of the
studio. A good example of the Republic family comedy product with an urban background and aimed at the neighborhood
theatres as well as small towns was the Higgins Family series. The Weaver Brothers and Elviry films were a variation, stressing a rural family in a comedy musical format
which appealed first to rural audiences and secondarily to
the urban trade. Perhaps the best and most famous of the
rural comedy musical type of film at any studio was the Judy
Canova series at Republic. The latter was especially successful, was sometimes considered more than a B product,
had a little extra message beneath the merriment, and is
still remembered.

The Higgins Family series was nothing more or less
than Republic's competition for the higher budgeted Hardy
and Jones series at Metro Goldwyn Mayer and Twentieth
Century-Fox respectively. While the Higgins entries always
relied a bit more heavily on physical humor, this was entirely natural in that Republic's advantage lay in action and
pacing while the writing department at the studio frequently
was a weak area. Nonetheless, the Higgins Family films
like their competitors contained the message, often delivered
without subtlety, that family unity was important. In these
films, it was a truism that goodness and family loyalty would
overcome stupidity and indiscretion on the part of the family
or greed and conniving on the part of the adversaries to ultimately deliver justice and satisfaction.

The series was originally directed by Gus Meins,

who received comedy training under Hal Roach, and starred
real life father, mother, and son, James, Lucille, and
Russell Gleason in film portrayals of that same relationship.
Well-known character actor Harry Davenport was the grand-
father, Tommy Ryan the younger son, while varying actresses
played the grown daughter.   The formula was quite simple
and basically situation comedy.   The father usually became
involved in an impossible situation through his wife's stupidity
and his own ignorance, pride, or lack of caution whereupon
the family would rally together, extricate themselves, and
save the situation in a finale frequently containing an element
of slapstick.   The plots were usually improbable and often
insane but the entertainment was there.   A few examples
will suffice.

The first movie The Higgins Family came in 1938 and
had the father after twenty years trying for success in advertising having his ambitions frustrated by family affairs including the inventive projects of his elder son and the romantic problems of his daughter.   Of course, it was worked
out successfully by the fadeout.   In My Wife's Relatives
(1939) the father was fired from a candy factory when he
quarreled with the owner because his daughter was going with
the owner's son.   Without a job he could not pay for an expensive ring he had purchased for his wife.   He went into
his own candy business and his wife lost the ring supposedly
in the chocolate mixing machine.   Here again the plot was
impossible but the family managed to pull through.   Photoplay found the film "acceptable" but did compliment the acting talents of the Gleasons. [1]*

Another entry included a similar theme of the dignity
of the common man.   Earl of Puddlestone, a 1940 release,
has Grandpa fighting the snobbery of the rich toward Betty,
his granddaughter, by creating imaginary royalty.   Betty
proves herself on her own merits thus delivering a blow for
democracy and rugged individualism as well as for family
unity. [2]   The series proceeded much along the same lines and
might have continued but for the death of Gus Meins. [3]

When Meins died in 1940 the series was furloughed
briefly and was revamped the following year with Roscoe
Karns and Ruth Donnelly replacing the leads.   However, it
was not particularly noteworthy or profitable at this point and

---

*Notes to Chapter VI begin on page 182.

was quietly cancelled. While there were only nine releases
possessing little that was unique, this family situation comedy was pleasant enough and did offer the comforting theme
of family support--always a strong middle American ideal
but especially attractive during the Depression and war years
of the thirties and early forties. As one author put it,"All
but forgotten now, the Gleason-Higgins family were nice
neighbors to meet at the neighborhood theatre".[4] It was basically a warmth series, not in the sense of the Hardys, but
with heavy doses of hectic comedy. The message was very
much subdued by the pacing and noise but it was obvious
that like the more prestigious Hardys, the Higgins' brought
comfort to its audience.

On the other hand, The Weavers were somewhat different in their appeal. They were definitely "down home"
rural folk with deliberate musical interludes. As such, their
attraction was closer to the Judy Canova series but contained
its own form of uniqueness. In fact, their major attraction
was that they were a proven hillbilly commodity. Republic
knew what it wanted with the group and just how to package
the series. The group made one earlier film for Warner
Brothers with Humphrey Bogart entitled Swing Your Lady
(1938) which moved Bosley Crowther to state that he was
sorry to see the "richly idiomatic folk humors" of the Weaver Brothers and Elviry reputed to be the funniest team in
vaudeville "subordinated to anybody".[5] However, the team
was really at home with Republic and their films were right
for the Republic rural audiences. They could have made
films more frequently but were well off from radio and vaudeville and chose not to do so.[6] Nevertheless, the eleven
films in their Republic series ran from 1938 to 1943 and
were filled with bucolic humor which, while sometimes less
acceptable to urban audiences, subtly brought home the message that simple rural folk by handling life decently and
straightforwardly could overcome and even derive benefits
from the sophisticated machinations of any greedy dehuman-
izing system. In all probability, urban viewers also appreciated the Weavers or Republic humor, but Republic aimed
the product at the rural and small town markets.

The team began in medicine shows, progressed to
vaudeville, and reached national stardom on the radio as
"The Arkansas Travelers."[7] The formula used by Republic
had Leon "Abner" Weaver as a small town philosopher supported by his brother Frank "Cicero" as a mute pantomimist,
and June "Elviry" as a musically talented country girl. Later

they were joined by Loretta, the daughter of Leon and June
who usually portrayed a wide-eyed innocent. They were all
musically inclined so each film contained interludes of hillbilly music including at least one number on the "musical"
saw. Actually, the Weaver success served as a prelude to
the national interest in country music in the mid forties
which continued to be revived periodically into the seventies.
Roy Rogers even played support in two of their films as a
young male lead early in his own career. [8]

    The first in the Republic series was Down in "Arkan-
saw" (1938) with orchestra leader and song writer Pinky
Tomlin and Ralph Byrd. It was an interesting mixture of
musical comedy and drama which carried a bit of obvious
propaganda. In the Arkansas backwoods, a government representative succeeded in making the hillbilly people understand the benefits they would derive from a dam which would
provide them with modern facilities. This basic plot, mixed
with romance, music, and comedy, was essentially a variation on the theme used in the Mesquiteers action/adventure
film, New Frontier. [9] At the same time, while the rural
elements benefited at the film's conclusion for the audience's
satisfaction, the picture argued more persuasively than the
Mesquiteers film in favor of the government's conservation
and rehabilitation projects. Defending their homesteads
against redevelopment, the Weavers were won over by the
clean-cut government agent's honesty and love for their daughter. By virtue of compromise and communication, just as
in the Mesquiteers, the backwoods people were vindicated and
both sides in the conflict were satisfied.

    In Old Missouri (1940) also brought out the value of
cooperation and the sagacity of rural wisdom. The Weavers
were impoverished sharecroppers but when they went to the
city, they found the landowner in equally bad straits. They
changed places and Pa Weaver was able to expose the landowner's crooked partners and make his family behave more
sensibly. The conditions of both the landowner and the sharecroppers were improved by the Weavers' handling of the situation.

    In Arkansas Judge (1941) the dishonesty of a spoiled
rich girl caused an innocent charwoman problems and led to
a family feud before Judge Weaver could set things right and
help justice triumph over the selfishness and thoughtlessness
of the rich girl. [10] The Old Homestead (1940) had small
town mayor Elviry handling big town gangsters as well as lo-

cal criminals. In the end, the Weavers ended crime in "Farm-
ington" as well as straightened out a romance. The circumstances changed from film to film but the music, the formula,
the attraction, and the message remained constant. Mountain
Rhythm (1943) added a liberal dose of World War II patriotism. The studio synopsis gives the plot, the atmosphere,
and the message of this film:

> The Weaver family chooses farming as their way
> of helping the national war effort. Their purchase
> of a West Coast acreage formerly owned by a Jap
> family bring them into conflict with the snobbish
> students of a nearby boys' school. The Weavers
> win the long-drawn-out tussel [sic] which ensues,
> the boys are converted to manual war-work, and
> the scoundrelly headmaster is exposed as a trouble-
> maker and an enemy agent and arrested. [11]

Thus, the appeal of the Weaver series was that of an honest
and dedicated rural family overcoming the artificial and dishonest sophisticates with an end result of vindication for
themselves and betterment for all except the forces of evil.
Served up with music and comedy, and in this case timely
and welcome patriotism, the Weavers series hit an appropriate chord in its designated audiences.

Judy Canova was unique in that her two series at Republic, while not really of A quality, were given better budgets by the studio than most of their B efforts. Canova had
early proved her talents and her films had special attraction.
She herself has said that she came to Republic as "a proven
commodity". [12] While mainly rural and small town in their
appeal, her musicals did play larger theatres much as the
"Special" Westerns of Autry and Rogers. [13] As such, Canova's films also received more notice upon occasion. Besides
the obvious theme of a rural innocent having basic decency
and folk wisdom to see her through her tribulations and conflicts with less honest and more pretentious adversaries, the
Canova series also relied heavily on a direct variant of an
archtypal folk story. In many of her pictures she started
out crude, clumsy, and seemingly unattractive. From the
bottom she rose to the top to become the well attired and
successful heroine in the finale. In other words, she portrayed again and again the Cinderella story. [14] The classic
story had the lowly heroine abused by her pretentious step-
relatives. Through outside help, super-natural in the folktale, she became the center of attention but was forced to

flee. The hero then searched her out and she was elevated
to a position of honor. The Canova variants frequently hit
most of these motifs with the supernatural aid being replaced
by self initiative or sympathetic friends. This parallel was
not a conscious effort for "significance" and can probably be
attributed to the universality of the tale. Its popularity was
simply adapted to the Canova formula.

Canova herself recognized this and attributed her movie success partially to this image. She also admitted that
there was a conscious effort to have her progress from
loser to winner in most of her films, another theme with
even more claim to universality. Canova was quite aware of
her appeal to her audience and knew her films might have
had a positive effect. She candidly commented, "Sure, they
[her pictures] were fairy tales that had a little upbeat lesson.
I started out as a plain Jane, an ugly duckling, and ended
up as a beautiful girl decked out in fancy dresses. I was
the heroine, the country bumpkin, honest and straightforward
who won out in the end. Republic had the best background
crews and production values for their kind of product ... but
I was a top money maker for Yates and I fought him on contracts... My shows were popular."[15]

Contrary to popular belief, Judy Canova was not simply a rural comedian portraying herself. Like Autry and
Rogers at the same studio, she picked and then molded her
image although in her case it was more of her own choosing
having been developed long before she received the attention
of the studio. Republic simply capitalized on the perfect
combination of the star's appeal and the tastes of the audience to which Republic directed its films. Canova was a
trained singer and could handle opera, but by her own ad-
mission early determined that her road to success lay in
hillbilly comedy. A born performer, she said that while the
chances of being successfully noticed as a straight or operatic singer were not high, she early decided that she could
garner attention with the comedy-musical approach and so
she deliberately worked to become a success in that field.
As she put it, "I wanted to be unique and set out to be the
best in the hillbilly field".[16]

Born in Florida, Canova attained her original success
along with her sister and two brothers in a family act in a
New York City Greenwich Village night spot in 1932. Then,
they were signed first by Rudy Vallee and later by Paul
Whiteman for their radio shows. The Canovas went on to

some vaudeville and a Broadway appearance in Calling All
Stars (1934). The New York Times said in part "The sketch
launched a quaint and enormously self-possessed girl named
Judy Canova apparently a Hill Billie herself... She has a
talent."[17] While not a success, the show led to a Warner
Brothers contract where she played supporting roles most
notably in the film In Caliente (1935), doing a hillbilly take
off on and immediate following a straight rendition of "The
Lady in Red" musical number. After additional solo stage
appearances, she returned with her family to Hollywood, this
time at Paramount in 1937 where she had fair supporting
roles in two films. After additional vaudeville and radio
stints, the family appeared on NBC-TV on May 3, 1939, in
an experimental broadcast which gave them the honor of being
the first televised hillbilly act.[18] Canova then had a starring role in the Broadway hit, Yokel Boy, which led to her
signing with Republic.

Canova maintained that she preferred the lead in low-
budget productions than to be a supporting player at a major
studio.[19] And this was her destiny at Republic. All told
she made thirteen films there in two series with a brief so-
journ at Columbia in between. Of varying merit, they all
were popular in the Republic strongholds because they cannily
read their audience and delivered both the message and the
required type of entertainment desired by their public.

Canova's first film in the Republic series was Scatterbrain (1940) and it included most of the elements which identified her successful movie formula. It was directed by Gus
Meins, the same comedy trained veteran who helmed the Higgins Family series. Scatterbrain had a rather complex plot.
A press agent planted a producer-director's girl friend with
an Ozark family in order to have her discovered as a natural
talent, play a hillbilly heroine in the producer's film, and
become a star. The actress was planted with Judy Canova
and her "pappy", only it was Judy who was signed by error.
The press agent and producer plan to marry her off and
thus get rid of the competition but finally her screen test
proved her true talent and they made her a real star.[20]

Canova started out loud, boisterous, and crude, wear-
ing calicos and pigtails. Although friendly and funny, she
was definitely at a disadvantage as the Hollywood schemers
tried various tricks to undo and discourage her. But she
and her cantankerous father were vindicated when she became
a sensation and everyone, including her previous adversaries,

recognized her worth. Elements of both the rural/city conflict and the Cinderella fantasy are obvious. The advertising
campaign incorporated both with the copy, "Here's Judy Canova, the hayseed glamour girl ... she's the mountain sugar
who raises cain," and "So, yer agoin' to that city of glam-
our--Hollywood? I figure it this way--what have those stars
got that I ain't got?"[21] A contemporary review pinpointed
the audience attraction of the picture, "Judy Canova displays
sufficient personality and ability in her backwoods character
to indicate sticking around for several pictures and possible
box office rating for the rural and family houses as time
goes on".[22] On the basis of this film's success, Yates
signed Canova to a five-year contract and she was considered
a major property.

For her second film with the studio, Republic utilized
as a springboard an old Broadway play, Sis Hopkins. Released in 1941, the film proved to be an outstanding success
and is the classic example of the Canova film formula. Canova, through naivete, assumed an uncle was penniless and
invited him to her farm. In reality he was wealthy and re-
tired. When she was burned out he reciprocated much to
the disdain of his socially conscious wife and selfish daughter.[23] Canova eventually proved her worth and was literally
the center of attention at the film's conclusion.

It was the perfect Cinderella theme complete with deg-
radation amongst plenty, evil pseudo-stepmother and daughter, fairy god uncle, flight from grace following her supposed
disgrace, and ultimate happy ending. The second theme was
also clearly present--the refreshingly honest underdog country bumpkin against the artificial city dwellers and collegiates
with the former proving her worth and receiving recognition.
Canova even sang a song entitled: "That Ain't Hay (It's the
U. S. A.)," a direct glorification of the rural American in
deflating the pretentious college boys.

The film was handsomely mounted for a B and included in its cast: Charles Butterworth, a well-known comedy
character actor; Susan Hayward, soon to achieve star status;
Bob Crosby, musical band leader turned actor; and Jerry
Colonna, the famous comedian, in its cast. It was reviewed
extensively for a Republic production and even the careful
New York Times found it acceptable although the reviewer
commented that the vehicle was quite old and ordinary.[24]
In addition to the comedy and pathos, the film included hillbilly, swing, and popular music and even one operatic selec-

tion for Canova. Sis Hopkins was extremely successful having been reissued four times. Its influence was felt throughout the entire series. It also led to Canova demanding and
receiving script, cast, and director approval and co-owner-
ship in her pictures--a development quite unusual at Republic
and shared only by John Wayne at a later date according to
Canova. 25

Canova's third release for Republic, Puddin' Head,
came only three months after Sis Hopkins and bore a resemblance to Scatterbrain. The story line involved the attempt
of a New York radio station to get Canova's farm through a
phony romance, a fake "haunting", and finally a specious radio contract. Of course Canova proved worthy of a proper
contract and achieved success complete with glamorous ap-
parel in the closing numbers. 26 She even proved to be a
better person than her tormentors by giving the conniving radio people the necessary land gratis. This film also had
most of the necessary elements to the Canova formula and
the mold was set. The Canova entries moved steadily if un-
surprisingly along the same proven track. Along with Wayne,
Rogers, and Autry, Canova was by this time part of Republic's established top lineup.

One other entry from Canova's first Republic series
should be mentioned in that it reflected that other major
theme so near and dear to Republic, Herbert Yates, and
their audience. Joan of Ozark (1942) co-starred another
wide and loud mouth comedy star, Joe E. Brown, and centered around Canova accidently shooting a pigeon carrying a
Nazi spy message, thereby becoming a national hero. 27 The
Nazis set out to kill her as an object lesson. She was lured
to a night club which was a Nazi front on the pretense of assisting G-men where she was to be killed. After the obligatory comedy mixups she turned the tables, uncovered the spy
ring, and even ended up destroying a Japanese submarine.
While played for laughs, the patriotic message was there.
One of Canova's songs was even entitled "The Lady at Lock-
heed" and the Republic synopsis of the film succinctly stressed
this emphasis. "The 'Ozark Thrush' became a national heroine by exposing the operations of a Nazi spy ring, her antics
proving a real nemesis to the Axis". 28 It is safe to say
that very few, if any, of the Republic series missed having
at least one patriotic entry in their course.

In 1942 and 1943, Canova turned out four films for
Republic and one on loanout to Paramount. Then for financial

and personal reasons she signed with Columbia where in 1946
she did three pictures. However, at Columbia her budgets
and production values were even less than at Republic where
the budgets for and support of her series had varied because
of personal conflicts within the studio.[29] As a result, Canova was off the screen until 1951 when Republic re-hired
her for six additional pictures through 1955. During the intervening period she kept busy with personal appearances,
troop entertainment, and her radio show which, if anything,
surpassed the success of her movies. It ran from 1943
through 1953 first on CBS and then NBC and she was voted
"Queen of the Air" in 1949.[30]

     Canova's second series at Republic was essentially
similar to her early pictures and is considered a second series only because of her intervening work at Columbia. She
was co-owner and, while the opening entries were in color,
black and white soon returned as budgets again were cut this
time in line with the prevalent policy at Republic in the fifties. Variety commented that Honeychile (1951), the first
entry, "figures as okay top-of-the-bill material for the smaller runs, particularly rural of small-town trade".[31] Apparently, Republic still knew the market as far as audience es-
timation was concerned. Basically, however, the later Canova vehicles were seen as second billing pictures in most
areas.

     The Canova formula and Republic's pacing held true
to the very end of her series. The final entry, Lay That
Rifle Down (1955), had Canova as the hillbilly drudge at her
greedy aunt's hotel. She took a charm course, invented an
imaginary prince charming, and took up with a confidence
man. He and his confederates attempted to take over a farm
upon which Canova had been supporting orphans. But Canova
converted him, captured his accomplices, and discovered that
there was oil on the property. The film blended both of Canova's attractions. It opened with the obvious Cinderella motif and shifted into the honest and charitable country girl out-
witting the slick city crooks for a happy ending.

     Always aware of the value of public exposure through-
out her career, Canova went on the road whenever possible
to retain her rapport with her audience. The New York
Times, in discussing how Republic retained a hold on its audience in competition with larger studios, noted, "Republic
has a[n] ... effective formula for making itself and its stars
known to audiences--the personal appearance tour--Judy Ca-

nova, a headliner in variety houses for years, makes personal appearances between her chores at the studio... To encourage its stars to keep up the good work Republic does not share in the proceeds from their outside engagements".[32] Her appearances were so popular that they sometimes made the papers when she was only passing through.[33] However, Canova was not only interested in the profits; she also understood the value of the publicity her shenanigans elicited. In 1941, she and Gene Autry appeared at the White House and Judy accepted a cigar after the luncheon, President Roosevelt even supposedly asking her if she wanted a light.[34] Apocryphal or not, the story fit Canova's image of the refreshingly direct hillbilly and solidified her appeal while bringing forth the desired publicity.

Canova controlled her image from the beginning and understood the attraction of her movies. A national magazine article at the height of Canova's popularity made much of the fact that she was the top hillbilly star and in demand in the Midwest and Southern markets.[35] Albert S. Rogell, who directed two of the Canova films, one at Republic and one at Columbia, is of the opinion that both aimed at the same audience but that Republic did a better job on this kind of film. He also states that while these films were simplistic they also contained "the teaching of the Church reduced to individual actions but the preachment was minimum and the pictures moved".[36] Barry Shipman, who wrote the last three of the second Canova series at Republic is a bit more pragmatic: "I even did a few of the Canova country-hick things. They weren't anything great. They were fairly set but they were a lot of fun."[37] However, Shipman also feels that much of this routine writing for the Westerns and other B's did have more effect than he or others realized at the time. He stoutly maintains, moreover, that any such audience effect was positive.

Following her successful career at Republic, Canova continued her personal and television appearances, did one other movie (Adventures of Huckleberry Finn, Metro Goldwyn Mayer, 1960), and spent a great deal of time in charitable activities, particularly the March of Dimes. She has been quite aware of the public acceptance of her screen personality from the very beginning, actively communicated with her audience during the height of her career, and even today can shift gears into the bucolic comedienne upon demand.[38]

The B comedy series usually with musical interludes

at Republic therefore did play not only a role in the studio's production schedules but also in the studio's image and the way in which it affected its audience. Whether it was a re-inforcement of family unity, a glorification of rural values, or a paeon to the efficacy of the Cinderella myth, the mes-sages were all related to the effectiveness of American tra-dition. For example, the continuing equation, especially at Republic, between conservative, rural common sense philos-ophy and flag waving patriotism versus the liberal urban at-mosphere of hollow cynicism and decadence often related to subversion or at least irreverence toward country was quite clear not only in the Canova and Weaver family vehicles but also in most of the Western series as discussed in the pre-vious chapter. The general beliefs of the middle American strata as interpreted by the studio were reflected in all B series at Republic because this type of entertainment was what their audience patronized. In the final analysis the B musical and comedy series were in much the same mold as the B Western series. The emphasis and the approach varied to fit the type of film but the overall aura was a restatement and a reinforcement of American values.

As demonstrated, the Republic studio excelled in the areas of serials, series Westerns, and rural comedy musi-cal series. These are the products which are so well re-membered by the fans and it is here that the impact which Republic had will be found. However, while these are the important group films, Republic also produced hundreds of individual B films, some of which were good, a few of which may have been excellent, and many of which were frankly routine. Although these films, along with the occasional A venture, were in most instances not as much a part of the image of Republic as the series, they still made up a signifi-cant part of the studio's output.

The Republic ventures into A production were summa-rized in Chapter I. The studio's main emphasis on a non-series B's fell into three general areas. First, there were many individual comedies. Secondly, the studio released several satisfactory non-series program musicals. Finally, and most important, Republic relied heavily on action, mys-tery, and melodrama in non-series productions. As one au-thority put it, "Action films were made at Republic, but not exclusively--they were trying anything, and everything, to grab the mass audience".[39] And some of these individual efforts proved quite effective.

In the areas of comedy and musical productions, Republic tried for solid family entertainment from the very beginning. In 1936 they released Follow Your Heart with opera star Marion Talley. It was light on comedy and heavy on music. In contrast, that same year they put out Sitting on the Moon starring Roger Pryor, minor leading man of the thirties, and Grace Bradley, a B leading lady, which was aimed at the popular music audience and concerned young lovers threatened by a blackmailing hussy. And in 1937 there was The Hit Parade with singer Frances Langford and big band names based on the famous weekly radio series. While basically a high budgeted B, this film was successful enough to merit followups such as Hit Parade of 1941, 1943, 1947, and 1951. All received fair to good although not sensational reviews in the New York Times save the last which was ignored.[40] This long string of productions might have qualified the "Hit Parade" as a series, but so much time elapsed between each and the plots and characters were for the most part unrelated. In addition, each production was later released under separate and unrelated titles for legal reasons thus destroying any series illusion.

Republic often utilized the services of actors and actresses on the decline in many of their B's. Jane Frazee, who ended up in Roy Rogers pictures, did occasional non-Western musicals for the studio such as Melody and Moonlight (1940), Moonlight Masquerade (1942), and Rosie the Riveter (1944).[41] Ruth Terry, B actress and character performer, also did musicals at the studio in addition to straight acting and starred in such routine musical vehicles as Sing, Dance, Plenty Hot (1940), Rookies on Parade (1941) with bandleader Bob Crosby, Youth on Parade (1942, and Pistol Packin' Mamma (1944). There were two Earl Carroll review musicals (1945 and 1946) and several Ice Capade entries starring the ice skating champion, Vera Hruba Ralston.[42]

Republic also put specialty acts from radio, fairs, and other local entertainment sources into their B musicals to boost box office returns and publicity in their areas of popularity. For example, Hoosier Holiday (1944) starred Dale Evans but included the musical group the Hoosier Hot Shots. The group was prominently emphasized, the advertisements were larger than normal, and the play dates were quite successful when the film was shown in such middle American locales as Indiana.[43] None of these B musicals

were epochal productions and few were more than light entertainment although many had heavy patriotic themes and sequences in keeping with the Yates dictum. Still they were
workmanlike productions and represented a minor emphasis
in the overall Republic schedule. Few of them contained elements of true "Stürm und Drang" and all carried the theme
that decent people doing right will end up happy.

        Even more effective among Republic's non-series film
programs were the various mystery melodramas produced
by the studio to fill its yearly schedules. Because these
films leaned heavily on action and pacing by their very nature, Republic seemed quite at ease in turning them out.
They not only predominated in the non-series area, but they
were usually more successful. For example, The President's
Mystery (1936) was written by the famous Nathanael West
and Lester Cole and based upon a suggestion by Franklin D.
Roosevelt for a series of stories in Liberty magazine. It
involved a man starting a new life but having to face up to
the old when his ex-wife was murdered. He did the right
thing and ended up happily with a new wife and a new life.
In the process of creating his new life, he became involved
with a strike bound factory in New England and the subject
of strikes was of course sensational given the state of the
economy and the union movements in the thirties. Nonetheless, the picture was not really outstanding, rather self-conscious, and the New York Times called it only "interesting."44
In his two years at Republic, West contributed to at least a
dozen films of which nine have been identified. While he
was never really committed to his writings there, he did ab-
sorb much of the background experiences which went into his
well-known pessimistic novel on Hollywood, The Day of the
Locust. 45

        Hearts in Bondage, a Civil War tale from 1936 was
the only directorial effort of actor Lew Ayres. It was not
remarkable but had fine special effects. Famed director
James Cruze, who handled such famous films as The Covered
Wagon (1923) and I Cover the Waterfront (1933), ended his
career at Republic with such journeymen but acceptable B
productions as The Wrong Road (1937), Prison Nurse, Gangs
of New York, and Come On Leathernecks (1938)--three crime
films and a military action piece. Cruze was an example that
the studio frequently used talented and well-known actors or
behind the scenes artists either on the way up or on the way
down the popularity scale.

As was true of all other Republic efforts these melodramas also made heavy use of the patriotic themes as wartime approached. Women in War (1940), starring the well
known British actress, Wendy Barrie, concerned a woman
who killed an officer to defend her honor and then vindicated
herself in nursing service. It was one of the early films
showing the London blackout under Nazi attack and contained
considerable pro-British feeling. Both Photoplay and Time
reacted favorably to its patriotism. [46] Pride of the Navy
(1939) with James Dunn utilized torpedo boats as a backdrop
for standard dramatics with a romantic triangle and was
complete fiction but foreshadowed in emphasis John Ford's
They Were Expendable at MGM six years later. Pride's patriotism was rampant and resembled a paid advertisement
for the Navy.

In the area of pure mysteries, Republic also had a
commendable record. The Leavenworth Case (1936) was
based on a detective story by famed mystery writer Anna
Katherine Green. Who Killed Aunt Maggie? in 1940 blended
both comedy and mystery and was quite well received in the
Republic strongholds according to famed character actor Walter Abel. [47] Republic also produced two Ellery Queen mys-
teries--one, The Spanish Cape Mystery (1935) with Donald
Cook, was acceptable and the second The Mandarin Mystery
(working title, The Chinese Orange Mystery) (1936) with
comic Eddie Quillan, was not, basically because Quillan was
a bug-eyed comedian type. [48] The studio also did three
rather mediocre "Mr. District Attorney" films based on the
popular radio series--Mr. District Attorney (1941), Mr. District Attorney in the Carter Case (1941) and Secrets of the
Underground (1942). [49] The last District Attorney entry was
a murder mystery but involved home front defense, counter-
feit war stamps, and the defeat of a major sabotage ring.
These "mini-series" were interesting experiments but Republic's mystery-melodrama strength really remained in its frequent individual releases.

In the period from late 1940 to early 1942, Republic
hit its stride and produced solid craftsmanlike B's for a
decade. The studio's professionalism showed in its individual products of the period as well as in its series. Most
of the entries were between fifty and sixty minutes in length
and were tailormade for the lower half of the double bill although an occasional film became a hit with the critics or
the public. The themes were, as usual, murder mysteries
or war oriented military melodramas. A typical example,

London Blackout Murders (1942), directed by George Sherman
and written by Curt Siodmak involved the systematic murders
of members of a Nazi spy organization. [50]

     With war, Republic's hundred percentism accelerated
as a major motif in single entry films. The plot to Remember Pearl Harbor was really nothing unusual and was used
on four other occasions at Republic. In many respects the
story line was secondary in that the film was rushed into
release in May, 1942, for its exploitation value--a fact recognized and criticized by the New York Times. [51] But the
blatancy of its message is obvious in its summary from the
studio's files: "The heroic sacrifice of a young American
soldier at the Philippine Army Post and his brilliant strategy
prevent the Japanese from landing reinforcements during
those fatal, first hours of the Pearl Harbor disaster." [52]
As would be expected, it played well in the traditional Republic strongholds. [53] My Buddy (1944), another rather unusual example of Republic's use of patriotism, portrayed a
World War I veteran portrayed by Don "Red" Barry forced
to turn to crime and eventually killed. The plight of returning veterans was the major theme and the prologue tied the
tale in neatly with the parallel situation facing the country
in 1944.

     Patriotism as related to the value of the American
way of life continued to be a major emphasis at Republic
even after World War II. The Red Menace (1949) was basically an exploitation film in which Yates took a special interest. [54] While a propaganda film aimed at a specific problem, the picture had further importance. The summary
from Republic's files illustrated how this film included all
the values that the studio emphasized through the years: "A
young war vet, resentful of the crooked deals he has had
from housing project crook promoters, joins the Communist
movement in the misguided belief that it will bring him re-
dress for his grievances. He soon discovers his mistake,
and, with the girl he loves, finds freedom and human toler-
ance in an American country town." [55] Rugged individualism,
sacrifice, the saving grace of honesty, evil city influence,
freedom in a rural environment, justice, law and order, and
patriotism were all apparent in an obvious but effective little
romantic melodrama.

     Message films are based on topical social issues and
hence are important gauges of popular social thought. [56]
Thus, The Red Menace was not only a good summary of Re-

public's interpretation of middle American values in general,
but was also a barometer of concerns of the United States
during the Cold War period of the late forties and early fifties. But, simply because the film tied in with the mentality of the mass audience of the era did not necessarily mean
that it was an effective film and some found its blatency of-
fensive. Bosley Crowther said in part:

> [I]t looks as though that studio, on the word of its
> president, Herbert Yates, meant it to be a solemn
> warning against 'insidious forces' that imperil our
> country from within. But the ineptitude of the
> plotting and the luridness with which it is played
> render the "menace" unimpressive and the perpe-
> trators oddly absurd. . . .
>   The most effective demonstration of charges
> against the Communists that the film provides is
> the disclosure of how the party allegedly abuses
> and intimidates those members who endeavor to
> break away. And for this, at least, the picture
> has a certain validity. [57]

Despite these reservations, The Red Menace had good playdates in the Midwest and South and adequately mirrored and
contributed to the McCarthy paranoia of the era. It mirrored the McCarthy mentality by the mere fact of being topical. It contributed by emphasizing the "menace" and reinforcing the message for those who were willing to accept it.

     These and many other similar entries from Republic
in the musical, mystery, melodrama, or military vein were
frequently ordinary and quickly forgotten but they were also
adequate and some were surprisingly good. They usually
had the same messages and the same audience appeal of the
Republic series but they lacked long term impact. The series and serials usually made more of an impression over
the long run because they were more identifiable and thus
more memorable. But, just as the series and serials declined in quality especially in the early fifties, so too did the
individual entries. While the subject matter remained the
same, production was rushed, short-cut techniques were
used, stock film was relied upon, and quality plots were less
noticeable. The actors were also an indication of the change.
In the heyday of the B films such well known actors and actresses as Ramon Novarro, Francis Lederer, Ethel Barry-
more, Edward Everett Horton, Richard Arlen, and Eric von
Stroheim made occasional singles for Republic while in the

declining days the stars were Rod Cameron, Robert Rockwell, Scott Brady, Don Megowan and similar performers
who rarely even got a chance at the majors.[58]

There were of course some good B's in the last
years such as Fair Wind to Java (1953) with Fred MacMur-
ray, Vera Ralston, and a good supporting cast. A seafaring
yarn in color and with good special effects, Republic would
have liked it to be A but the principals were miscast and it
became an acceptable B which was not a critical success.[59]
Stranger at My Door (1956) was an unusual little minister
versus outlaw morality play starring a B lead and A support actor MacDonald Carey and Skip Homier, a child actor
turned character actor. Directed by William Witney and
written by Barry Shipman, the story had an outlaw (originally
meant to be Jesse James but changed due to legal complica-
tions) fall in love with a preacher's young wife and help the
family while the preacher tried to convert the outlaw to the
path of God. While there were some fine action sequences,
the stress was on human emotions and conflicts. The spirit-
ual mood prevailed. The film brought forth good reviews in
Variety[60] and The Hollywood Reporter[61] and even unsolicited
letters of praise. One said in part, "This picture must appeal to people of all age groups and all religions. Without
a doubt this picture is worthy of more publicity and mention
[than] it has received so far... Why is it that millions can
be spent for overated [sic] pictures, when here in our own
back yard [the letter came from Glendale, California] someone can make a picture for 'Peanuts', so to speak, and have
the so-called spectaculars beat a thousand ways".[62] This
film was representative of what is meant by a B "sleeper",
a routine offering that became more popular than was pre-
dicted.

But such "sleepers" as well as even nominally good
B movies became less and less frequent as the production
schedule at Republic decreased. Good, bad, or indifferent,
the individual B pictures at Republic went the way of the B
series, but they were all a part of the Republic schedule and
continually presented positive interpretations on life in a variety of formats.

Notes

1. L111 (May, 1939), p. 63.
2. "Republic Productions, Inc. Produced Properties", p. 30.

3. Other examples include The Covered Trailer (1939) emphasizing family cooperation and loyalty, Grandpa Goes to Town (1940) concerning the family's good reputation, and Meet the Missus (1940) with Grandpa even considering a loveless marriage to save the son from disgrace. "Republic Productions, Inc. Produced Properties", pp. 30, 62, 102.
4. Miller, B Movies, P. 108.
5. New York Times, January 27, 1938.
6. New York Times, February 2, 1941.
7. Charles K. Stumpf, "The Weaver Brothers and Elviry", Film Collector's Registry, V (May, 1973), p. 10.
8. Jeepers Creepers (1939) and Arkansas Judge (1940).
9. See p. 133. This was also an obvious theme of Autry's Rovin' Tumbleweed (1939), p. 143 and Rogers' Under Western Stars (1938), p. 150.
10. Atlanta Constitution, February 20, 1942.
11. "Republic Productions Inc. Produced Properties", p. 107
12. Interview by Professor Milton Plesur, State University of New York at Buffalo, and author with Judy Canova, Los Angeles, California, May 15, 1976.
13. For example in Kokomo, Indiana Canova's pictures played one of the two larger theaters out of six available on their initial run normally. See Kokomo Tribune, March 30, 1944.
14. Stith Thompson, The Folktale (New York: Dryden Press, 1951), pp. 126-28. Cinderella (Type 510A) is probably the best known of all folktales and more than five hundred versions have been collected in Europe alone.
15. Interview with Judy Canova, Los Angeles, California, May 15, 1976.
16. Interview with Judy Canova, Los Angeles, California, May 15, 1976.
17. December 14, 1934.
18. Variety, May 4, 1939. The Canova's were not singled out as a special group however. The network was simply using whatever acts were available in these early broadcasts, and the family happened to be in New York City thus becoming the first television hillbillys by accident.
19. Interview with Judy Canova, Los Angeles, California, May 15, 1976.
20. "Republic Productions, Inc. Produced Properties", p. 147.
21. Elwood [Indiana] Call-Leader, October 1, 1946 and October 3, 1946. Reissue booking.
22. Variety, August 4, 1040.
23. Although she was ridiculed by the family and unhappy in

her surroundings, he stood by her and enrolled her in his snobbish daughter's college. Because of her talent, Canova was given a major role in the college musical and the daughter's role was cut proportionately. The daughter, in an attempt at sabotage, involved the innocent hillbilly in a burlesque show but her expulsion from college was cancelled when the uncle came to her aid. Canova was the hit of the college show and even wore fancy clothing in the finale.

24. May 1, 1941.
25. Interview with Judy Canova, Los Angeles, California, May 15, 1976.
26. Elwood [Indiana] Call-Leader, January 20, 1949. Reissue booking.
27. Elwood [Indiana] Call-Leader, October 20, 1942.
28. "Republic Productions, Inc. Produced Properties", p. 83.
29. Interview with Judy Canova, Los Angeles, California, May 15, 1976. Yates took a personal interest in Canova and when she did not reciprocate, she indicated that he had her budgets cut. Actually, the budgets on five of her first seven pictures increased slightly but the personal conflicts were apparently real. Had she not been so popular, he would have taken other steps she feels.
30. Richard Gertner, ed., International Television Almanac (New York: Quigley Publishing, 1976), p. 37.
31. Undated clipping in the Judy Canova clipping file of the Margaret Herrick Library at the Academy of Motion Picture Arts and Sciences, Los Angeles, California.
32. February 2, 1941.
33. Atlanta Constitution, January 19, 1942 noted "Atlanta Gets Brief Look at J. Canova" when she made a half hour stopover there. Atlanta, though a large city, reflected Southern interest and gave Republic stars good coverage.
34. James Robert Parish, The Slapstick Queens (New York: Castle Books, 1973), p. 214.
35. Kyle Crichton, "Hillbilly Judy", Colliers, CIX (May 16, 1942), p. 17.
36. Interview with Albert S. Rogell, Los Angeles, California, May 5, 1976.
37. Interview with Barry Shipman, San Bernardino, California, May 11, 1976.
38. Interview with Judy Canova, Los Angeles, May 15, 1976.
39. Miller, B Movies, p. 106.
40. May 31, 1937; August 18, 1940; April 16, 1943; May 5, 1947. The ads from the 1943 entry with John Carroll

and Susan Hayward offered, "Gay Tunes! Sparkling
Comedy! blended into the season's brightest hit!",
Kokomo [Indiana] Tribune, June 11, 1943.
41. The last named film was a lighthearted but patriotic
musical based on a real event of the war. The plot
had to do with housing shortages, war production,
and romantic entanglements. Rosina B. (Bonavita)
Hickey, the real Rosie the Riveter, has commented,
"It was such a different world then. Jennie [her part-
ner] and I were the same as all the people we knew.
We worked hard because that's how we were brought
up and because we believed in what our country was
fighting for. We were very patriotic. Everyone was."
[Richard Lamparski, Lamparski's Whatever Became
Of ...? (New York: Bantam, 1976), p. 271.] The
Elwood [Indiana] Call-Leader gave the patriotic theme
a big emphasis, August 22, 1944.
42. The first entry, Ice Capades, listed her a Vera Hruba,
her Czech name, in a supporting role. Atlanta Constitution, Thursday, January 1, 1942. However, she
soon attained star status both in ice skating movies
and other vehicles at Republic. See Chapt. I, pp. 20-22.
43. Elwood [Indiana] Call-Leader, Tuesday, May 9, 1944;
Wednesday, May 10, 1944; and Thursday, May 11,
1944.
44. October 4, 1936.
45. Tom Dardis, Some Time in the Sun (New York: Charles
Scribner's Sons, 1976), p. 154.
46. Photoplay, LIV (July, 1940), p. 61, and Time XXXV
(June 17, 1940), p. 86.
47. Interview with Walter Abel by Professor Milton Plesur,
New York City, March 1, 1976.
48. Miller, B Movies, p. 113.
49. "Republic Productions, Inc. Produced Properties", pp. 105,
149.
50. Commonweal, XXXVII (January 22, 1943), p. 351.
51. June 4, 1942.
52. "Republic Productions, Inc. Produced Properties", p. 134.
53. Elwood [Indiana] Call-Leader, November 20, 1942.
54. A publicity brochure was released with this B picture
which shows Republic's and Yates' patriotic motivation. Although lacking subtlety, Yates' statement
shows much about the man, his studio, and the times.

The picture, "The Red Menace," was produced
by Republic Productions, Inc., as our effort to
assist in the fight against Communism and any other

"Ism", whose purpose is to destroy our form of
government by force and violence, bloodshed and
terror.

It must be evident to every sincere American
citizen that our country and our American way of
life are being imperiled by insidious forces from
within and from without. Not long ago, one great
American stated: "The Communists Have Been,
Still Are and Always Will Be a Menace to Freedom,
to Democratic Ideals, to the Worship of God, and
to America's Way of Life."

Within the past two weeks, another great American has declared:

"The Communist Party and the Communist World
Movement Have a Fixed Objective. That Objective
Is World Domination Through Revolution. It Is a
Long Range Objective, That Objective Will Never
Change, Because If It Did, Communism Would Die."

It is to combat this evil that was produced.
Even though the picture was made behind closed
doors, and there has been no public showing to
date, Republic Studios and the Writer Have Already
Been Attacked by the Daily People's World, a
Communist Paper Published in San Francisco, and
the Daily Worker, A Communist Paper Published
in New York.

The attack is more than an open threat. It is
an effort to intimidate Republic Pictures and to
stifle its right of freedom of speech. We accept
the challenge of The Communist Party and its Fellow Travelers, and we declare that the Republic
organization will do everything in its power, regardless of expense or tribulations, to make certain that "The Red Menace" Is Shown in Every City,
Town and Village in The United States of America
and Other Countries Not Under Communist Control.

Herbert J. Yates
President
Republic Productions, Inc.

55. "Republic Productions, Inc. Produced Properties", p. 133.
56. White and Averson, The Celluloid Weapon, book jacket re-
     phrased, p. 260. The Red Menace is given as an ex-
     ample of the anti-Communist film of the period on
     pp. 123-24.
57. New York Times, June 27, 1949.
58. These were good actors but lacked the popularity or

versatility of earlier Republic stars. For example
Rod Cameron remained a B Western lead and television star (State Trooper) for most of his career;
Robert Rockwell is best remembered as a supporting
actor in Our Miss Brooks on television. Brady fared
better but was reduced to playing character supporting
roles on Police Story and in television movies in the
Sixties and Seventies. Don Megowan was a stuntman
who played in inexpensive science fiction films such
as The Werewolf (1956) and occasional guest roles on
The Lucy Show on television.

59. New York Times, August 28, 1953.

60. Variety, April 14, 1956, "Republic has an exceptionally
     well-done family trade offering ... strong inspirational
     values ... raise it considerably above ... the average
     program entry."

61. The Hollywood Reporter, April 14, 1956, "... a theme
     that lifts it well out of the ordinary class and into a
     niche where it deserves to be considered with very
     special interest."

62. Letter to the author from Barry Shipman, February 1,
     1976. Shipman sent the original studio issued circu-
     lar on this film. The trade reviews, testimonials,
     and fan letter were included. Witney also recalls
     this film as his favorite because it dealt with "rela-
     tionships." Francis M. Nevins, Jr., "William Wit-
     ney", Films in Review, p. 538.

Chapter VII

THE REPUBLIC LEGACY: SUMMARY AND CONCLUSIONS

In the present study the importance of the B film and
the philosophy of Republic Pictures as demonstrated in the
output of such movies has been examined. As the largest
and most efficient of the independent studios Republic probably had a major influence on a segment of the great American audience and while it did not contribute dramatically to
the film industry in a major way, the studio did at the same
time make a subtle but significant contribution through the
years.

Leo Rosten, perceptive observer of the Hollywood
scene, recognized the basic contribution of the movie colony
in its heyday. "Our values are extended to the strident and
the unmistakable in Hollywood's way of life. It is for this
reason that a study of Hollywood can cast the profile of American society into sharper relief."[1]* Thus, in other words,
its values reflect those of the wider culture. But in addition to reflection, the movies also serve as a reinforcement
factor. Rosten pointed out that the very success of Hollywood lies both in the skill with which it reflects the assump-
tions, the fallacies, and the aspirations of an entire culture
and also that through movies, it reinforces "our typologies ...
with overpowering repetitiveness."[2]

Herein lies the importance and significance of Republic and its product. It mirrored and, in doing so, reinforced
the values of a large segment of the American people in
terms and stories which they could understand, appreciate,
and enjoy for entertainment's sake. Thus it can be said that
while Republic perhaps did not have a major role in reflecting or influencing American culture as a whole, it did reinforce certain values for a particular audience and was particularly well received in the "Bible Belt". The Republic
product at its best served as a cultural document—certainly
not in terms of reflecting the West, the War, the policework,

*Notes to Chapter VII begin on page 198.

or rural life as it was--but rather in mirroring the artificial
excitement, the slick action, and the escapist fantasies that
its audience, especially the young and unsophisticated, wanted
from their entertainment in the thirties and forties. Simultaneously and because of their success with this type of product, Republic reinforced the ethical and moral standards of
the times and reinforced the value system which the audience
needed and which supported them during those two decades
of instability.

Undoubtedly, Republic's understanding of the power of
the B film was most evident in its excellent serials and the
genre leading Autry, Rogers, and Canova movies. After
1939, John Wayne provided some strength for the studio's
ventures into A's but not with the consistency of their thrust
into the B area since Wayne, while under exclusive contract,
was loaned out regularly at very profitable rates.

Photoplay, which in the thirties and forties was the
most astute fan magazine, recognized the Republic contribution when it discussed the potency of Gene Autry in 1938 as
the studio was solidifying its program:

> ... Gene and his quiet staggering success is both
> a lesson and a promise. The lesson is never
> again to forget the down-to-earth people upon whom
> the movies have always depended. The promise is
> the unlimited rewards to come from pictures pre-
> pared to please them... A Gene Autry can sell
> many stars far more famous than himself in more
> territories than you ever imagined. He can swell
> the returns from their pictures and build their
> names, too, in that now very respectable orphans'
> home of the movies--the once lowly sticks. [3]

Given this Republic impact upon the B audience, what
were the specific values that the studio's films so successfully promulgated? Obviously, Republic religiously followed
the dictates of the Motion Picture Production Code. [4] Good
always won out and there was no confusing good and evil in
a Republic production. The studio couched it in action and
comedy but the message was always prominent. But, as has
been consistently shown, Republic went well beyond the simple guidelines of good over evil. A combination of President
Yates' convictions, the desires and needs of the audience,
and the accepted beliefs of the era all meshed to provide
other messages, usually outright but sometimes slightly less
immediately obvious.

These messages permeated the entire spectrum of Republic productions from serials to A films. A final comparative example will illustrate that the message was observable throughout the firm's entire output although perhaps more obvious in the B segment. Whatever message any film had was most concentrated in the thirty-second to two-minute trailer created to attract the audience and to give that audience a massive dose of whatever the film had to offer in a short period. With this factor in mind, compare select passages from the "coming attractions" of two representative Republic films of the same year. One is an example of Republic's specialty; the other is from a Republic prestige production. The first is from the last meritorious serial in terms of new ideas and production values released in 1949 before the final decline of that genre--King of the Rocket Men. That same year the studio also released one of its more successful and well-known A productions, a John Wayne vehicle entitled Sands of Iwo Jima.

The trailer for King of the Rocket Men was very loud, very brassy, and designed to take away the breath of the audience. It opened with four different shots of the film's best special effects showing the hero flying through the air while the titles emblazoned across the screen: "He's Coming Your Way... The Jet-Propelled Phantom of the Sky! Fearless Enemy of Spies and Saboteurs! King of the Rocket Men." The scene changed to a fight sequence between three heavies, two heroes, and the heroine while a deep-voiced narrator intoned, "When a gang of foreign agents plot to kill the leading scientists of the world ... Jeff King, thunderbolt of the air ... wrecks their plans by his heroic action ..." during which the visual returned to the flying hero in exciting shots of him flying close to the ground. [5]   And this was merely the first seven shots of the short trailer. The emphasis was blasted out with an unsubtle blatancy which was nonetheless effective in reaching its audience. The action continued on for a total of twenty-three separate shots but the opening seven with accompanying titles and narration give the serial's drift sufficiently--an action-packed paeon to self reliance, rugged individualism, patriotism, and the fight for law and order.

In comparison, the Sands of Iwo Jima trailer, while naturally striving to hold the attention, was much more subdued and aimed at adult viewers but the themes were surprisingly similar. It opened with a shot of a marine camp and the hero and his squad marching out to an offscreen chorus singing the Marine Hymn while the titles rolled up

the screen proclaiming: "Republic Studios Proudly Dedicates
One of the Truly Great Motion Pictures Ever to Reach the
Screen ... To the Fighting'est Most Lovable Bunch of Guys
in the World...." A few scenes later, John Wayne as Stryker was seen standing in the center of his squad saying, "I'm
gonna ride ya tell ya can't stand up, but when ya do stand
up, you're gonna be Marines!" Over scenes of Marine train-
ing, the narrator came in, "These are your boys ... whom
John Wayne, as Sergeant Stryker, forged into fighting men...."
The trailer concluded with scenes of Marine combat, inter-
spersed with Wayne in an action shot, the sound of punctu-
ated gunfire, and the Titles stating: "An Inspiring Human
Story Makes the Mightiest of Motion Pictures! ... Starring
John Wayne ... His Greatest Performance! ... His Biggest
Picture! ... 'Sands of Iwo Jima' ... A Republic Production."
The final visual showed Marines and tanks at the foot of Suri-
bachi with the Marine flag superimposed over the whole
scene. 6

    This trailer was a bit less brassy and fast paced and,
in keeping with its "class," was more complex. But the
similarity in values is evident. Even with the example recounting only about half the content, this excerpt showed that
the Republic A's included the same ideals--patriotism, self
reliance, rugged individualism, defense of the American way
of life. Of course, as would be expected, in the A productions there were also other values in addition to the basics
and all were presented with more maturity and therefore perhaps more subtlety than in a B. For example, in Sands,
war is presented not only for patriotic effects and action sequences but also with much more realism and with more consideration of its effects on human emotions than would be
usual in a formula B. And the hero was a flawed man with
personal problems. 7

    Sophistication, maturity, and expense aside, the Re-
public A's were not that different from Republic B's in terms
of basic message. Indicatively, the audience for the Republic B's could usually appreciate the Republic A. While the
basic themes remained the same, each B genre developed
different approaches and emphases.

    The serials first and foremost brought out the virtues
of self reliance and rugged individualism as the hero/heroine
battled against overwhelming odds to overcome the usually
much more imaginative and always more aggressive forces
of evil. The tribulations also frequently underwrote the value

of leadership and initiative.   The whole point could be summarized as integrity.   Secondly, the serials drew deeply
upon the virtue of patriotism and self sacrifice for one's com-
panions and country.   Finally, the chapter plays relied upon
the themes of justice and law and order.

The Western series emphasized much the same messages as the serials but in a different priority and with a
few additions.   The main theme in Republic Westerns seemed
to be justice and law and order coupled with rugged individu-
alism--but individualism tempered with cooperation when appropriate.   There was also a strong undercurrent of the importance of defending the underdog--rarely emphasized in the
serials.   Of course, the Westerns also utilized patriotic materials whenever possible, perhaps not as much as serials
but worthy of comment nonetheless.   Lastly, the glorification
of rural values was clear in the studio's Western output.

The series comedies shared some of the preceding
themes, but given the different mood, the approach was usually altered.   The comedies tended to stress domestic and
social values rather than the aggressive life and death strug-
gles prevalent in the other two genres.   The primary message of the comedy tended to be integrity but integrity through
family unity.   Rural values were a strong second priority.
Also, honesty seemed to be singled out more than in Westerns
and serials.   Much has been made of the Cinderella theme
and, in some respects this is another description for the defense of the underdog and the belief in the strength of the
common man.   Finally, the comedies did not escape the inclusion of patriotic plots and themes although they were presented in a lesser degree than in serials and Westerns.

There were of course other messages in the Republic
product and even occasional lapses and contradictions in
those listed above, but these were the primary themes.   These
values, packaged to reach the Republic audience, also fit the
needs of the times--the insecurity and dehumanization of the
Great Depression, the normal and even commendable chauvinism of the Second World War, and the paranoia of the
McCarthy era--altered slightly to fit each period.   It was
good versus evil with a heavy dose of patriotism and, when
all of the themes and examples are summarized, it came
down to the fact that the message of Republic, and Hollywood,
was a politicized version of the Protestant Ethic, a major
force in American history.

Secondarily, the studio offered a contribution to the industry as a training ground for professionals which functioned as a "baptism of fire". Republic may not have been a power within the Hollywood hierarchy, but it did provide certain significant services to the other studios under the contributions of journeymanship, craftmanship, and technical excellence. It was indirect, unplanned, and perhaps even unsuspected at the time but was quite identifiable in retrospect. This fact has been acknowledged by many movie people on both sides of the camera.

Character actor I. Stanford Jolley, who appeared in over five hundred films, many of which were for Republic, summed up the value of Republic in teaching efficiency within the industry:

> ... serials and the budget westerns were such
> wonderful training grounds for actors and directors
> alike. You had to learn fast to stay in the busi-
> ness; you had to learn well. To help you better
> understand what I am saying, allow me to illus-
> trate. The high professionalism and teamwork at
> a small studio like Republic, with limited finances,
> could result in up to 100 scenes a day. While over
> at, say, MGM, if they got 10 scenes a day it was
> a small miracle![8]

In other words, Republic's schedule resulted in professional productions and technical excellence under pressure. But the studio taught more than just speed. Republic's rapid schedule, low budgets, and areas of specialization taught its actors and technical crews basic fundamentals valuable throughout the industry. John Wayne, whose recognition of Republic's value to his career has been cited previously, also admitted the value of the B's as a training ground. He felt that the essential ability to handle dialogue was the most valuable lesson he received from his B career. "The quickie westerns taught me how to speak lines ... straight lines.... The biggest difference between a B western and an A western is in how they tell the story. The B picture has to do it with stretches of talk, straight exposition. Every once in a while they stop the action and the hero or somebody explains the background or why somebody came to town."[9]

On the other side of the camera, director Joseph Kane, who received his start at Republic and became the "house director", observed that he and others learned the value of

the ability to make decisions at Republic. "Action takes
quite a lot of time... You have to know exactly what you're
going to do... So you don't waste any time. As soon as you
say, 'Cut! Print!' you move to the next setup right away.
You don't hesitate. And you don't change your mind. As
soon as you set something up, the whole damn crew leaps at
it and starts getting it ready... They're working hard and
you don't want to fool around... And keep going, keep moving."[10] Kane credited his action-oriented years at Republic
with making possible his later transition to television, which
also thrives on pressure and speed.

Another B director who frequently worked at Republic
stressed that the studio taught teamwork. After recounting
how he worked with the actors and technicians to make an
action sequence in a Red Ryder vehicle (Sheriff of Las Vegas,
Republic, 1944) more interesting and out of the ordinary,
Lesley Selander pointed out, "Now this might not seem like
anything on a little Western. But it showed the care, interest, and, family-like attitude we all had then. We were a
team, even on a budget Western it made no difference."[11]

In the area of writing, Barry Shipman, who wrote
Westerns and other B's at Republic, saw the Western format
as a creative form of writing and valuable to his career.
"The Western writer, that is, one who makes a career of
writing outdoor action films, is a breed all his own... To
me it offers the challenge that faces any writer of fiction and
actually has more fulfillment for my creative instinct than any
other form of film. Besides, it allows me more freedom."[12]
Shipman still feels that his years with Republic where he
started writing serials and progressed through all B genres,
were valuable professionally.[13] Although it seems a contradiction, the formula writing on B pictures did provide creative freedom within the format and it taught discipline.

In a realm of movie technology--that of special effects--
the Lydecker brothers at Republic were considered to be the
best. Ted Lydecker was very enthusiastic about his Republic
career:

> My business was the most fantastic there was.
> Everything was new everyday. You were your own
> little world of explosions and miniature cars and
> planes. People don't understand or realize what
> we did, Howard and I. It was kind of like Walt
> Disney when he first started. Everything he did

> was your own way. I wish we could do that kind
> of stuff today. It was wonderful and nerve-wrack-
> ing! We worked on a weekly schedule for the se-
> rials. The miniatures and climaxes were all done
> at the last minute. We never got a complete script
> in advance. We would make up a budget but there
> were always changes. On features, the effects
> were always done after the picture was completed. [14]

In certain respects, the special effects people controlled the
end product and the scheduling. Ted Lydecker elaborated on
another occasion that although they worked well with the other
Republic personnel, the brothers and their assistants knew
that acceptable special effects took time especially when the
budget was limited. Therefore, since the effects were done
last, the special effects people exerted a great deal of influence on the final product. [15] Regardless of their status, the
effects of Republic were highly rated and the Lydeckers delivered on time when it was a crucial factor.

Even in the field of music, Republic made a contribution by training young musicians. Music was important at
Republic and added a gloss and excitement lacking in other
inexpensive productions. The studio made it a practice to
score serials, Westerns, and other B films heavily. This
meant that the music was frequently mass produced or drawn
from stock. Stanley Wilson, who became Executive Musical
Director at Universal and who was a well-known cinema composer, said of his Republic period, "We were a very good
highly overworked underpaid group of dedicated people... It
was the best training anyone ever had." [16]

Finally, in the field of stuntwork Republic utilized the
best craftsmen and afforded them the opportunity to develop
techniques. Not only did these men gain experience at Republic and train others in their field, but the major studios
benefited also from their expertise. David Sharpe, one of
the best who worked on innumerable Republic pictures, pointed out that his crew of stuntmen and second unit directors
moved freely between the independents and the majors since
Warners, MGM, Twentieth, etc. could not afford to keep action units on the payroll constantly. This meant the action
sequences in most of the major studio productions were clear
and obvious reflections of the state of the art in B films, the
primary environment for action sequences. [17] The film credits
of many quality movies from the most prestigious studios reflects the inter-relationship between major and minor studios
through the good offices of the action units. [18]

In the year 1943, Republic produced fifty-five films
compared with MGM's twenty-seven and Warner Brothers'
nineteen. With such a production schedule and its demonstrated technical excellence, it is no surprise that Republic
offered its personnel a complete course in pragmatic film
making. As further proof, it can be pointed out that when
the market for the B film declined in the early fifties, many
of the Republic personnel moved directly over to the fast
paced, rapid delivery field of weekly television series.[19]
Republic trained people remained in demand. In fact, Don
Barry called Republic "a university for television production".[20]

Finally, Republic personnel not only had staying power,
but many became leaders in their field of specialization. In
addition to the actors who have been mentioned frequently in
earlier chapters, representative Republic workers who received recognition for their contributions included executive
Michael Frankovich, who became a well-known production
company head, and Robert Beche, who went on to the popular and long-lasting television series, Gunsmoke. Director
William Witney, the famous serial director, is still making
action films for both theaters and television. Republic stal-
wart Allan Dwan was highly acclaimed by contemporary Peter
Bogdanovich, and Edward Ludwig is yet another rediscovered
director, having been discussed in Take One[21] and other
scholarly film magazines. Academy Award winning stunt co-
ordinator Yakima Canutt was still active until the early seventies and another excellent stuntman David Sharpe was until
recently very active in television. Cameramen Bud Thackery
and Jack Marta still do superior camerawork in television
and are recognizable by their distinctive styles. Broadway
musical composer Cy Feuer and multi-talented musician Victor Young both are Republic alumni as was television composer Stanley Wilson.

Thus, many Republic personnel are still active or remained so until retirement at the few studios which maintained a full schedule. Universal and Buena Vista for example utilized Republic trained people. As Ted Lydecker said,
"My brother and I trained most of the special effects people
who are now over at Universal".[22] These sentiments are
echoed by a number of ex-Republic staff.

Republic and its product have undergone a rediscovery
and appreciation over the last decade and there appears to
be a continuing interest in its B output. Much of it is ad-

mittedly nostalgic but this does not remove the phenomenon
from serious consideration. In a 1976 survey of serial favorites, thirty to forty years after they were released, eight
out of the top ten and seventeen out of the top twenty were
released by Republic.[23] Periodicals such as Film Collector's Registry, Serial World, and Yesterday's Saturdays
are devoted to Westerns and serials and invariably rank Republic highly. Serious publications such as Films in Review
and Take One devote space to the B revival. The Republic
products are favorites at film conventions and are in continual television release, either in their original formats or in
re-edited versions such as Roy Rogers Presents the Great
Movie Cowboys. Republic stars, supporting players and
even behind-the-scenes personnel are also in demand at film
conventions.

Peggy Stewart, Republic serial and B Western heroine,
summed up the various reasons for Republic's appeal:

> It's kind of hard to say, the majority of people at
> the conventions that I've talked to, they love the
> memory. It's memorable, happy memories, good
> memories even if you didn't have a childhood that
> you particularly liked. You find people saying how
> they enjoyed that portion of their childhood.
> A lot of folks too have talked about the fact that
> there are no places to send their kids on Saturdays,
> no matinees so they have shown their Westerns to
> satisfy their kids. To give them shows, good
> shows, the Westerns and serials, show them right
> from wrong, the goodies and the baddies, the white
> hats and the black hats on Saturdays and it enter-
> tains them for a week.
> I also think the interest is because of morality.
> The Westerns and serials, particularly the Westerns
> had morality in them. People like this and they
> liked to be left on an affirmative note, not a nega-
> tive note.[24]

Stewart covered the ground well--memories, straightforward
entertainment, morality, affirmation. Republic filled a need
and filled it well. It is true that other producers of B films
also contributed both to the audience and to the industry to
some degree. But Republic by all criteria made the most of
the B niche. Would American society have been different
without it? Perhaps not, but it might have been poorer.
The existence of Republic and its role in the lives of at least
two generations of moviegoers cannot be ignored.

Notes

1. Hollywood: The Movie Colony, The Movie Makers (New York: Harcourt Brace and Company, 1941), p. 5.
2. Rosten, p. 360.
3. Kirkley Baskette, "Pay Boy of the Western World", Photoplay, L11 (January, 1938), p. 327.
4. Olga J. Martin, Hollywood's Movie Commandments: A Handbook for Motion Picture Writers and Reviewers (New York: H. W. Wilson Company, 1937; reprint ed., Arno Press, 1977), p. 99.
5. "King of the Rocket Men" Trailer Cutting Continuity in Republic Studio Shooting and Continuity Scripts, Collection 979 in the Special Collections Library, University of California at Los Angeles.
6. "Sands of Iwo Jima" Cross Plug Trailer Cutting Continuity in Republic Studio Shooting and Continuity Scripts, Collection #979 in the Special Collections Library, University of California at Los Angeles.
7. For elaboration on the cinematic value of Sands, see Eyles, John Wayne and the Movies, pp. 119-20.
8. Jim Schoenberger, "An Interview with I. Stanford Jolley", Film Collector's Registry, VI (March, 1974), p. 4.
9. Zolotow, Shooting Star: A Biography of John Wayne, p. 113.
10. Quoted in McCarthy and Flynn, Kings of the Bs, p. 322.
11. Jon Tuska, ed. Close Up: The Contract Director (Metuchen, New Jersey: Scarecrow Press, 1976), p. 247.
12. Hollywood Citizen-News, July 21, 1952.
13. Interview with Barry Shipman, San Bernardino, California, May 11, 1976.
14. Dan Daynard, "The Lydeckers, Masters of Miniature Mayhem", The New Captain George's Whizzbang, III (n.d.), p. 7.
15. Interview with Theodore Lydecker, Los Angeles, California, May 17, 1976.
16. Dan Daynard, "The Film Music of Stanley Wilson", The New Captain George's Whizzbang, IV (n.d.), p. 15.
17. Interview by Mark Hall, California State University at Chico, with David Sharpe, August, 1976, sponsored by the American Film Institute.
18. Undated letter from Mark Hall, August, 1976.
19. Robert Sklar, Movie Made America, p. 282.
20. Interview with Donald Barry, Los Angeles, California, May 6, 1976.

21. Alan Collins, "Edward Ludwig: The Quiet Revolutionary", Take One, IV (May-June, 1972), pp. 27-28; John H. Dorr, "Allan Dwan", Take One, IV (May-June, 1972), pp. 8-9; and Peter Bogdanovich, Allan Dwan: The Last Pioneer (New York: Praeger, 1971).

22. Interview with Theodore Lydecker, Los Angeles, California, May 17, 1976.

23. "Spy Smasher Tops Serial Poll", Film Collector's Registry, No. 61 (February, 1976), p. 4.

24. "An Interview with Peggy Stewart", Western Corral, No. 1, p. 18.

Appendix A

REPUBLIC SERIALS

Darkest Africa (1936)
Undersea Kingdom (1936)
The Vigilantes Are Coming (1936)
Robinson Crusoe of Clipper Island (1936)
Dick Tracy (1937)
The Painted Stallion (1937)
SOS Coast Guard (1937)
Zorro Rides Again (1937)
The Lone Ranger (1938)
Fighting Devil Dogs (1938)
Dick Tracy Returns (1938)
Hawk of the Wilderness (1938)
The Lone Ranger Rides Again (1939)
Daredevils of the Red Circle (1939)
Dick Tracy's G-Men (1939)
Zorro's Fighting Legion (1939)
Drums of Fu Manchu (1940)
Adventures of Red Ryder (1940)
King of the Royal Mounted (1940)
Mysterious Doctor Satan (1940)
Adventures of Captain Marvel (1941)
Jungle Girl (1941)
King of the Texas Rangers (1941)
Dick Tracy Vs. Crime Inc. (1941)
Spy Smasher (1942)

Perils of Nyoka (1942)
King of the Mounties (1942)
G-Men Vs. The Black Dragon (1943)
Daredevils of the West (1943)
Secret Service in Darkest Africa (1943)
The Masked Marvel (1943)
Captain America (1944)
The Tiger Woman (1944)
Haunted Harbor (1944)
Zorro's Black Whip (1944)
Manhunt of Mystery Island (1945)
Federal Operator 99 (1945)
The Purple Monster Strikes (1945)
The Phantom Rider (1946)
King of the Forest Rangers (1946)
Daughter of Don Q (1946)
The Crimson Ghost (1946)
Son of Zorro (1947)
Jesse James Rides Again (1947)
The Black Widow (1947)
G-Men Never Forget (1948)

Dangers of the Canadian
  Mounted (1948)
Adventures of Frank and
  Jesse James (1948)
Federal Agents Vs. Under-
  world, Inc. (1949)
Ghost of Zorro (1949)
King of the Rocket Men (1949)
The James Brothers of Mis-
  souri (1950)
Radar Patrol Vs. Spy King
  (1950)
The Invisible Monster (1950)
Desperadoes of the West (1950)
Flying Discman from Mars
  (1951)
Don Daredevil Rides Again
  (1951)

Government Agents Vs.
  Phantom Legion (1951)
Radar Men from the
  Moon (1952)
Zombies of the Strato-
  sphere (1952)
Jungle Drums of Africa
  (1953)
Canadian Mounties Vs.
  Atomic Invaders (1953)
Trader Tom of the China
  Seas (1954)
Man with the Steel Whip
  (1954)
Panther Girl of the
  Kongo (1955)
King of the Carnival
  (1955)

Appendix B

REPUBLIC'S THREE MESQUITEER SERIES

The Three Mesquiteers
(1936)
Ghost Town Gold (1936)
Roarin' Lead (1936)
Riders of the Whistling
Skull (1937)
Hit the Saddle (1937)
Gunsmoke Ranch (1937)
Come On Cowboys (1937)
Range Defenders (1937)
Heart of the Rockies (1937)
Trigger Trio (1937)
Wild Horse Rodeo (1937)
Purple Vigilantes (1938)
Call the Mesquiteers (1938)
Outlaws of Sonora (1938)
Riders of the Black Hills
(1938)
Heroes of the Hills (1938)
Pals of the Saddle (1938)
Overland Stage Raiders (1938)
Santa Fe Stampede (1938)
Red River Range (1938)
Night Riders (1939)
Three Texas Steers (1939)
Wyoming Outlaw (1939)
New Frontier (1939)
Kansas Terrors (1939)
Cowboys from Texas (1939)
Heroes of the Saddle (1940)
Pioneers of the West (1940)
Covered Wagon Days (1940)

Rocky Mountain Rangers
(1940)
Oklahoma Renegades (1940)
Under Texas Skies (1940)
Trail Blazers (1940)
Lone Star Raiders
(1940)
Prairie Pioneers (1941)
Pals of the Pecos (1941)
Saddlemates (1941)
Gangs of Senora (1941)
Outlaws of the Cherokee
Trail (1941)
Gauchos of El Dorado
(1941)
West of Cimarron (1941)
Code of the Outlaw (1942)
Raiders of the Range
(1942)
Westward Ho! (1942)
Phantom Plainsmen
(1942)
Shadows on the Sage
(1942)
Valley of Hunted Men
(1942)
Thundering Trails
(1943)
Blocked Trail (1943)
Santa Fe Scouts (1943)
Riders of the Rio Grande
(1943)

Appendix C

GENE AUTRY'S REPUBLIC APPEARANCES

Tumbling Tumbleweeds
(1935)
Melody Trail (1935)
The Sagebrush Troubadour
(1935)
The Singing Vagabond (1935)
Red River Valley (1936)
Comin' Round the Mountain
(1936)
The Singing Cowboy (1936)
Guns and Guitars (1936)
Oh Susannah! (1936)
Ride, Ranger, Ride (1936)
The Big Show (1936)
The Old Corral (1936)
Round-Up Time in Texas
(1937)
Git Along Little Doggies
(1937)
Rootin' Tootin' Rhythm
(1937)
Yodelin' Kid from Pine
Ridge (1937)
Public Cowboy No. 1 (1937)
Boots and Saddles (1937)
Manhattan Merry-Go-Round
(1937) [guest appearance]
Springtime in the Rockies
(1937)
The Old Barn Dance (1938)
Gold Mine in the Sky (1938)
Man from Music Mountain
(1938)
Prairie Moon (1938)
Rhythm of the Saddle (1938)
Western Jamboree (1938)
Home on the Prairie (Ridin'
the Range) (1939)

Mexicali Rose (1939)
Blue Montana Skies
(1939)
Mountain Rhythm (1939)
Colorado Sunset (1939)
In Old Monterey (1939)
Rovin' Tumbleweeds
(1939)
South of the Border
(1939)
Rancho Grande (1940)
Gaucho Serenade (1940)
Carolina Moon (1940)
Ride, Tenderfoot, Ride
(1940)
Melody Ranch (1940)
Ridin' on a Rainbow
(1941)
Back in the Saddle (1941)
The Singing Hills (1941)
Sunset in Wyoming
(1941)
Under Fiesta Stars
(1941)
Down Mexico Way (1941)
Sierra Sue (1941)
Cowboy Serenade (1942)
Heart of the Rio Grande
(1942)
Home in Wyoming
(1942)
Stardust on the Sage
(1942)
Call of the Canyon
(1942)
Bells of Capistrano
(1942)
Sioux City Sue (1946)

Trail to San Antone (1947)   Saddle Pals (1947)
Twilight on the Rio Grande   Robin Hood of Texas
  (1947)   (1947)

ROY ROGERS' REPUBLIC APPEARANCES

Tumbling Tumbleweeds
(1935)--Autry
The Big Show (1936)--Autry
The Old Corral (1936)--Autry
Wild Horse Rodeo (1937)--
Three Mesquiteers
The Old Barn Dance (1938)-
Autry
Under Western Stars (Washington Cowboy) (1938)
[first starring role]
Billy the Kid Returns
(1938)
Come On, Rangers (1938)
Shine On, Harvest Moon
(1938)
Rough Riders' Round-up
(1939)
Frontier Pony Express
(1939)
Southward Ho! (1939)
In Old Caliente (1939)
Wall Street Cowboy (1939)
The Arizona Kid (1939)
Jeepers Creepers (1939) -
Weaver Brothers and
Elviry
Saga of Death Valley (1939)
Days of Jesse James (1939)
Young Buffalo Bill (1940)
Dark Command (1940)
[first A film appearance]
Carson City Kid (1940)
The Ranger and the Lady
(1940)
Colorado (1940)

Young Bill Hickok (1940)
The Border Legion
(1940)
Robin Hood of the Pecos
(1941)
Arkansas Judge (1941)--
Weaver Brothers and
Elviry
In Old Cheyenne (1941)
Sheriff of Tombstone
(1941)
Nevada City (1941)
Bad Men of Deadwood
(1941)
Jesse James at Bay
(1941)
Red River Valley (1941)
The Man from Cheyenne
(1942)
South of Santa Fe (1942)
Sunset on the Desert
(1942)
Romance on the Range
(1942)
Sons of the Pioneers
(1942)
Sunset Serenade (1942)
Heart of the Golden
West (1942)
Ridin' Down the Canyon
(1942)
Idaho (1943)
King of the Cowboys
(1943)
Song of Texas (1943)
Silver Spurs (1943)
The Man from Music

Mountain (1943)
Hands Across the Border (1944)
The Cowboy and the Senor-
ita (1944)
Yellow Rose of Texas (1944)
Song of Nevada (1944)
San Fernando Valley (1944)
Lights of Old Santa Fe
(1944)
Brazil (1944) [guest appear-
ance]
Lake Placid Serenade (1944)
[guest appearance]
Utah (1944)
Bells of Rosarita (1945)
The Man from Oklahoma
(1945)
Sunset in El Dorado (1945)
Don't Fence Me In (1945)
Along the Navajo Trail
(1945)
Song of Arizona (1946)
Rainbow Over Texas (1946)
My Pal Trigger (1946)
Under Nevada Skies (1946)
Roll On, Texas Moon (1946)
Home in Oklahoma (1946)
Out California Way (1946)
[guest appearance]
Helldorado (1946)
Apache Rose (1947)
Hit Parade of 1947 (1947)
[guest appearance]
Bells of San Angelo (1947)
Springtime in the Sierras

(1947)
On the Old Spanish Trail
(1947)
The Gay Ranchero (1948)
Under California Stars
(1948)
Eyes of Texas (1948)
Night Time in Nevada
(1948)
Grand Canyon Trail (1948)
Far Frontier (1948)
Susanna Pass (1949)
Down Dakota Way (1949)
The Golden Stallion
(1949)
Bells of Coronado
(1950)
Twilight in the Sierras
(1950)
Trigger, Jr. (1950)
Sunset in the West
(1950)
North of the Great Di-
vide (1950)
Trail of Robin Hood
(1950)
Spoilers of the Plains
(1951)
Heart of the Rockies
(1951)
In Old Amarillo (1951)
South of Caliente
(1951)
Pals of the Golden
West (1951)

Appendix E

OTHER REPUBLIC SERIES DISCUSSED

The Higgins Family Series
  The Higgins Family (1938)
  My Wife's Relatives (1939)
  Should Husbands Work? (1939)
  The Covered Trailer (1939)
  Money to Burn (1939)
  Grandpa Goes to Town (1940)
  Earl of Puddlestone (1940)
  Meet the Missus (1940)
  Petticoat Politics (1941)

Weaver Brothers and Elviry Series
  Down in "Arkansaw" (1938)
  Jeepers Creepers (1939)
  In Old Missouri (1940)
  Grand Ole Opry (1940)
  Friendly Neighbors (1940)
  Arkansas Judge (1941)
  Mountain Moonlight (1941)
  Tuxedo Junction (1941)
  Shepherd of the Ozarks (1942
  The Old Homestead (1942)
  Mountain Rhythm (1943)

Judy Canova Series
  Scatterbrain (1940)
  Sis Hopkins (1941)
  Puddin' Head (1941)
  Sleepytime Gal (1942)
  Joan of Ozark (1942)
  Chatterbox (1943)
  Sleepy Lagoon (1943)
  Honeychile (1951)
  Oklahoma Annie (1952)
  The Wac from Walla Walla (1952)
  Untamed Heiress (1954)
  Caroline Cannonball (1955)
  Lay That Rifle Down (1955)

BIBLIOGRAPHY

MANUSCRIPTS AND ORIGINAL REPUBLIC
PICTURES, INC. MATERIAL

Collections

Academy of Motion Picture Arts and Sciences. Los Angeles.
Vertical File. Republic Studios and related headings.

"Republic Pictures Studio: The Fastest Growing Organization in Film Industry." The Hollywood Reporter, 1938.

American Film Institute. Los Angeles. Vertical File. Republic Studios and related headings.

National Telefilm Associates. Los Angeles, Republic collection.
"History of Republic Pictures." n.d. Manuscript. 4 pp.
Ten Years of Progress: Republic Pictures Corporation
10th Anniversary. Los Angeles: Republic Pictures Corporation, [1945].

New York Public Library. Theatrical Section. Vertical File.
Republic 1935-36 Attractions Now Available! Los An-
geles: Republic Pictures, 1935.
Republic Pictures Pressbook. 1935. (Microfilm reel
ZAN-T8, reel 33).

University of California at Los Angeles Special Collections
Library. Collection 979. Republic Continuity
Scripts and Shooting Scripts.
Dick Tracy's G-Men. Continuity Script. No. 896. Au-
gust, 1939.
The Fighting Devil Dogs. Continuity Script. No. 1740.
April, 1938.
"King of the Rocket Men" Trailer Cutting Continuity.
"Sands of Iwo Jima" Cross Plug Trailer Cutting Continu-
ity.

Stranger at My Door. Shooting Script.

University of California at Los Angeles Theater Arts Library. "Producer-Interest Stories; SWG Credits; Story Purchases; Pictures Cleared." Hollywood: Republic Pictures Corporation, 1957 [?]. "Republic Productions, Inc. Produced Properties". Story Department. January 1, 1951. "Summaries on: Unproduced Autrys, Produced Rogers [etc.]: Themes on: Unproduced Westerns; Produced Properties." Hollywood: Republic Pictures Corporation, 1953 [?].

University of Wyoming Library. Collection 5189. Duncan Renaldo Collection. The Lone Ranger Rides Again. Shooting Script. No. 1009. January, 1939. Secret Service in Darkest Africa. Shooting Script. No. 1295. June, 1943.

OTHER REPUBLIC PICTURES, INC. MATERIAL WITH LOCATIONS

Pressbooks. Published by studio for theater use.

Heart of the Golden West. Hollywood: Republic Pictures, 1942. Jack Mathis. Northbrook, Illinois.
Heroes of the Saddle. Hollywood: Republic Pictures, 1940. Jack Mathis. Northbrook, Illinois.
Spoilers of the Plains. Hollywood: Republic Pictures, 1951. Jack Mathis. Northbrook, Illinois.

Still Manuals. Published by studio for theater use.

Bells of Rosarita. Hollywood: Republic Pictures, 1945. Jack Mathis.
Canadian Mounties Vs. Atomic Invaders. Hollywood: Republic Pictures, 1953. Jack Mathis.
Captain America. Hollywood: Republic Pictures, 1944. Jack Mathis.
The Crimson Ghost. Hollywood: Republic Pictures, 1946. Jack Mathis.
Dangers of the Canadian Mounted. Hollywood: Republic Pictures, 1948. Jack Mathis.
Drums of Fu Manchu. Hollywood: Republic Pictures, 1940. Jack Mathis.

G-Men Never Forget. Hollywood: Republic Pictures, 1948.
     Jack Mathis.
G-Men Vs. The Black Dragon. Hollywood: Republic Pic-
     tures, 1943. Jack Mathis.
Government Agents Vs. Phantom Legion. Hollywood: Repub-
     lic Pictures, 1951. Jack Mathis.
The James Brothers of Missouri. Hollywood: Republic Pic-
     tures, 1950. Jack Mathis.
Jesse James Rides Again. Hollywood: Republic Pictures,
     1947. Jack Mathis.
In Old Monterey. Hollywood: Republic Pictures, 1939.
     Jack Mathis.
King of the Cowboys. Hollywood: Republic Pictures, 1943.
     Jack Mathis.
King of the Mounties. Hollywood: Republic Pictures, 1942.
     Jack Mathis.
King of the Rocket Men. Hollywood: Republic Pictures,
     1949. Jack Mathis.
Manhunt of Mystery Island. Hollywood: Republic Pictures.
     1945. Jack Mathis.
The Masked Marvel. Hollywood: Republic Pictures, 1943.
     Jack Mathis.
My Pal Trigger. Hollywood: Republic Pictures, 1946. Jack
     Mathis.
The Purple Monster Strikes. Hollywood: Republic Pictures,
     1945. Jack Mathis.
Rovin' Tumbleweeds. Hollywood: Republic Pictures, 1939.
     Jack Mathis.
Secret Service in Darkest Africa. Hollywood: Republic Pic-
     tures, 1943. Jack Mathis.
South of the Border. Hollywood: Republic Pictures, 1939.
     Jack Mathis.
Springtime in the Sierras. Hollywood: Republic Pictures,
     1947. Jack Mathis.
Spy Smasher. Hollywood: Republic Pictures, 1942. Jack
     Mathis.
Zombies of the Stratosphere. Hollywood: Republic Pictures,
     1952. Jack Mathis.

Miscellaneous Republic Pictures, Inc. Material.

Republic Pictures: 16 MM Program. Hollywood: Republic
     Pictures, [1950]. Author's collection.
Republic Reporter, The. Company journal. I (April 11,
     1939): 11 to I (January 9, 1940): 37. Alan
     Barbour. Kew Gardens, New York.
Wood, Thomas. "Corn in the Can". Manuscript. 1941.

In the Serials clipping file at the Margaret Herrick
Library of the Academy of Motion Picture Arts
and Sciences. Los Angeles.
Yates, Herbert J. The Red Menace. Promotional brochure.
Hollywood: Republic Pictures, 1949. Author's
collection.
Yates, Herbert J. Republic Pictures Corporation Annual Re-
port. January 31, 1951. Hollywood: Republic
Pictures, 1951. Author's collection.

FILMS VIEWS
(Listed chronologically within subject)

Serials

Undersea Kingdom (1936).
SOS Coast Guard (1937).
Fighting Devil Dogs (1938).
Daredevils of the Red Circle (1939).
Dick Tracy's G-Men (1939).
Zorro's Fighting Legion (1939).
Mysterious Doctor Satan (1940).
Adventures of Captain Marvel (1941).
Spy Smasher (1942).
Perils of Nyoka (1942).
G-Men Vs. the Black Dragon (1943).
The Masked Marvel (1943).
Captain America (1944).
The Tiger Woman (1944).
Manhunt of Mystery Island (1945).
The Purple Monster Strikes (1945).
Daughter of Don Q (1946).
The Black Widow (1947).
King of the Rocket Men (1949).
Flying Disc Man from Mars (1951).
Zombies of the Stratosphere (1952).
Canadian Mounties Vs. Atomic Invaders (1953).
Panther Girl of the Kongo (1955).

'B' Series Films

Hit the Saddle--Three Mesquiteers (1937).
New Frontier--Three Mesquiteers (1939).
Tumbling Tumbleweeds--Gene Autry (1935).
The Big Show--Gene Autry (1936).
In Old Monterey--Gene Autry (1939).

Sioux City Sue--Gene Autry (1946).
Under Western Stars--Roy Rogers (1938)
Bells of Rosarita--Roy Rogers (1945).
Don't Fence Me In--Roy Rogers (1945).
My Pal Trigger--Roy Rogers (1946).
Home in Oklahoma--Roy Rogers (1946).
Scatterbrain--Judy Canova (1940).
Roy Rogers Presents the Great Movie Cowboys. Syn-
    dicated television series of B Western movies
    shown on WNED-TV. Buffalo, New York. Fall
    1976--Spring 1977. National Telefilm Associates.

'A' Films

Man of Conquest (1939).
Dark Command (1940).
Wake of the Red Witch (1948).
Macbeth (1948).
Sands of Iwo Jima (1949).
The Quiet Man (1952).
Johnny Guitar (1954).

SOUNDTRACK TAPES
(Listed chronologically)

Adventures of Captain Marvel. (1941). Tape of soundtrack
    in author's collection.

Spy Smasher. (1942). Tape of soundtrack in author's col-
    lection.

G-Men Vs. the Black Dragon. (1943). Tape of soundtrack
    in author's collection.

D Day on Mars (feature version of The Purple Monster
    Strikes). (1945). Tape of soundtrack in author's
    collection.

Lost Planet Airmen (feature version of King of the Rocket
    Men). (1949). Tape of soundtrack in author's
    collection.

Missile Monsters (feature version of Flying Disc Man from
    Mars). (1951). Tape of soundtrack in author's
    collection.

INTERVIEWS

Abel, Walter. Actor. New York. Interview by Milton Plesur, Professor of History, State University of New York at Buffalo and author. March 1, 1976.

Abrams, Morris R. Republic script supervisor and assistant director. Los Angeles. May 17, 1976.

Alyn, Kirk. Republic actor. Los Angeles. May 11, 1976.

Barry, Donald "Red". Republic actor. Los Angeles. May 6, 1976.

Bennet, Spencer G. Republic director. Los Angeles. May 10, 1976.

Bennett, Bruce. Republic actor. Los Angeles. Telephone interview. May 7, 1976.

Bernds, Edward. Columbia director. Los Angeles. May 6, 1976.

Canova, Judy. Republic actress. Los Angeles. Interview by Milton Plesur, Professor of History, State University of New York at Buffalo and author. May 15, 1976.

Chapman, Marguerite. Republic actress. Los Angeles. Interview by Milton Plesur, Professor of History, State University of New York at Buffalo and author. May 15, 1976.

Glut, Donald F. Movie historian and television writer. Los Angeles. May 10, 1976.

Hagner, John. Stuntman director of Stuntman's Hall of Fame. Los Angeles. Telephone interview. May 10, 1976.

Hall, Mark. Instructor, Chico State College. Los Angeles. May 15, 1976.

Harmon, Jim. Writer. Los Angeles. May 10, 1976.

Hills, Rowland "Dick". Republic business office manager. Los Angeles. May 13, 1976.

Kirkpatrick, Ernest. National Telefilm Associates, Techni-
    cal Services and Republic's Hollywood Television
    Service Division. Los Angeles. May 12, 1976.

Lamparski, Richard. Writer. Los Angeles. Telephone in-
    terview. May 6, 1976.

Livingston, Robert. Republic actor. Los Angeles. Tele-
    phone interview. May 8, 1976.

Lydecker, Theodore. Republic special effects expert. Los
    Angeles. May 17, 1976.

Nibley, Sloan. Republic writer. Los Angeles. May 4, 1976.

Ralston, Vera Hruba (Mrs. Charles Alva). Republic ac-
    tress. Santa Barbara, California. Telephone in-
    terview. May 10, 1976.

Rogell, Albert S. Republic director. Los Angeles. May 5,
    1976.

Rush, Art. Roy Rogers' manager. Los Angeles. Tele-
    phone interview. May 6, 1976.

Sharpe, David. Republic stuntman. Los Angeles. Inter-
    view by Mark Hall for the American Film Insti-
    tute. August, 1976.

Shipman, Barry. Republic writer. San Bernardino, Cali-
    fornia. May 11, 1976.

Siegel, Sol C. Republic producer. Los Angeles. Telephone
    interview. May 5, 1976.

Slide, Anthony. Film scholar. American Film Institute.
    Buffalo, New York. January 18, 1975.

Stewart, Peggy. Republic actress. Los Angeles. May 18,
    1976.

Stirling, Linda. Republic actress. Los Angeles. May 13,
    1976.

Waggoner, Rex. National Telefilm Associates, Publicity
    Director. Los Angeles. May 12, 1976.

White, William. Associate Professor, Chico State College.
    Chico, Calif. May 15, 1976.

NEWSPAPER ARTICLES

"Allege 18 Vera Ralston Films Flopped: Movie Head Sued
    Over Actress-Wife", New York Herald Tribune,
    October 30, 1956.

"Asks Receiver for Republic Film Studio", New York Post,
    August 20, 1958.

"Atlanta Gets Brief Look at J. Canova", Atlanta (Georgia)
    Constitution, January 19, 1942.

Buckley, Tom, " 'The Day of the Locust': Hollywood, by
    West, by Hollywood", New York Times Magazine,
    June 2, 1974, pp. 10-13.

"C. B. S. Buys Studio", New York Times, February 24, 1967.

"C. B. S. Gets 10-Year Lease on Coast Republic Studio",
    New York Times, May 4, 1963.

"Carr, Johnston Leaving Outfit", Variety, December 18, 1936.

Darst, Stephen, "Old Film Serial Director Decries Sex and
    Violence in Movies of Today", St. Louis Review,
    n.d. [1975].

"Exhibs Seize on Serials to Woo Tots Away from Telesets",
    Variety, November 9, 1950.

"Exit (As Expected) of Republic from MPEA First in O'Seas
    Body's History", Variety, December 11, 1957.

"Fading, Fading--One-Man Rule; Yates' Republic Exit Latest
    Instance", Variety, July 8, 1959.

"Figure Skating Bug Hits Republic Head", New York Morning
    Telegraph, June 14, 1941.

"Film Group Changes Its Corporate Name", New York Times,
    April 13, 1935.

"Film Guilds Warn Republic Studios", New York Times, Janu-
    ary 22, 1958.

"Film Partners in Quick Rise", New York World-Telegraph, April 27, 1935.

"Fred Brannon" (Obituary), Variety, April 15, 1953.

"Gene Autry of Westerns Goes Over Big with Fans", New York World-Telegraph, May 14, 1938.

"Gene Autry's Advice to Youth in Wartime". Unidentified Sunday supplement article, circa 1942. In the Theatrical Section of the New York Public Library.

Greenbaum, Lucy, "Sinatra in a Sombrero", New York Times Magazine, November 4, 1945, p. 42.

Haber, Joyce, "Roy's Not Ready to Ride into the Sunset", Los Angeles Times, Calendar, April 21, 1974.

Hanna, David, "The Little Acorn Has Grown", New York Times, February 2, 1941.

Haugland, Vern, "Don Barry Is Western Star No. 5 After Short, Swift Rise in Films". Unidentified newspaper, November 8, 1942. In the Donald Barry clipping file at the Theatrical Section of the New York Public Library.

"Hedda Hopper's Hollywood", Los Angeles Times, May 31, 1942.

"Herbert Yates" (Obituary), Variety, February 9, 1966.

"Herbert Yates, Founder of Republic Pictures" (Obituary), New York Herald Tribune, February 5, 1966.

"Herbert Yates of Republic Films, Developer of Cowboy Stars, Dies" (Obituary), New York Times, February 5, 1966.

Hirshey, Gerri, "Roy Rogers Rides Again", The New York Sunday News, Leisure, December 28, 1975.

"Home, Home on the Ranch", Atlanta (Georgia) Constitution, This Week, June 14, 1942, p. 14.

"I-deas: Spy Smasher Triumphs Again", Edwardsville, (Illinois) Intelligencer, November 29, 1973.

"In the Big Time", New York Times, September 7, 1941.

"Investors Sue Yates", New York Times, October 30, 1956.

" 'King of the Serials' to do 100th Film", New York Herald
    Tribune, October 31, 1952.

Levitas, Louise, "A Stranger in Pitchman's Gulch: Roy
    Rogers, the Cowboy Star, Gets Not a Tumble,
    Despite Full Regalia", PM, May 20, 1941.

"Little Dogies Git Along", New York Times, August 4, 1940.

Martinez, Al, "Roy Rogers and Gene Autry: Two Old-Time
    Cowboy Stars Reflect a Heroic Age", Los Angeles
    Times, February 27, 1977, sec. CC, Part II,
    pp. 3, 5-6.

"Myers, Rembusch Blast Rep on Plan for Selling to TV",
    Variety, June 13, 1951.

"New Suit Seeks Liquidation of Republic Pic", Variety, Au-
    gust 27, 1958.

"New Supplier of 'Kid Matinee' Pics", Variety, July 12, 1974.

"News of the Screen", New York Sun, July 8, 1936.

Parsons, Louella O., "In Hollywood--Vera Ralston", New
    York Journal American, February 8, 1943.

Pelswick, Rose, "Republic Steps Up with Texas Epic", New
    York Journal American, April 23, 1939.

"Plastics the Charmer in Bettered Earnings Picture for Re-
    public", Variety, October 12, 1960.

Redelings, Lowell E., "The Hollywood Scene: Men Behind
    the Scenes", Hollywood Citizen-News, July 21,
    1952.

"Rep's Old Pix in 'New' Dress", Variety, February 10, 1954.

"Rep's Sale to TV Cues Interest in Wall Street", Variety,
    June 13, 1951.

"Republic Aims Its Films at Heart of America", Variety,
    Ninth Anniversary Edition, October 29, 1942.

"Republic Doubles Budget for '52-53", New York Times,
    July 23, 1952.

"Republic Enters Field of Feature Pictures", New York World
    Telegraph, July 13, 1938.

"Republic Film Plans", New York Times, October 3, 1953.

"Republic Is Adding Four Sound Stages", New York Times,
    June 16, 1953.

"Republic Okays Old Films for Tele; Editing, Rescoring to
    Fit TV Needs", Variety, June 13, 1951.

"Republic Pictures Plans 50 Features in Season", New York
    Herald Tribune, April 6, 1939.

"Republic Pictures to Spend $2,500,000", New York Times,
    February 18, 1942.

"Republic Pictures Upheld in Autry, Rogers Suits", Wall
    Street Journal, June 9, 1954.

"Republic Plans Major Scale Return to TV Productions;
    Seeks Key Men", Variety, August 9, 1959.

"Republic Raises Production List", New York Times, Feb-
    ruary 3, 1955.

"Republic Sets Biggest Slate", New York Morning Telegraph,
    March 4, 1941.

"Republic Sets Budget for Features, Westerns, Serials", New
    York Sun, February 28, 1941.

"Republic Starts Cutback in Staff", New York Times, May 23,
    1956.

"Republic Stepping High", Variety, Tenth Anniversary Edition
    October 29, 1943, p. 455.

"Republic Studio to Resume Work", New York Times, Janu-
    ary 8, 1957.

"Republic Studios Continue to Grow", New York Times, Au-
    gust 17, 1954.

"Republic Studios Expanding Plant", New York Times, June 14, 1957.

"Republic to Make 22 'De Luxe' Films", New York Times, January 14, 1954

"Republic to Offer Independents Aid", New York Times, September 11, 1953.

"Republic to Rent Top Films to TV", New York Times, January 13, 1956.

"Republic Will Turn Out Escape Films, Says Yates", New York World-Telegraph, September 9, 1939.

"Republic's Bright New Outlook; Carter Quips About Old Nepotism", Variety, November 30, 1960.

"Republic's Chief, H. J. Yates Discusses Independent Pix", New York Post, May 2, 1939.

Roberts, William, "Cliffhangers", Los Angeles Times, November 20, 1946.

"Serials: Continued This Week", Los Angeles Times, January 20, 1965.

Shlyen, Ben, "For Present and Future", Box Office, January 15, 1968.

"62 Feature Films Listed by Republic", New York Times, May 30, 1940.

"Stockholder Sues to Close Republic Films", New York Daily News, August 20, 1958.

"Strongly Reported, Flatly Denied: Richard Altschuler Denies Republic Closedown of Domestic Branches", Variety, February 12, 1958.

"Studio Enjoins Gene Autry: Says 'Horse Opera' Star Ran Away to Go on the Stage", New York Herald Tribune, February 4, 1938.

"Suit Calls Film Tycoon's Wife 9-1 Floperoo", New York Daily News, October 30, 1956.

"Theatrical Cliffhanger Serials of Yesteryear Still Sell 'Far
        Out' ", Variety, February 12, 1964.

Thirer, Irene, "It's Vera Ralston Now--Republic's Queen
        Takes 'Rib' ", New York Post, June 4, 1946.

"30 Writers Working at Repub, New High", Variety, Au-
        gust 16, 1939.

Thomas, Bob, "Roy Rogers Finds Happy Trails Far from
        the Movie Industry", Los Angeles Times, Janu-
        ary 6, 1975.

"200G Rep Deal Releasing 104 Pix for TV Seen Breaking Log
        Jam", Variety, December 17, 1952.

"Two Old Cowboys Still Ride High", Buffalo Courier-Express,
        March 1, 1977.

"TV-Movie Tie-Ins Remain Confused", New York Times,
        May 15, 1952.

"Vera Ralston Finds Court's for Courting", New York World
        Telegram and Sun, June 15, 1962.

Whalen, David B., "Republic Pictures", The Film Daily Cav-
        alcade, 1939, pp. 176-182. In the Republic Pic-
        tures clipping file at the Margaret Herrick Li-
        brary of the Academy of Motion Picture Arts and
        Sciences. Los Angeles.

Wood, Thomas, "The Sad State of the Serial", New York
        Times, December 22, 1946.

"Writers Strike Versus Republic on TV Residuals", Variety,
        February 19, 1958.

Yates, Herbert J., "Top-Cost Pix Shed", Variety, January 7,
        1953.

"Yates Wants Better B's from Republic," Variety, Febru-
        ary 22, 1939.

NEWSPAPER USE OF REPUBLIC ADVERTISEMENTS
FOR SPECIFIC FILMS.

Elwood (Indiana) Call-Leader, October 15, 1942; October 20,

1942; November 20, 1942; December 16, 1943;
February 4, 1944;   April 21, 1944; May 9, 10,
11, 1944; July 27, 1944; August 22, 1944; November 9, 1944; August 23, 1945; February 14, 1946;
October 1, 1946; October 3, 1946; November 21,
1946; December 13, 1946; February 14, 1947;
January 20, 1949.

Kokomo (Indiana) Tribune, June 10, 1943; June 11, 1943;
December 16, 1943; March 30, 31, 1944; May 4,
1944; June 22, 23, 24, 1944; June 12, 1947; October 9, 1947; November 13, 1947; February 12,
1948; June 9, 1949; January 5, 1951; January 19,
1952.

REVIEWS OF MOVIES

Apache Rose. New York Times, July 23, 1947.

Arkansas Judge. Atlanta (Georgia) Constitution, February 20,
1942.

Boots and Saddles. New York Times, November 8, 1937.

Call the Mesquiteers. New York Times, March 12, 1938.

Calling All Stars (Broadway theatrical play). New York
Times, December 14, 1934.

Chatterbox. New York Times, July 2, 1943.

Crowther, Bosley. My Pal Trigger. New York Times, August 17, 1946.

Crowther, Bosley. The Red Menace. New York Times,
June 27, 1949.

Crowther, Bosley. Sis Hopkins. New York Times, May 1,
1941.

Crowther, Bosley. Swing Your Lady. New York Times,
January 27, 1938.

Fair Wind to Java. New York Times, August 28, 1953.

Hartung, Philip T. London Blackout Murders. Commonweal.
XXXVIII (January 22, 1943): 351.

Heart of the Golden West. Box Office, November 16, 1942.

Heart of the Golden West. Variety, November 16, 1942.

Hi Ho Silver. New York Post, July 25, 1940.

Hit Parade. New York Times, May 31, 1937.

Hit Parade of 1941. New York Times, August 18, 1940.

Hit Parade of 1943. New York Times, April 16, 1943.

Hit Parade of 1947. New York Times, May 5, 1947.

Hit the Saddle. Variety, August 4, 1957.

Honeychile. Variety, 1951. Undated clipping in the Judy
     Canova clipping file at the Margaret Herrick Li-
     brary of the Academy of Motion Picture Arts and
     Sciences. Los Angeles.

Ice Capades. Atlanta (Georgia) Constitution, January 1, 1942.

In Old Monterey. Variety, August 4, 1939.

King of the Cowboys. Box Office, April 5, 1943.

London Blackout Murders. Commonweal. XXXVIII (Janu-
     ary 22, 1943): 351.

Manhattan Merry-Go-Round. New York Times, December 31,
     1937.

Melody Ranch. New York Times, December 26, 1940.

Mishkin, Leo, Rookies on Parade. New York Morning Tele-
     graph, May 22, 1941.

Mortimer, Lee, Remember Pearl Harbor. New York Daily
     Mirror, June 4, 1942.

My Wife's Relatives. Photoplay. LII (May, 1939): 63.

The President's Mystery. New York Times, October 4,
     1936.

Rags to Riches. New York News, November 8, 1941.

Remember Pearl Harbor. New York Times, June 4, 1942.

Rovin' Tumbleweeds. Motion Picture Herald, November 25,
    1939.

Santa Fe Stampede. New York Times, April 26, 1939.

Scatterbrain. Variety, August 4, 1940.

Sioux City Sue. New York Times, July 23, 1947.

South of the Border. Motion Picture Herald, December 16,
    1939.

Stranger at My Door. Hollywood Reporter, April 14, 1956.

Stranger at My Door. Variety, April 14, 1956.

Three Texas Steers. Variety, July 2, 1939.

Under Western Stars. New York Times, June 25, 1938.

Utah. New York Times, March 12, 1945.

Winsten, Archer, Rocky Mountain Rangers. New York Post,
    June 27, 1940.

Winsten, Archer, The Sombrero Kid. New York Post, Sep-
    tember 30, 1942.

Women in War. Photoplay, LIV (July, 1940): 61.

Women in War. Time, XXXV (June 17, 1940): 86.

JOURNAL AND PERIODICAL ARTICLES

Adams, Leo, Ed. Yesterday's Saturdays. No. 1 (1972) to
    No. 6 (1975).

Barbour, Alan G., ed. Screen Ads Monthly. I (October,
    1967): 1 to I (January, 1968): 4.

Barbour, Alan G. Screen Nostalgia Illustrated. No. 1 to
    No. 8 (1975).

Barbour, Alan G. Serial Pictorial. No. 1 to No. 8 (n.d.).

Barbour, Alan G., ed. Serial Quarterly. No. 1 (January-March, 1966) to No. 7 (July-September, 1967).

Baskette, Kirkley. "Pay Boy of the Western World". Photoplay. LII (January, 1938): 327-328.

Beaumont, Charles. "Don't Miss the Next Thrilling Chapter!" Show Business Illustrated. I (March, 1962): pp. 52-56, 78-80.

Black, Gregory and Koppes, Clayton R. "OWI Goes to the Movies: The Bureau of Intelligence's Criticism of Hollywood, 1942-43". Prologue: The Journal of the National Archives. VI (Spring, 1974): 44-59.

Blair, Earl W., Jr. "Meanwhile ... at Republic". Film Collector's Registry. No. 70. (November, 1976): 12-13.

Blair, Earl W., Jr. "Reminiscing with Henry Brandon". Those Enduring Matinee Idols. II (December, 1972-January, 1973): 291-292.

Blair, Earl W., Jr. "Republic Today!" Film Collector's Registry. No. 68 (September, 1976): 11.

Blair, Earl W., Jr. "Rocketman Flies Again". Film Collector's Registry. No. 69 (October, 1976): 11-13.

"A Chill in Hollywood". Newsweek. XLVIII (November 12, 1956): 116.

Cocchi, John. "The Films of Allan Lane". Screen Facts. No. 19. IV (1968): 50-58.

Cocchi, John. "The Films of Roy Rogers and Gene Autry". Screen Facts. No. 5. I (1963): 47-61.

Cohen, Joan. "The Second Feature: The Rise and Fall of the B Movie". Mankind. V (June, 1976): 26-35.

Collins, Alan. "Edward Ludwig: The Quiet Revolutionary". Take One. IV (May-June, 1972): 27-28.

Connor, Edward. "The First Eight Serials of Republic". Screen Facts. No. 7. II (1964): 52-61.

Connor, Edward. "The Golden Age of Republic Serials".
Screen Facts. No. 17. III (1968): 48-61.

Connor, Edward. "The Golden Age of Republic Serials
(Part 2)". Screen Facts. No. 18. III (1968):
20-35.

Connor, Edward. "The Three Mesquiteers". Screen Facts.
I (1964): 52-61.

"Continued Next Week". Screen Thrills Illustrated. I (June,
1962): 16-29.

Coons, Minard. "An Interview with Peggy Stewart". Film
Collector's Registry. No. 57 (November, 1975):
5-9.

Coons, Minard, and Easterling, Allan. "The Jolley Villain:
An Interview with I. Stanford Jolley". Film Collector's Registry. No. 67 (September, (1976); 3-6.

Crichton, Kyle. "Hillbilly Judy". Colliers. CIX (May 16,
1942): 17, 62-63.

Davy, Daryl. "Davy on 16 MM: William Elliott". Film
Fan Monthly. No. 94 (April, 1969): 17.

Danard [sic], Donald. "Bennet's Serials". Films in Review.
XIV (October, 1963). 8: 509.

Daynard, Don. "The Film Music of Stanley Wilson". The
New Captain George's Whizzbang. No. 17 (n.d.):
15.

Daynard, Don. "The Lydeckers: Masters of Miniature
Mayhem". The New Captain George's Whizzbang.
No. 16 (n.d.): 2-8.

Daynard, Don. "Master of Miniature Mayhem: Chapter Two".
The New Captain George's Whizzbang. No. 17
(n.d.): 28-29.

Daynard, Don. "The Perils of Linda". The New Captain
George's Whizzbang. No. 18 (n.d.): 8-14.

Daynard, Don. "Roy Barcroft--Best of the Badmen". The
New Captain George's Whizzbang. No. 7 (n.d.): 2-5.

Daynard, Don. "Shooting Down Some B-Western Myths".
     The New Captain George's Whizzbang. No. 18
     (n. d.): 32.

Dorr, John H. "Allan Dwan". Take One. IV (May-June,
     (1972): 8-9.

"Double Mint Ranch". Time Magazine. XXXV (January 15,
     1940): 47-48.

Dyer, Peter John. "Those First Rate Second Features".
     Films and Filming. II (September, 1956): 17-18.

Eisenberg, Michael T. "A Relationship of Constrained Anx-
     iety: Historians and Film". History Teacher.
     VI (1973) 553-568.

Elkin, Frederick. "The Psychological Appeal of the Holly-
     wood Western". The Journal of Educational So-
     ciology. XXIV (October, 1950): 72-86.

Emery, F. E. "Psychological Effects of the Western Film:
     A Study in Television Viewing". Human Relations.
     XII (1959): 195-231.

Everson, William K. Review of B Movies, by Don Miller.
     Films in Review. XXV (November, 1974): 564-
     565.

Everson, William K. "Serials with Sound". Films in Re-
     view. IV (June-July, 1953): 270-276.

Everson, William K. "Stunt Men". Films in Review. VI
     (October, 1955): 394-402.

"Fallen Republic". Time Magazine. LXXXIX (April 14,
     (1958): 56.

Farber, Manny. "Movie in Wartime". New Republic. CX
     (January 3, 1944): 18-20.

Fernett, Gene. "An Interview with Theodore Lydecker".
     Film Collector's Registry. V (November, 1973):
     1, 6.

Fernett, Gene. "Jack English Looks Back". Classic Film
     Collector. No. 21 (Summer, 1968): 52, 55.

Fernett, Gene. "Nat Levine: The Serial King". Views and
    Reviews. I (Summer, 1969): 22-31.

Fernett, Gene. "Spencer Gordon Bennett [sic] Biography
    Off the Press". Classic Film Collector. No. 36
    (Fall, 1972): 63.

Folsom, James K. "Western Themes and Western Films".
    Western American Literature. II (1967): 195-203.

Friedman, Norman L. "Studying Film Impact on American
    Conduct and Culture". Journal of Popular Film.
    III (Spring, 1974): 173-181.

Geltzer, George. "40 Years of Cliffhanging". Films in Re-
    view. VII (February, 1957): 60-68.

"Gene Autry's Cowboy Dictionary". TV Guide. I (October 2,
    1953): 8-9.

Glut, Don. "Interview: Tom Steele". The Tom Crier. I
    (n. d.): 2.

Goodman, Mark. "The Singing Cowboy". Esquire. LXXIII.
    (December, 1975): 154-155, 240, 245-248.

Hagner, John G. , ed. Falling for Stars Newsletter. I (Jan-
    uary, 1965): I to IV (January, 1968): 1.

Hagner, John G. , ed. News and Views: The Hollywood
    Stuntmen's Hall of Fame. I (June 10, 1976): 10
    to I (Fall, 1976): 15.

Hagner, John G. "Yak: Super Stuntman". Classic Film
    Collector. No. 18 (Summer, 1967): 13.

Harper, Mr. "After Hours: Falling Idol". Harpers. CC
    (January, 1950): 99-101.

Hewetson, Alan. "Comics in Cinema". Cinema. V (1969):
    2-7.

Hoffman, Eric. "Saturday Matinee Spy Hunters of World
    War Two". Serial World. No. 1 (1974): 8-9.

Hoffman, Eric. "The Screen Avengers: The Comic Heroes
    of the Cliffhangers". Mediascene. No. 19 (May-
    June, 1976): 4-19.

Hoffman, Eric. "Undersea Kingdom". Those Enduring Matinee Idols. I (December, 1970-January, 1971): 90-93.

Hoffman, Eric, and Malcomson, Bob. "Drums of Fu Manchu". Those Enduring Matinee Idols. II (December, 1972-January, 1973): 284-290.

Hughes, Albert H. "Outlaw with a Halo". Montana: The Magazine of Western History. XVII (1967): 60-75.

Hughes, William. "The Propagandist's Art". Film and History. IV (September, 1974): 11-15.

Jackson, Greg., Jr. "Serial World Interviews Rocketman Tris Coffin". Serial World. No. 10 (Spring, 1977): 3-9.

Jameux, Charles. "William Witney and John English". Positif. No. 88 (October, 1967).

Johnston, Alva. "Tenor on Horseback". Saturday Evening Post. CCXII (September 2, 1939): 18-19, 74-75.

"Judy Comes Down the Hill". Newsweek. XXVI (December 17, 1945): 102-103.

Kelez, Steve. "Captain America". Film Fan Monthly. No. 61/62 (July/August, 1966): 25-26.

King, Barbara. "Through the Looking Glass". Liberty. I (Spring, 1974): 8.

"King of the Cowboys". Newsweek. XXI (March 8, 1943): 74-75.

Knauth, Percy. "Gene Autry, Inc." Life. XXIV (June 28, 1948): 88-100.

Koppes, Clayton R., and Black, Gregory D. "What to Show the World: The Office of War Information and Hollywood, 1942-1945". The Journal of American History, LXIV (June, 1977): 87-105.

Lackey, Wayne. "Sunset Carson". Film Fan Monthly. No. 92 (February, 1969): 20.

Langley, W. D. "William Witney". Films in Review.
    XXVII (June, 1976): 381.

"Linda Stirling's Fond Memories of the Serials". The New
    Captain George's Whizzbang. No. 18 (n.d.): 15.

Malcomson, Robert M. "The Sound Serial". Views and Re-
    views. III (Summer, 1971): 12-26.

Malcomson, Robert M. "Sound Serials of Yesteryear". Yes-
    teryear. No. 1 (n.d.): 2-6.

Malcomson, Robert, ed. Those Enduring Matinee Idols. I
    (October-November, 1969): 1 to III (Chapter 29,
    1974): 9.

Malcomson, Bob, and Hoffman, Eric. "King of the Royal
    Mounted". Those Enduring Matinee Idols. III
    (n.d.): 338-340.

Martin, Pete. "Cincinnati Cowboy". Saturday Evening Post.
    CCXVII (June 9, 1945): 26-27, 78, 80-81.

Meyer, Jim. "Vera Hruba Ralston". Film Fan Monthly.
    No. 83 (May, 1968): 3-8.

Michael, Earl. "The Serials of Republic". Screen Facts. I
    (1963): 52-64.

Miller, Don. "Roy Rogers". The New Captain George's
    Whizzbang. No. 14 (n.d.): 18-21.

Nevins, Francis M., Jr. "Ballet of Violence: The Films
    of William Witney". Films in Review. XXV`
    (November, 1974): 523-545.

Nevins, Francis M., Jr. Review of Kings of the B's, edited
    by Todd McCarthy and Charles Flynn. Films in
    Review. XXVI (October, 1975): 499-500.

Oates, Stephen B. "Ghost Riders in the Sky". Colorado
    Quarterly. XXIII (Spring, 1974): 67-74.

Oehling, Richard A. "Germans in Hollywood Films: The
    Changing Image, 1914-1939". Film and History.
    III (May, 1973): 1-10, 26.

Oehling, Richard A. "Germans in Hollywood Films: The
        Changing Image, The Early Years, 1939-1942".
        Film and History. IV (May, 1974): 8-10.

Page, Alan. "Mixed Bag". Sight and Sound. VII (Autumn,
        1938): 126.

"The Painted Stallion". Those Enduring Matinee Idols. I
        (April-May, 1971): 121-123.

Parkhurst, C. M. "Parky". "The Lone Ranger Rides Again".
        Those Enduring Matinee Idols. II (April-May,
        1972): 218-221.

Powdermaker, Hortense. "An Anthropologist Looks at the
        Movies". Annals of the American Academy of
        Political and Social Science. CCLIV (Novem-
        ber, 1947): 80-87.

Powdermaker, Hortense. "Hollywood and the U. S. A."
        In Mass Culture: The Popular Arts in America,
        pp. 278-293. Edited by Bernard Rosenberg and
        David Manning White, New York: The Free Press,
        1957.

Prylock, Calvin. "Front Office, Box Office, and Artistic
        Freedom: An Aspect of the Film Industry 1945-
        1969". Journal of Popular Film. III (Fall, 1974):
        294-305.

Rainey, Buck. "A Conversation with Linda Stirling, Sensu-
        ous Siren of the Serials". Film Collector's Reg-
        istry. No. 71 (December, 1976): 3-7.

Reid, Ashton. "Hero on Horseback". Colliers. CXXII
        (July 24, 1948): 27, 62-65.

"Republic Pictures Celebrates Its Tenth Anniversary". The
        Independent. (June 23, 1945): 22-24, 30.

Sanford, Harry. "Joseph Kane: A Director's Story, Part 1".
        Views and Reviews. V (September, 1973): 31-38.

Sanford, Harry. "Joseph Kane: A Director's Story, Con-
        cluded". Views and Reviews. V (December,
        1973): 17-25.

Schlesinger, Arthur, Jr. "When Movies Really Counted".
    Show: Magazine of the Arts. I (April, 1963):
    77-78, 125.

Scott, Diane. "Memory Wears Carnations". Photoplay.
    LXXII (May, 1949): 34-36.

Seeley, Wallace. "A Fond Look at Movie Stuntmen". The
    New Captain George's Whizzbang. No. 11 (n. d.):
    8-12.

"Serial Discussion Panel". Those Enduring Matinee Idols.
    III (n. d.): 350-355.

Shain, Russell E. "Cold War Films, 1948-1962: An Anno-
    tated Filmography". Journal of Popular Film.
    III (Fall, 1974): 365-372.

Shain, Russell E. "Hollywood's Cold War". Journal of
    Popular Film. III (Fall, 1974): 334-350.

Sherman, Sam. "Republic Studios: Hollywood Thrill Fac-
    tory". Screen Thrills Illustrated. I (January,
    1963): 24-31.

Sherman, Sam. "Republic Studios: Hollywood Thrill Fac-
    tory". Screen Thrills Illustrated. II (October,
    1963): 12-17.

Shipley, Glenn. "King of the Serial Directors: Spencer
    Gordon Bennet". Views and Reviews. I (Fall,
    1969): 5-22.

Shoenberger, Jim. "A Final Visit with Reed Hadley".
    Film Collector's Registry. VII (January, 1975):
    5, 9.

Shoenberger, Jim. "An Interview with I. Stanford Jolley".
    Film Collector's Registry. VI (March, 1974): 1,
    4.

Sklar, Robert. "A Broad Mosaic on the Social Screen".
    American Films. II (June, 1976): 73-74.

Small, Melvin. "Motion Pictures and the Study of Attitudes:
    Some Problems for Historians". Film and His-
    tory. II (February, 1972): 1-5.

Smith, H. Allen. "King of the Cowboys". Life. XV (July
    12, 1943): 47-54.

Spears, Jack. "2nd-Unit Directors". Films in Review. VI
    (March, 1955): 108-112.

"Spy Smasher Tops Serial Poll". Film Collector's Registry.
    No. 61. (February, 1976): 4.

Stephenson, Ron. "Concerning Serials and Trends". Those
    Enduring Matinee Idols. III (n. d.): 444-446.

Stumpf, Charles. "Judy Canova". Film Collector's Regis-
    try. V (July, 1973): 5-6.

Stumpf, Charles. "Weaver Brothers and Elviry". Film Col-
    lector's Registry. V (May, 1973): 10.

Thomas, Bob. "Hollywood's General of the Armies". True.
    XXX (July, 1966): 47-48, 86-90.

Townsend, Shepherd. "William Whitney [sic]". Films in Re-
    view. XXVII (March, 1976): 190-191.

Trewin, J. C. "One Thing After Another: Being a Discourse
    on Serials". Sight and Sound. XVI (Autumn,
    1947): 106-107.

Tuska, Jon. "From the 100 Finest Westerns: Dark Com-
    mand". Views and Reviews. I (Winter, 1970):
    48-53.

Tuska, Jon. "From the 100 Finest Westerns: The Light-
    ning Warrior". Views and Reviews. II (Spring,
    1971): 49-55.

Tuska, Jon. "In Retrospect: Tim McCoy, Last of Four
    Parts". Views and Reviews. II (Spring, 1971):
    12-41.

Tuska, Jon. "Overland with Kit Carson--A Cinematography".
    Those Enduring Matinee Idols. II (June-July,
    1971): 146-148.

Tuska, Jon. "Overland with Kit Carson--A Cinematography".
    Those Enduring Matinee Idols. II (August-Septem-
    ber, 1971): 163-165.

Tuska, Jon. "The Vanishing Legion". Views and Reviews.
        III (Fall, 1971): 16-33.

Tuska, Jon. "The Vanishing Legion". Views and Reviews.
        III (Winter, 1972 [1971]): 10-26.

Tuska, Jon. "The Vanishing Legion". Views and Reviews.
        III (Spring, 1972): 22-39.

Tuska, Jon. "The Vanishing Legion". Views and Reviews.
        IV (Fall, 1972): 56-79.

Tuska, Jon. "The Vanishing Legion". Views and Reviews.
        IV (Winter, 1972): 34-52.

Tuska, Jon. "The Vanishing Legion". Views and Reviews.
        IV (Spring, 1973): 28-47.

Tuska, Jon. "The Vanishing Legion". Views and Reviews.
        IV (Summer, 1973): 64-68.

Van Hise, James. "Spy Smasher". Film Collector's Regis-
        try. VII (February, 1972): 9-13.

Walton, Jeff, ed. Serial World. No. 1 (1974) to No. 10
        (Spring, 1977).

Woll, Allen L. "Hollywood's Good Neighbor Policy: The
        Latin Image in American Film, 1939-1946".
        Journal of Popular Film. III (Fall, 1974): 278-
        293.

Woll, Allen L. "Latin Images in American Films, 1929-
        1939". Journal of Mexican American History.
        IV (Spring, 1974): 28-40.

Zeitlin, David. "The Great General Slays 'Em Again".
        Life. XLII (May 27, 1966): 93-98.

BOOKS

Adventures of Captain Marvel. Cliffhanger Ending and Es-
        cape Pictorial. Northbrook, Illinois: Jack Mathis
        Advertising, n. d.

Adventures of Red Ryder. Cliffhanger Ending and Escape

Pictorial. Northbrook, Illinois: Jack Mathis Advertising, n.d.

Allen, Frederick Lewis. Since Yesterday: The 1930s in America: September 3, 1929-September 3, 1939. New York: Harper and Row, 1939.

Alyn, Kirk. A Job for Superman. Los Angeles: by the author, Hollywood, California, 1971.

Barbour, Alan G. Cliffhanger: A Pictorial History of the Motion Picture Serial. New York: A and W Publications, 1977.

Barbour, Alan G. Days of Thrills and Adventure. New York: Macmillan and Company, 1970.

Barbour, Alan G., ed. Days of Thrills and Adventure. 2 Vols. Kew Gardens, New York: Screen Facts Press, 1968-1969.

Barbour, Alan G., ed. Great Serial Ads. Kew Gardens, New York: Screen Facts Press, 1965.

Barbour, Alan G., ed. High Roads to Adventure. Kew Gardens, New York: Screen Facts Press, 1971.

Barbour, Alan G., ed. Hit the Saddle. Kew Gardens, New York: Screen Facts Press, 1969.

Barbour, Alan G., ed. Movie Ads of the Past, No. 1: The B Western. Kew Gardens, New York: Screen Facts Press, 1966.

Barbour, Alan G., ed. Old Movies 1: The B Western. Kew Gardens, New York: Screen Facts Press, 1969.

Barbour, Alan G., ed. Old Movies 2: The Serial. Kew Gardens, New York: Screen Facts Press, 1969.

Barbour, Alan G., ed. Old Movies 3: The B Western. Kew Gardens, New York: Screen Facts Press, 1970.

Barbour, Alan G., ed. Old Movies 4: The Serial. Kew Gardens, New York: Screen Facts Press, 1970.

Barbour, Alan G., ed. The Serial. 4 Vols. Kew Gardens, New York: Screen Facts Press, 1967-1971.

Barbour, Alan G., ed. Serial Favorites. Kew Gardens, New York: Screen Facts Press, 1971.

Barbour, Alan G., ed. Serial Showcase. Kew Gardens, New York: Screen Facts Press, 1968.

Barbour, Alan G. The Serials of Columbia. Kew Gardens, New York: Screen Facts Press, 1967.

Barbour, Alan G. The Serials of Republic. Kew Gardens, New York: Screen Facts Press, 1965.

Barbour, Alan G. A Thousand and One Delights. New York: Collier Books, 1971.

Barbour, Alan G., ed. A Thousand Thrills. Kew Gardens, New York: Screen Facts Press, 1971.

Barbour, Alan G., ed. Thrill After Thrill. Kew Gardens, New York: Screen Facts Press, 1971.

Barbour, Alan G. The Thrill of It All. New York: Collier Books, 1971.

Barbour, Alan G., ed. Trail to Adventure. Kew Gardens, New York: Screen Facts Press, 1971.

Barbour, Alan G., ed. The Wonderful World of B-Films. Kew Gardens, New York: Screen Facts Press, 1968.

Baxter, John. STUNT: The Story of the Great Movie Stunt Men. Garden City, New York: Doubleday and Company, Inc., 1974.

Behlmer, Rudy, ed. Memo from David O. Selznick. New York: The Viking Press, 1972.

Behlmer, Rudy, and Thomas, Tony. Hollywood's Hollywood: The Movies About the Movies. Secaucus, New Jersey: The Citadel Press, 1975.

Bergman, Andrew. We're in the Money: Depression America and Its Films. New York: Harper and Row, 1971.

Blair, Earl, ed. Western Corral. No. 1. Houston, Texas:
     by the author, 1976.

Blum, Daniel. Screen World 1949. New York: Greenberg
     Publisher, 1950.

Blumer, Herbert, and Hauser, Philip M. Movies, Delin-
     quency, and Crime. The Payne Fund Studies
     Series. New York: The Macmillan Company:
     reprint ed., New York: Arno Press and the New
     York Times, 1970.

Bogdanovich, Peter. Allan Dwan: The Last Pioneer. New
     York: Praeger, 1971.

Bogdanovich, Peter. Fritz Lang in America. New York:
     Frederick A. Praeger, Inc., 1967.

Brosnan, John. James Bond in the Cinema. London: The
     Tantivy Press, 1972.

Brosnan, John. Movie Magic: The Story of Special Effects
     in the Cinema. New York: St. Martin's Press,
     1974.

Calder, Jenni. There Must Be a Lone Ranger: The Ameri-
     can West in Film and in Reality. New York:
     Taplinger Publishing Company, 1975.

Captain America. Cliffhanger Ending and Escape Pictorial.
     Northbrook, Illinois: Jack Mathis Advertising,
     n.d.

Cawelti, John G. The Six-Gun Mystique. Bowling Green,
     Ohio: Bowling Green University Popular Press,
     1975.

Corneau, Ernest N. The Hall of Fame of Western Film
     Stars. North Quincy, Massachusetts: The Chris-
     topher Publishing House, 1969.

Dardis, Tom. Some Time in the Sun. New York: Charles
     Scribner's Sons, 1976.

Daredevils of the Red Circle. Cliffhanger Ending and Escape
     Pictorial. Northbrook, Illinois: Jack Mathis Ad-
     vertising, n.d.

Daredevils of the West. Cliffhanger Ending and Escape Pic-
        torial. Northbrook, Illinois: Jack Mathis Adver-
        tising, n.d.

Drums of Fu Manchu. Cliffhanger Ending and Escape Pic-
        torial. Northbrook, Illinois: Jack Mathis Adver-
        tising, n.d.

Everson, William K. The Bad Guys: A Pictorial History of
        the Movie Villain. New York: Bonanza Books,
        1964.

Everson, William K. A Pictorial History of the Western
        Film. New York: The Citadel Press, 1969.

Eyles, Allen. John Wayne and the Movies. Cranbury, New
        Jersey: A. S. Barnes, 1976.

Eyles, Allen. The Western. Cranbury, New Jersey: A. S.
        Barnes and Company, 1975.

Fenin, George N., and Everson, William K. The Western:
        From Silents to Cinerama. New York: Bonanza
        Books, 1962.

Fernett, Gene. Next Time Drive off the Cliff! Cocoa, Flor-
        ida: Cinememories Publishing Company, 1968.

Fernett, Gene. Poverty Row. Satellite Beach, Florida:
        Coral Reef Publications, Inc., 1973.

Film Daily Yearbook of Motion Pictures: 1944. New York:
        Film Daily, Inc., 1945.

Film Daily Yearbook of Motion Pictures: 1946. New York:
        Film Daily, Inc., 1947.

Forman, Henry James. Our Movie Made Children. The
        Payne Fund Studies Series. New York: The Mac-
        millan Company, 1935; reprint ed., New York:
        Arno Press and the New York Times, 1970.

Freulich, Roman, and Abramson, Joan. Forty Years in Hol-
        lywood: Portraits of a Golden Age. Cranbury,
        New Jersey: A. S. Barnes, 1971.

Gertner, Richard, ed. 1975 International Motion Picture

Almanac. New York: Quigley Publishing Com-
     pany, 1975.

Gertner, Richard, ed. 1975 International Television Almanac.
     New York: Quigley Publishing Company, 1975.

Golden Age of Serials, The. Catalog No. 474. New York: Ivy
     Film, n. d.

Greenberg, Harvey R. The Movies on Your Mind. New York:
     Saturday Review Press, 1975.

Hagner, John G. Falling for Stars. Vol 1. Los Angeles:
     El' Jon Publications, 1964.

Hagner, John G. The Greatest Stunts Ever. Los Angeles:
     El' Jon Publications, 1967.

Handel, Leo A. Hollywood Looks at Its Audience: A Report
     of Film Audience Research. Urbana, Illinois:
     The University of Illinois Press, 1950.

Harmon, Jim, and Glut, Donald F. The Great Movie Se-
     rials: Their Sound and Fury. Garden City, New
     York: Doubleday and Company, Inc., 1972.

Harris, Charles W., and Rainey, Buck, ed. The Cowboy:
     Six-Shooters, Songs, and Sex. Norman, Oklaho-
     ma: University of Oklahoma Press, 1975.

Horwitz, James. They Went Thataway. New York: E. P.
     Dutton and Company, Inc., 1976.

Jowett, Garth. Film: The Democratic Art. Boston: Little,
     Brown and Company, 1976.

Karpf, Stephen Louis. The Gangster Film: Emergence,
     Variation and Decay of a Genre 1930-1940. Dis-
     sertations on Film Series. New York: Arno
     Press, 1973.

King of the Mounties. Cliffhanger Ending and Escape Pic-
     torial. Northbrook, Illinois: Jack Mathis Adver-
     tising, n. d.

Kitses, Jim. Horizons West: Anthony Mann, Budd Boet-
     ticher, Sam Peckinpah: Studies on Authorship

Within the Western. Bloomington, Indiana: Indiana University Press, 1969.

Lahue, Kalton C. Bound and Gagged: The Story of the
Silent Serials. New York: Castle Books, 1968.

Lahue, Kalton C. Continued Next Week: A History of the
Moving Picture Serial. Norman, Oklahoma: University of Oklahoma Press, 1964.

Lahue, Kalton C. Riders of the Range: The Sagebrush
Heroes of the Sound Screen. New York: Castle
Books, 1973.

Lamparski, Richard. Lamparski's Whatever Became of ...?
Giant 1st Annual. New York: Bantam Books,
1976.

Lamparski, Richard. Whatever Became of ...? I and II.
New York: Crown Publishers, Inc., 1967.

Lamparski, Richard. Whatever Became of ...? The New
Fifth Series. New York: Bantam Books, 1974.

Lingeman, Richard R. Don't You Know There's a War On?
The American Home Front 1941-1945. New York:
G. P. Putnam's Sons, 1970.

Lupoff, Dick, and Thompson, Don, ed. All in Color for a
Dime. New Rochelle, New York: Arlington
House, 1970.

Lynd, Robert S., and Lynd, Helen Merrell. Middletown:
A Study in American Culture. New York: Harcourt, Brace and World, Inc., 1929.

Maltin, Leonard. The Great Movie Shorts. New York:
Crown Publishers, Inc., 1972.

Maltin, Leonard. Movie Comedy Teams. New York: The
New American Library, Inc., 1970.

Maltin, Leonard, ed. The Real Stars: Articles and Inter-
views on Hollywood's Great Character Actors.
The Curtis Film Series. New York: Curtis
Books, 1969.

Maltin, Leonard, ed. The Real Stars #2: Articles and In-
    terviews on Hollywood's Great Character Actors.
    The Curtis Film Series. New York: Curtis
    Books, 1972.

Manchester, William. The Glory and the Dream: A Narra-
    tive History of America 1932-1972. Boston: Little,
    Brown and Company, 1973.

Martin, Olga J. Hollywood's Movie Commandments: A Hand-
    book for Motion Picture Writers and Reviewers.
    New York: H. Wilson, 1937; reprint ed., New
    York: Arno Press, 1975.

Mathis, Jack. Valley of the Cliffhangers. Northbrook, Illi-
    nois: Jack Mathis Advertising, 1975.

McCarthy, Todd, and Flynn, Charles, ed. Kings of the Bs:
    Working Within the Hollywood System: An An-
    thology of Film History and Criticism. New York:
    E. P. Dutton and Company, Inc., 1975.

McClure, Arthur F., and Jones, Ken D. Heroes, Heavies
    and Sagebrush: A Pictorial History of the "B"
    Western Players. Cranbury, New Jersey: A. S.
    Barnes and Company, Inc., 1972.

Michael, Paul, ed. The American Movies Reference Book:
    The Sound Era. Englewood Cliffs, New Jersey:
    Prentice-Hall, Inc., 1969.

Munsterberg, Hugo. The Film: A Psychological Study: The
    Silent Photoplay in 1916. New York: D. Apple-
    ton and Company, 1916; reprint ed., New York:
    Dover Publications, 1970.

Mysterious Doctor Satan. Northbrook, Illinois: Jack Mathis
    Advertising, n.d.

Nachbar, Jack, ed. Focus on the Western. Englewood Cliffs,
    New Jersey: Prentice-Hall, Inc., 1974.

1956 International Motion Picture Almanac. New York:
    Quigley Publishing Company, 1956.

Nye, Russel. The Unembarrassed Muse: The Popular Arts
    in America. New York: The Dial Press, 1970.

Parish, James Robert, and Stanke, Don E. The Glamour
       Girls. New Rochelle, New York: Arlington House
       Publishers, 1975.

Parish, James Robert, ed. The Great Movie Series. Cran-
       bury, New Jersey: A. S. Barnes and Company,
       Inc., 1971.

Parish, James Robert, ed. The Slapstick Queens. New
       York: Castle Books, 1973.

Parkinson, Michael, and Jeavons, Clyde. A Pictorial His-
       tory of Westerns. London: Hamlyn, 1972.

Perrett, Geoffrey. Days of Sadness, Years of Triumph:
       The American People 1939-1945. New York
       Coward, McCann and Geoghegan, Inc., 1973.

The Purple Monster Strikes. Northbrook, Illinois: Jack
       Mathis Advertising, n. d.

Ricci, Mark, Zmijewsky, Boris, and Zmijewsky, Steve.
       The Films of John Wayne. New York: Citadel
       Press, 1970.

Rosenberg, Bernard, and White, David Manning, ed. Mass
       Culture: The Popular Arts in America. New
       York: Free Press, 1964.

Rosten, Leo C. Hollywood: The Movie Colony, the Movie
       Makers. New York: Harcourt, Brace and Com-
       pany, 1941.

Rothel, David. Who Was That Masked Man? The Story of
       the Lone Ranger. Cranbury, New Jersey: A. S.
       Barnes and Company, Inc., 1976.

Seldes, Gilbert. The Great Audience. New York: Viking
       Press, 1950.

Sklar, Robert. Movie Made America: A Social History of
       American Movies. New York: Random House,
       1975.

Smith, Paul, ed. The Historian and Film. New York:
       Cambridge University Press, 1976.

Spears, Jack. HOLLYWOOD: The Golden Era. New York:
    Castle Books, 1971.

Spy Smasher. Cliffhanger Ending and Escape Pictorial.
    Northbrook, Illinois: Jack Mathis Advertising, n.d.

Stedman, Raymond William. The Serials: Suspense and
    Drama by Installment. Norman, Oklahoma: Uni-
    versity of Oklahoma Press, 1971.

Stott, William. Documentary Expression and Thirties Amer-
    ica. New York: Oxford University Press, 1973.

Thompson, Stith. The Folktale. New York: Dryden Press,
    1951.

Tuska, Jon, ed. Close-Up: The Contract Director. Me-
    tuchen, New Jersey: The Scarecrow Press, Inc.,
    1976.

Tuska, Jon. The Filming of the West. Garden City, New
    York: Doubleday and Company, 1976.

Warshow, Robert. The Immediate Experience. Garden City,
    New York: Doubleday, 1962.

Weiss, Ken, and Goodgold, Ed. To Be Continued.... New
    York: Crown Publishers, Inc., 1972.

White, David Manning, and Averson, Richard. The Cellu-
    loid Weapon: Social Comment in the American
    Film. Boston: Beacon Press, 1972.

Wilson, Robert, ed. The Film Criticism of Otis Ferguson.
    Philadelphia: Temple University Press, 1971.

Wise, Arthur, and Ware, Derek. Stunting in the Cinema.
    New York: St. Martin's Press, 1973.

Wofenstein, Martha, and Leites, Nathan. Movies: A Psycho-
    logical Study. New York: The Free Press, 1950;
    reprint ed., New York: Hafner Publishing Com-
    pany, 1971.

Wood, Michael. America in the Movies or "Santa Maria,
    It Had Slipped My Mind". New York: Basic
    Books, 1975.

Wright, Will. Six Guns and Society: A Structural Study of
        the Western. Berkeley: University of California
        Press, 1975.

Zinman, David. Saturday Afternoon at the Bijou. New Ro-
        chelle, New York: Arlington House, 1973.

Zolotow, Maurice. Shooting Star: A Biography of John
        Wayne. New York: Simon and Schuster, 1974.

Zorro's Fighting Legion. Cliffhanger Ending and Escape
        Pictorial. Northbrook, Illinois: Jack Mathis
        Advertising, n. d.

INDEX